ACCESS YOUR ONLINE RESOURCES

Nurturing Compassionate Connections is accompanied by a number of printable online materials designed to ensure this resource best supports your professional needs.

Go to https://resourcecentre.routledge.com/speechmark and click on the cover of this book.

Answer the question prompt using your copy of the book to gain access to the online content.

NURTURING COMPASSIONATE CONNECTIONS

In a profession where empathy and compassion form the bedrock of impactful interactions, yet remain relatively unexplored, this book endeavours to be a beacon of inspiration and guidance.

The book explores what compassionate relationships might look like and translates extensive research into actionable steps that practitioners can easily integrate into their routines. Chapters:

- Include guidance for fostering effective, empathetic relationships with colleagues and young children, as well as extending empathy to parents and carers
- Offer suggestions for supporting and promoting positive behaviour, with guidance on embracing empathy in challenging situations
- Prioritise practitioner wellbeing and include real-life case studies of nurturing connections, recognising both the demands and satisfaction of the profession
- Are full of reflective prompts and activities to reshape the narrative of early years practice and equip practitioners to navigate challenges with resilience.

Nurturing Compassionate Connections advocates a strengths-based approach and aspires to redefine the landscape of compassionate practice, enriching the journey of those who care for young children. It is essential reading for all early years practitioners and allied professionals.

Angela Hodgkins is Senior Lecturer and Course Leader for BA (Hons) Integrated Working with Children and Families at the University of Worcester. She has had a varied 20-year career in early years, working across both special and mainstream settings, as well as advising on early years inclusion. Angela has recently completed a PhD in investigating the practice of empathy in the early years profession.

NURTURING COMPASSIONATE CONNECTIONS

A Guide to Practitioner Empathy in the Early Years

Angela Hodgkins

Designed cover image: Getty Images

First published 2026
by Routledge
4 Park Square, Milton Park, Abingdon, Oxon OX14 4RN

and by Routledge
605 Third Avenue, New York, NY 10158

Routledge is an imprint of the Taylor & Francis Group, an informa business

© 2026 Angela Hodgkins

Some figures in this book have been created by the author using Canva

The right of Angela Hodgkins to be identified as author of this work has been asserted in accordance with sections 77 and 78 of the Copyright, Designs and Patents Act 1988.

All rights reserved. No part of this book may be reprinted or reproduced or utilised in any form or by any electronic, mechanical, or other means, now known or hereafter invented, including photocopying and recording, or in any information storage or retrieval system, without permission in writing from the publishers.

Trademark notice: Product or corporate names may be trademarks or registered trademarks, and are used only for identification and explanation without intent to infringe.

British Library Cataloguing-in-Publication Data
A catalogue record for this book is available from the British Library

ISBN: 978-1-032-73536-8 (hbk)
ISBN: 978-1-032-73535-1 (pbk)
ISBN: 978-1-003-46468-6 (ebk)

DOI: 10.4324/9781003464686

Typeset in Interstate
by Apex CoVantage, LLC

Access the Support Material: https://resourcecentre.routledge.com/speechmark

To early years practitioners everywhere: Your work is among the most vital in the world, nurturing the youngest members of our society. This book is a tribute to the countless empathic, caring, and passionate professionals who dedicate their days to providing young children and their families with the best possible start in their care and educational journeys. Your efforts are truly remarkable.

And to my grandson, Louis Arthur Smart. You are my pride, my joy, and my inspiration for the future.

CONTENTS

Acknowledgements	x
1 Introducing the philosophical foundations of this book	1
2 Understanding empathy and compassion	16
3 Building empathic relationships with young children	34
4 Extending empathy and compassion to parents, carers, and families	50
5 Fostering empathic and supportive teams	68
6 Supporting and promoting positive behaviour	86
7 Embracing empathy and compassion in challenging situations	102
8 Developing and enhancing empathy skills	121
9 Understanding and managing empathic distress	139
10 Experiencing satisfaction through positive empathy and compassion	158
11 Guided reflections and future directions	175
Index	*187*

ACKNOWLEDGEMENTS

I would like to express my heartfelt gratitude to the participants known in this book as Aadiya, Andrea, Cheryl, Debbie, George, Harriet, Jake, Joel, and Mel. These early years practitioners, managers, and teachers took part in the empathy research project between 2019 and 2023. Thank you all for your generosity of time and your openness throughout the project.

A special thank you to my wonderful editor and editorial assistant at Routledge, Clare Ashworth and Molly Kavanagh. Your positivity and encouragement provided the motivation I needed to complete this book. Your support has been invaluable.

1
Introducing the philosophical foundations of this book

Chapter objectives

- To position the view of early years practice in this book
- To outline the philosophical approach for this book
- To discuss the value of examining a personal philosophy
- To summarise a research project examining early years practitioners' perceptions of empathy
- To identify chapter reflective features

The aim of this first chapter is to introduce the philosophy underpinning this book. Early years practice is constantly changing as governments change and new legislation and policies inform practice. In the 21st century, there are many challenges, including an enduring lack of appreciation of the profession, staff recruitment difficulties, the Covid-19 recovery process, and the current cost of living crisis. However, there are also many opportunities to shape the lives of young children, and the career can be very rewarding.

In this chapter, a research investigation which focussed on empathy within early years practice (Hodgkins, 2023) is introduced. This comprehensive piece of research is revisited in every chapter, with vignettes and voices of early years practitioners working in the UK. These voices aim to illustrate the themes of the book using real life scenarios.

This book is intended to be useful for anyone working in the early years sector or in allied fields with young children and families. Whether you are a student, a researcher, a tutor, a practitioner, or an early years manager, there will be useful content and exercises designed to support the development of compassionate and empathic practice. Reflective activities for individuals will support you in analysing your own views and practice, whilst group activities are useful tools for staff meetings, CPD, and training.

Early years practice today

The childcare profession in the UK has undergone many changes since the first formal training, the 'training for ladies as children's nurses' began at the Norland Institute in 1892 (Wright, 1999). The main aim of the training then was to offer,

> a career opportunity for women of genteel birth who could not cope with the intellectual rigours of teacher training, but had empathy with, and an awareness of, the needs of young children.
>
> (p. 7)

Early years practitioners are no longer seen as less intellectual than teachers (hopefully!), but they are still predominantly female. Despite efforts to encourage males into early years as a career (Thorpe et al., 2020), the workforce remains 97% female (Haux et al., 2022). The traditional perception is that working with young children is a role undertaken by women, the assumption being that caring for others is a maternal, female role (Fairchild and Mikuska, 2021).

In the United States, formal childcare first began when the Quaker movement set up provision for poor families during the Great Depression to allow women to go out to work (Feeney et al., 2022). However, in both societies, the predominant view when childcare became available was that children were better cared for in the home by their parents. In the UK and in the USA, the childcare and education model that we see today developed as the number of working women increased in the 1950s and 1960s.

Developments in qualifications, the professionalisation of the workforce, and a move towards graduate leadership have resulted in more pressures for childcare workers, with no change to status, increase in pay, or improvement in conditions. Practitioners have been increasingly required to 'perform professionalism and be judged against an external set of criteria' (Osgood, 2010, p. 120). As a result, staff turnover within the profession is high. An Australian study by Thorpe et al. (2020) identified this as having an emotional cost to relationships within settings. The study worryingly recognised reduced responsiveness to young children as an effect of additional stresses on practitioners. The profession has experienced an escalation in work stress and emotional exhaustion in the past decade (Jena-Crottet, 2017; OECD, 2019). The additional pressures of the Covid-19 pandemic have contributed to high levels of stress and emotional exhaustion (Eadie et al., 2021). These factors have resulted in a huge number of practitioners leaving the profession, as the figures in Table 1.1 show.

Explanations given from all three nations identified in the table are identical: low pay, high workload, poor career progression, and lack of recognition. So why do people stay in the profession? The organisation Teacher Active (2024) identifies five reasons why early years work is one of the most rewarding careers. The first of these is the reward of setting children up for a future of success, knowing that you are having a positive impact on a young child's future. The second reason is that no two days are the same, as you support children in exploring the world. The third reason given is the fact that working with young children

Introducing the philosophical foundations of this book 3

Table 1.1 Number of practitioners leaving the profession

UK	USA	Australia
* 10,000 practitioners have left the profession since 2019 (Hill, 2023) * More than half of early years practitioners in the UK plan to leave in the next year (Oxtoby, 2023)	* 100,000 early childhood workers have left the profession since the Covid pandemic (Goldstein, 2022) * A third of early childhood educators plan to leave the profession (Bryant et al., 2023)	* There is currently a shortage of 7,300 early childhood educators (Hendy, 2022) * 75% of early childhood educators plan to leave the profession within the next three years (Dent, 2021)

means that you will see the world in a different way and learn alongside the children. A focus on creative learning is the fourth of the reasons given, learning through play and exploration, and encouraging imagination. The final reason given by Teacher Active is the scope for progression within the profession. This is in direct contrast with the poor career progression identified previously, but there are opportunities for advancement, both within childcare settings and into other professions, with qualifications in teaching, for example, becoming more accessible. In the research detailed later in this chapter (Hodgkins, 2023), the positives about working in early years are identified in Figure 1.1.

 Reflective prompt – Think about your own experience of working in early years; reflect on the driving and resisting forces within your role. Think about your inspiration, beliefs, values, and people.

Figure 1.1 Positives about working in the early years

Figure 1.2 Driving and resisting forces. FreePik

The underpinning philosophy of this book

The philosophy underpinning this book is a strength-based, positive one. Throughout my professional career, I have met many wonderful people: compassionate practitioners, caring and dedicated students, inspirational leaders, and supportive managers. It is my view that people generally go into careers working with children and families because they care and because they want to make a difference. Providing an encouraging and supportive environment for young children can be instrumental in preparing them for exploration, learning, and development. In early years practice, we have a real opportunity to set children on the path to success and happiness. As practitioners, carers, and teachers, we have a significant influence on the young children we work with. We are role models; children will copy what they see and will learn to treat others as they see us treat them. As such, I believe that empathy and compassion should serve as the foundation for all aspects of care and education.

My views and philosophy for working with young children are informed by my own background and experiences, which have culminated in the research and writing of this book. Qualifying as an NNEB nursery nurse in 1984, I had a 20-year career working with children across various settings and contexts. I worked as a nanny, a childminder, in pre-schools, primary schools and special schools, playschemes, and out-of-school care. I was involved in setting up one of the first SureStart centres in the early 2000s and worked as an early years inclusion advisor for the Local Education Authority. In 2004, I gained adult teaching qualifications and moved into lecturing at a further education college, moving on to my current role as a senior lecturer at the University of Worcester. In addition to my work with young children, I also trained as a counsellor and worked as a volunteer counsellor in victim support, for a GP surgery and for the charity Childline.

Both of my careers, as an early years practitioner and as a counsellor, have centred around person-centred practices. Person-centred practice is an approach that puts the person at the centre, working with the person to help them achieve what they want. The approach uses three 'core conditions' to build a relationship built on trust and positivity. These 'core conditions' are empathy, congruence, and unconditional positive regard, and they were first conceived by Carl Rogers in 1957 as a therapeutic approach to use in counselling. Rogers identified six core conditions in total but saw these three conditions as useful for any interpersonal relationship. Rogers believed that by providing these core conditions, people would grow and develop and help themselves to succeed. He explains,

> In my early professional years, I was asking the question: How can I treat, or cure, or change this person? Now I would phrase the question in this way: How can I provide a relationship which this person may use for his own personal growth?
>
> (Rogers, 1961)

To be congruent, we need to be genuine in our dealings with people. Being true to ourselves, being true to our personal values, means that we are being authentic. Rogers believed that a person's ideal self and their actual experience should be the same, or similar, to be completely congruent. However, this rarely happens; therefore, most people have a certain amount of incongruity in their lives. For example, imagine that you are ambitious and very driven to succeed. If you are working for a company with no advancement opportunities for you, you will be in a state of incongruence. If you strongly believe that babies need to be cuddled and carried, but you work in a nursery with a supervisor who disapproves, you would need to stick to your values and stand up for what you think is right for you to remain congruent. Congruence in working with children means staying true to your values and beliefs, even when this is difficult or challenged by others.

Unconditional positive regard means acceptance and support for others, regardless of what the person says or does. In any profession involving work with people, anti-discriminatory practice is a guiding principle. Regardless of any personal prejudices, which everyone has, we treat people equally and with respect. Unconditional positive regard is treating people positively, regardless of nationality, sex, race, etc. But more than this, it is treating people with respect regardless of what they may say or do. If the parent of a child at your setting makes a complaint and speaks to you in a hostile manner, you would treat that person with respect and positivity. Doing so is likely to help to diffuse any tension and anger.

Empathy is arguably the most important of the core conditions and is the fundamental concept of this book. Empathy is usually understood as a willingness to put yourself in the position of another person, to try and imagine how it must be to be in that person's position. Chapter 2 encompasses an in-depth study of empathy.

> **Individual activity**
>
> Choose one of the following children:
>
> - Stefania is a 4-year-old child who is partially sighted. Her family has recently moved to the area and is starting at your nursery. You are told that she can see large objects, furniture, and people but not small details like facial expressions and writing.
> - Ibrahim is a shy, quiet 3-year-old child who is usually on his own and does not play with the other children.
> - Bobby is a looked-after child who lives with a foster family. He was removed from his family due to neglect but seems to have settled into his new home well.

Imagine that you and the rest of the practitioners at your setting practice the core conditions. You empathise with the child, trying to put yourself in the child's position and understand what it must be like for them. You are honest and authentic in your interactions with the child and the child's family. You accept the child unconditionally and want to provide the best care possible for this child. How might this look in practice? How do you think this person-centred approach would impact the child? Can you see the benefits of the approach?

Ethics

It is important, at this point, to clarify that all practitioners and children detailed in the activities in this book are fictional, although many are loosely based on children I have known/worked with in the past. In the empathy research, all practitioners have been given pseudonyms, and no children or places are identified. All children, families, and practitioners must be afforded privacy; they have a right to confidentiality and anonymity (BERA, 2024).

A strength-based approach

A previous book that I co-authored focussed on strength-based practice, an approach that is relevant to this book too. Relationships are at the forefront of this book, a view that parallels one of the cornerstones of a strength-based approach: a secure relationship built on trust. Within an early years setting, the relationship between practitioner and child is probably the most crucial aspect of practice, hence the significance of having a named key person for each child (Hodgkins and Prowle, 2023). This is discussed in detail in Chapter 3. In the strength-based approach, there is a belief that there will be strengths within the most challenging of situations. Identifying these strengths leads to empowerment and builds resilience. For example, in a family experiencing poverty and deprivation, there may be strength in supportive, loving family relationships; a child with challenges due to a significant disability may have a talent in a particular area, which builds their self-esteem and gives them strength. Nurturing others to identify their strengths builds resilience and self-belief, encourages people to view obstacles as challenges, and promotes people's ability to 'bounce back' from adversity. Strength-based practice sees people as resourceful and promotes self-actualisation. As Maslow maintained in his 'hierarchy of human needs' (1943), the basic need for security must be met before any further development can take place. If a child does not feel secure, then they cannot learn. Children's sense of security is achieved by building compassionate, empathic relationships.

Critically reflective practice

Reflective practice has been an essential cornerstone of early years care and education for some time (Schön, 1991) and has recently become a clear focus for Ofsted inspections, with reports of outstanding settings emphasising the importance of reflection in improving practice (Edwards, 2019). Reflecting on our practice is important as a tool for self-improvement and development. We can become better practitioners when we learn from our reflections and gain insight. However, *critical* reflective practice is more than learning from experience; 'critical reflective practice must include an honest, introspective critique of ourselves, which challenges our views, values and core beliefs' (Ayres, 2013). Critical reflection involves more than thinking, 'this is what went well, so this is what I will do differently next time'; it is about thinking more deeply and considering the underpinning values at the root of practice. Critical reflective practice, which includes discussion with colleagues can play a powerful role in 'authentic and meaningful early care and education' (Shin and Recchia, 2023, p. 626). Argyris (2002) calls this 'double-loop learning', which includes the adaptation of goals in the light of experience. The first loop uses the goal, and the second loop enables their modification, hence 'double loop'. Double-loop learning recognises that the way a problem is defined and solved can be a source of the problem. In double-loop learning, if something goes wrong, we examine the underlying causes, e.g. policies, assumptions, informal practices, and individuals' motives. Here is an example of reflective practice compared with critically reflective or 'double-loop' practice (Figure 1.3).

Reflective practice is closely associated with empathy, so it is very relevant to this book. Research by Lynch et al. (2019) identified higher levels of empathy among child and family social workers who engaged in regular reflective practice. McNaughton's (2016) research with early years students also recognised the value of reflective practice in developing empathy. Reflective practice is advantageous in helping people manage their emotions. In the Social Work profession, for example, there is a reflective approach to supervision. Social workers are encouraged to talk freely and openly about the emotions experienced during their work. Shea's (2019) research into reflective practice for social workers indicated an increased awareness of the social and emotional impact of the work when reflective practice skills are developed within a relationship context. These results, therefore, advocate for group reflective supervision.

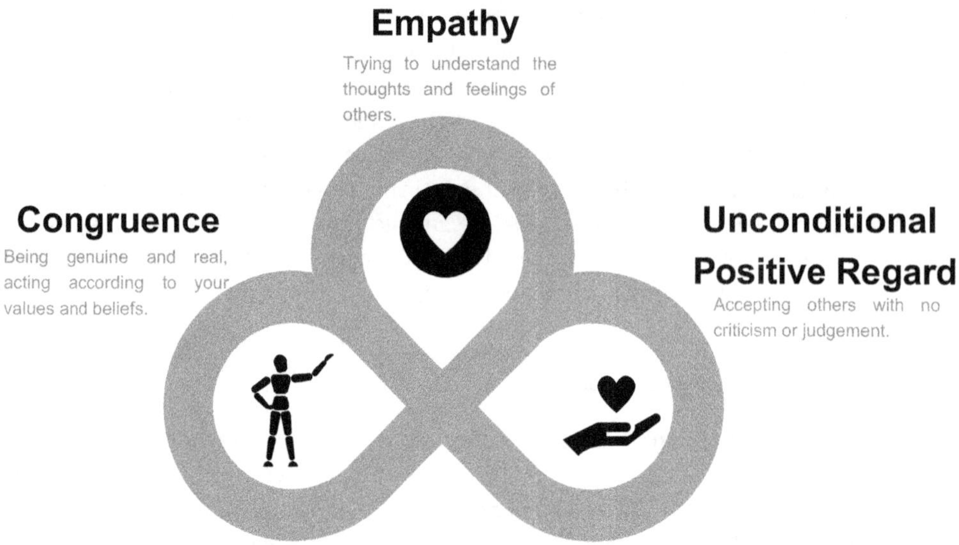

Empathy
Trying to understand the thoughts and feelings of others.

Congruence
Being genuine and real, acting according to your values and beliefs.

Unconditional Positive Regard
Accepting others with no criticism or judgement.

Figure 1.3 The Core Conditions

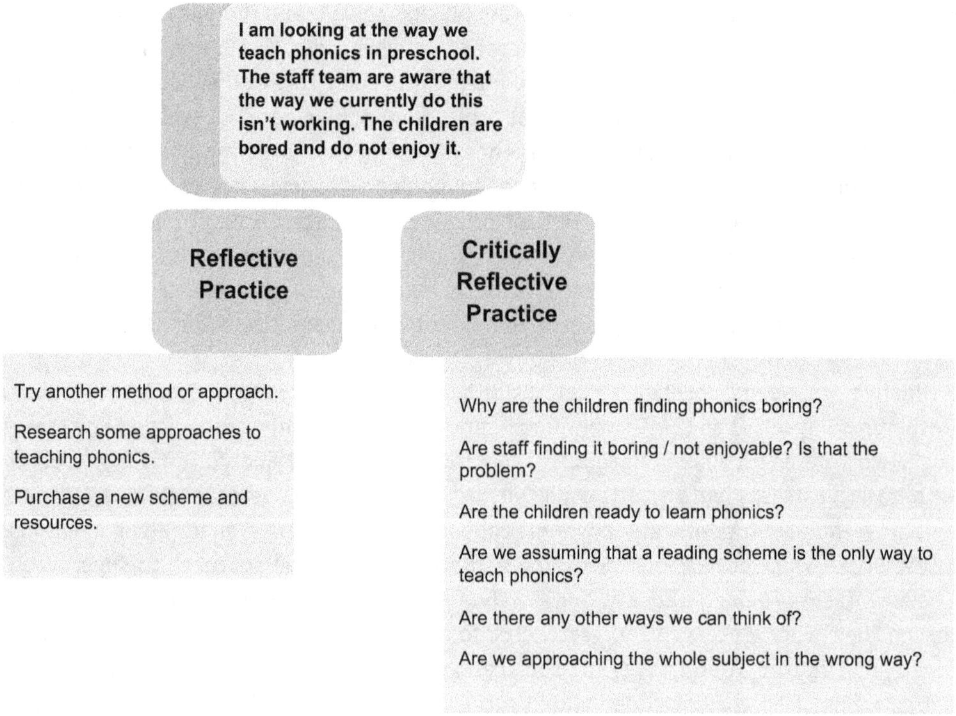

I am looking at the way we teach phonics in preschool. The staff team are aware that the way we currently do this isn't working. The children are bored and do not enjoy it.

Reflective Practice

Critically Reflective Practice

Try another method or approach.

Research some approaches to teaching phonics.

Purchase a new scheme and resources.

Why are the children finding phonics boring?

Are staff finding it boring / not enjoyable? Is that the problem?

Are the children ready to learn phonics?

Are we assuming that a reading scheme is the only way to teach phonics?

Are there any other ways we can think of?

Are we approaching the whole subject in the wrong way?

Figure 1.4 Critically reflective practice

> **Group activity**
>
> Discuss how reflective practice is practised in your setting and use these questions to reflect on the usefulness of group reflection.
>
> - Is reflective practice carried out formally or informally in your setting? Which is best? Or do you need both?
> - When and how does each individual person reflect on their work?
> - What might be the benefits of group reflection?
> - How might it support group relationships?
> - How might it benefit children and families?
> - How, when, and where might you be able to do this?
> - What are the challenges/barriers?
> - How might these be overcome?

Developing a personal philosophy

A personal philosophy is a framework that helps you understand who you are and make sense of your life. It is made up of your thoughts, values, beliefs, concepts, and attitudes about everything, the core of who you are as a person and as a professional. Although we may behave differently in our personal lives to the way we are in practice, our core values are the same.

In this chapter so far, I have described some of my own values and beliefs, which make up my personal philosophy. My philosophy is based on:

- My personality (e.g. empathic, introvert)
- My values (e.g. relationships, compassion, security)
- My professional training in early years and counselling
- My experiences in working with children
- My experiences of working with adults
- My early years – my upbringing, background, and culture (e.g. working class, Black Country)
- My reading and studies, theories that I agree with (e.g. Rogers)
- Influences of people around me – family, friends, students, and colleagues
- My experience as a parent and grandparent

All of these things have made me who I am today, and they influence my daily life and my work. Sometimes, an incident or a specific experience can stay with you and influence your practice, a child you have worked with, a book you have read, or something that a teacher said to you. These 'critical incidents' form an important part of who you are and how you work. You may already have a personal philosophy as an early years practitioner. Try the following activity to see if it helps you to consolidate this.

> **Individual activity**
>
> Examine your own personal philosophy for practice. Create an image of your own personal philosophy for practice, identifying what has influenced this.

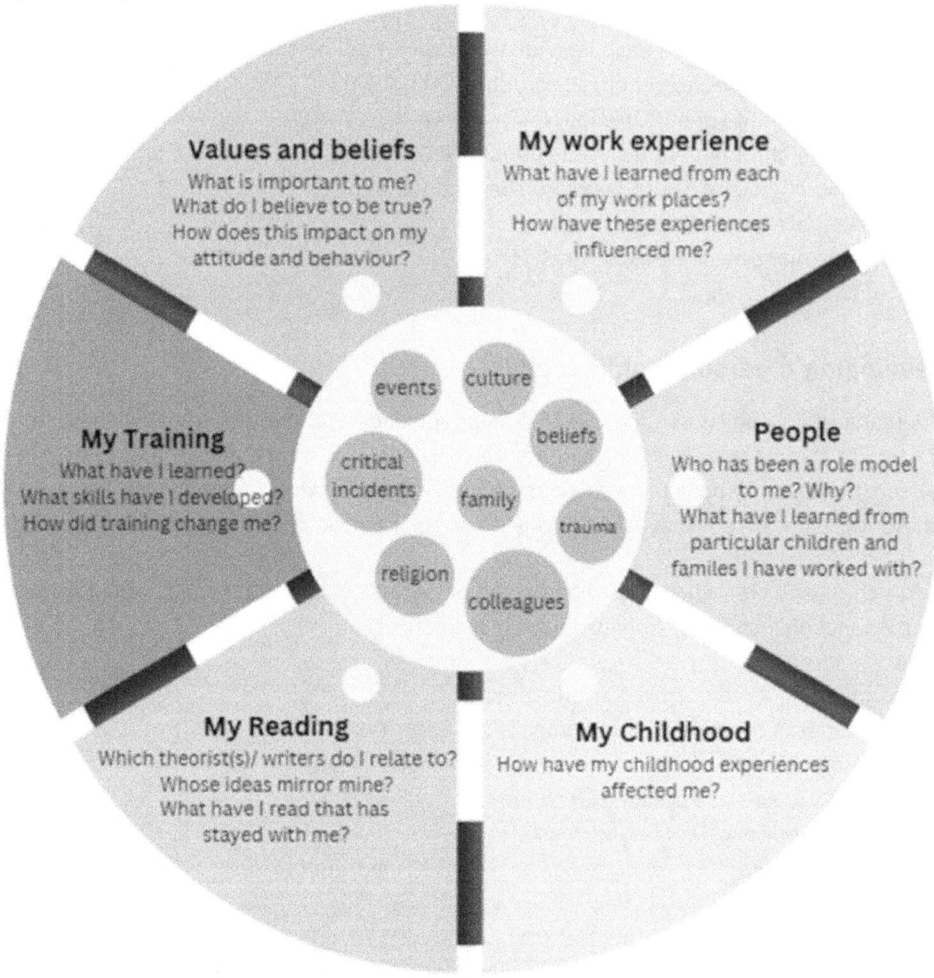

Figure 1.5 Personal philosophy exercise

The empathy research

This book was written following a substantive research investigation which examined empathy in early years practice. The importance of empathy for anyone working with people surely cannot be contested, and in work with young children in the early years profession, it is of the utmost significance.

In early years practice, the development of close personal relationships between practitioners and young children is paramount. Practitioners need empathy to 'tune into' children to understand their needs. Despite this, empathy is generally not explicitly included in job descriptions or training specifications. Although there has been an increase in research into emotion within early years practice over the last decade, none had examined empathy in particular before this one (Hodgkins, 2023). The research drew on theories of empathy (for example, Rogers, 1957) and investigated types of empathy seen in early years practice. The aim and objectives of the research were to investigate how practitioners perceived empathy within their practice, to identify types of empathy being demonstrated, and to understand the impact, if any, on practitioners' wellbeing.

Reflective diaries were completed by nine practitioners in England, followed by semi-structured interviews to further examine diary content. Analysis of diaries and interview transcripts illustrated practitioners' close empathic relationships with children, colleagues and parents/carers. Practitioners demonstrated cognitive and affective empathy in their interactions, affective empathy in particular, influencing their lives outside of work. The study illuminated the exhaustion and emotional cost of empathic interactions for early years practitioners.

The findings of the project recommended acknowledgement of the emotional impact of the role and preparation for this in education and training. It called for improved reflective supervision for practitioners who report an impact upon their own wellbeing daily.

Ethical research

Empathy is central to early years practice, and so it is equally important in early years research. The research discussed in this book (Hodgkins, 2023) was carried out with the utmost regard for the feelings of the people involved: the staff, children, and families in the early years' settings. The intention of the research was to make a difference in future early years practitioners' lives, to understand and appreciate the demands of the role and the skills they were using. Beneficence is a fundamental principle in research with people and is particularly important as the subject being studied is an emotional one, with empathy and emotion being intrinsically linked (Andreychik, 2019). The intention was to go further than simply doing no harm (Hugman et al., 2011); it was to bring about good (Bogolub, 2010). It was hoped that a greater understanding of the emotional demands of early years practice would provide awareness of the responsibilities of the role and should support training and supervision, which will benefit practitioners. Stern (2016) terms this 'virtuous research': using the researcher's qualities of honesty and kindness throughout the research process. I would add empathy to the list of qualities, as empathy for the practitioners as participants is vital and adds another layer to the research story.

How to use this book

This book is not necessarily intended to be read from cover to cover, it is intended to be useful, in a tangible way, for people working with young children. The book aims to be a transformational tool – a practical guide tailored to early years practitioners and students.

It aims to encapsulate messages and wisdom gleaned from research into actionable steps that practitioners can readily incorporate into their routines. By prioritising empathic and compassionate relationships with young children, the book aims to rekindle the passion and enthusiasm that attracted professionals to this field in the first place. Each chapter includes examples from participants' diaries and interviews drawn from the empathy research. Real world examples of early years practice are used to inspire, provoke, and prompt discussion. Each chapter aims to guide, inspire, and transform practice through the use of critically reflective activities for individual practitioners and groups.

Case studies - Each chapter includes case studies that showcase real-life examples from practitioners working in early years care and education. These case studies illustrate practical interactions and offer opportunities to reflect on real-world situations.

Reflective prompts - These are brief opportunities to stop and think about the points made in the chapter. They can be used by individuals very informally, or they may be used in the same way as the individual or group activities described later. They are invitations to take a moment to consider how the content may apply to their own practice. These reflective moments will encourage a growth-oriented mindset.

Individual activities

These activities are designed to improve your understanding of your own individual values and beliefs and strengthen your personal philosophy for early years practice. They are opportunities to spend some time considering how you personally feel about the content of the book and to empower you to actively apply theories and concepts within your setting.

Group activities

These activities have been designed to be used with small groups, as there is much evidence that collaborative reflection can be transformative (Elfer, 2012; Basford, 2019). The interactive activities may be useful for early years practitioners to discuss in a staff meeting, to prompt discussion, or they could form part of an in-house training session to analyse practice and devise strategies for improvement.

Introducing the philosophical foundations of this book 13

The activities are also useful for students of early years in class. It is hoped that, in this case, this experiential learning may help to prepare students for the profession or to revitalise practice in those engaged in continuing professional development.

Chapter summary

This chapter began with an exploration of the contemporary landscape of early years practice, a profession with significant challenges and stresses underscored by a history of low pay, poor conditions, and a lack of recognition. The rewards, however, can be just as significant. The intrinsic satisfaction derived from nurturing relationships with children, witnessing their accomplishments, and fostering an environment of enjoyment and creativity serves as a counterbalance to the profession's adversities.

The philosophy of this book has been laid out; it is grounded in empathy and compassion alongside the fundamental principles of reflective practice, core conditions, and a strength-based approach. Defining and describing your own philosophy for practice not only reinforces individual values and motivations but also serves as a guide to navigating the complexities of early years practice.

The narrative of this book revolves around a research inquiry into empathy within early years practice, featuring excerpts extracted from practitioners' reflective diaries and interviews. These authentic accounts of professional experiences, conveyed in the practitioners' own words, serve to underpin the messages, themes, and insights within the book. Each chapter incorporates individual and group reflective activities designed to facilitate deeper engagement with the material and to empower readers to instil empathy and compassion into every facet of their professional practice.

Key messages

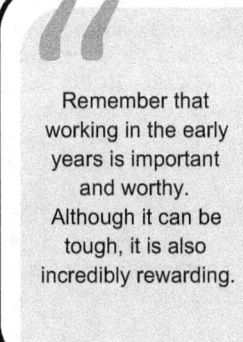
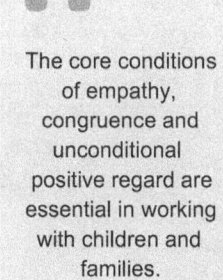
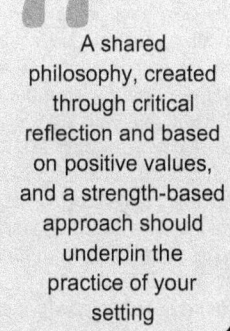

Figure 1.6 Chapter 1 key messages

References

Andreychik, M. (2019) 'Feeling your joy helps me to bear feeling your pain: Examining associations between empathy for others' positive versus negative emotions and burnout', *Personality and Individual Differences*, 137, pp. 147–156.

Argyris, C. (2002) 'Double-loop learning, teaching and research', *Academy of Management Learning & Education*, 1(2), pp. 206–218.

Ayres, D. (2013) 'Reflective practice', *Learning and Teaching Blog*, available at: https://danieljayres.blogspot.com/2013/05/reflective-practice.html (accessed 19th January 2024).

Basford, J. (2019) 'Being a graduate professional in the field of Early Childhood Education and Care: Silence, submission and subversion', *Education*, 47(7), pp. 862–875.

Bogolub, E. (2010) 'The obligation to bring about good in social work research', *Qualitative Social Work*, 9(1), pp. 9–15.

British Educational Research Association (BERA). (2024) *Ethical guidelines for educational research*, 4th edn, available at: www.bera.ac.uk/publication/ethical-guidelines-for-educational-research-2018-online#intro (accessed 29th February 2024).

Bryant, J., Ram, S., Scott, D. and Williams, C. (2023) *K-12 teachers are quitting. What would make them stay?* McKinsey and Company, available at: www.mckinsey.com/industries/education/our-insights/k-12-teachers-are-quitting-what-would-make-them-stay

Dent, G. (2021) '73% of early educators plan to leave the sector within three years', *Women's Agenda*, available at: https://womensagenda.com.au/latest/73-of-early-educators-plan-to-leave-the-sector-within-three-years/ (accessed 9th January 2024).

Eadie, P., Levickis, P., Murray, L., Page, J., Elek, C. and Church, A. (2021) 'Early childhood educators wellbeing during the COVID-19 pandemic', *Early Childhood Education Journal*, 49(5), pp. 903–913.

Edwards, C. (2019) '100 Ofsted reports – Part 1: Vision, reflection, evaluation and drive for improvement', *Foundation Stage Forum*, available at: https://eyfs.info/articles.html/leadership-and-management/100-ofsted-reports-part-1-vision-reflection-evaluation-and-drive-for-improvement-r264/#:~:text=It%20listens%20to%20staff%2C%20parents,work%20well%20as%20a%20team

Elfer, P. (2012) 'Emotion in nursery work: Work discussion as a model of critical professional reflection', *Early Years*, 32(2), pp. 129–141.

Fairchild, N. and Mikuska, E. (2021) 'Emotional labor, ordinary affects, and the early childhood education and care worker', *Gender, Work and Organization*, 28(3), pp. 1177–1190.

Feeney, S., Moravcik, E. and Nolte, S. (2022) *Who am I in the lives of children? An introduction to early years education*, 12th edn, Pearson.

Goldstein, D. (2022) 'Why you can't find child care: 100,000 workers are missing', *New York Times*, available at: www.nytimes.com/2022/10/13/us/child-care-worker-shortage.html#:~:text=The_shortage_contributing_to_the_Bureau_of_Labor_Statistics

Haux, T., Butt, S., Rezaian, M., Garwood, E., Woodbridge, H., Bhatti, S., Woods-Rogan, R., Davies, H., Bain, E. and Hunnikin, L. (2022) 'Early years recruitment, retention and business planning during the Coronavirus pandemic research report: A summary of findings', *Government Social Research*, available at: https://assets.publishing.service.gov.uk/media/62695faae90e0746cd3f0f9c/Early_years_recruitment__retention_and_business_planning_during_the_Coronavirus_pandemic.pdf

Hendy, N. (2022) 'Numbers don't add up for childcare workers or parents', *Australian Financial Review*, available at: www.afr.com/companies/infrastructure/numbers-don-t-add-up-for-childcare-workers-or-parents-20221126-p5c1gx

Hill, J. (2023) 'Too few workers leaves childcare "revolution" in peril', *FE Week*, available at: https://feweek.co.uk/too-few-workers-leaves-childcare-revolution-in-peril/ (accessed 9th January 2024).

Hodgkins, A. (2023) *Exploring early childhood practitioners' perceptions of empathic interactions with children and families*. PhD thesis, University of Worcester, available at: https://eprints.worc.ac.uk/13525/

Hodgkins, A. and Prowle, A. (2023) *Strength-based approaches with children and families*, St. Albans: Critical Publishing.

Hugman, R., Pittaway, E. and Bartolomei, L. (2011) 'When "do no harm" is not enough: The ethics of research with refugees and other vulnerable groups', *The British Journal of Social Work*, 41(7), pp. 1271–1287.

Jena-Crottet, A. (2017) 'Early childhood teachers' emotional labour', *New Zealand International Research in Early Childhood Education*, 20(2), pp. 19-33.

Lynch, A., Newlands, F. and Forrester, D. (2019) 'What does empathy sound like in social work communication? A mixed-methods study of empathy in child protection social work practice', *Child & Family Social Work*, 24(1), pp. 139-147.

Maslow, A. (1943) 'A theory of human motivation', *Psychological Review*, 50(4), pp. 370-396.

McNaughton, S. (2016) 'Developing pre-requisites for empathy: Increasing awareness of self, the body and the perspectives of others', *Teaching in Higher Education*, 21(5), pp. 501-515.

OECD. (2019) *Providing quality early childhood education and care: Results from the starting strong survey 2018*, available at: https://www.oecd.org/publications/providing-quality-early-childhood-education-and-care-301005d1-en.htm (accessed 2nd June 2023).

Osgood, J. (2010) 'Reconstructing professionalism in ECEC: The case for the "critically reflective emotional professional"', *Early Years*, 30(2), pp. 119-133.

Oxtoby, K. (2023) 'More than half of nursery staff are considering quitting the sector, research finds', *Early Years Educator*, available at: www.earlyyearseducator.co.uk/news/article/more-than-half-of-nursery-staff-are-considering-quitting-the-sector-research-finds (accessed 6th November 2023).

Rogers, C. (1957) 'The necessary and sufficient conditions of therapeutic personality change', *Journal of Consulting Psychology*, 21, pp. 95-103.

Rogers, C. (1961) *On becoming a person*, New York: Mifflin.

Schön, D. (1991) *The reflective practitioner: How professionals think in action*, London: Routledge.

Shea, S. (2019) 'Reflective supervision for social work field instructors: Lessons learned from infant mental health', *Clinical Social Work Journal*, 47(1), pp. 61-71.

Shin, M. and Recchia, S. (2023) 'Nurturing the nurturer: Enacting transformative infant-toddler teacher preparation through reflective practice', *Early Years*, 43(3), pp. 626-640.

Stern, J. (2016) *Virtuous educational research: Conversations on ethical practice*, Oxford: Peter Lang.

Teacher Active. (2024) *Five reasons why early years teaching is one of the most rewarding careers*, available at: www.teacheractive.com/media-post/five-reasons-why-early-years-teaching-is-one-of-the-most-rewarding-careers

Thorpe, K., Jansen, E., Sullivan, V., Irvine, S., McDonald, P. and The Early Years Workforce Study Team. (2020) 'Identifying predictors of retention and professional wellbeing of the early childhood education workforce in a time of change', *Journal of Educational Change*, 21(4), pp. 623-647.

Wright, B. (1999) *A history of the National nursery examination board*, London: Council for Awards in Childcare and Education.

2
Understanding empathy and compassion

> **Chapter objectives**
> - To explore the definitions and connections between empathy and compassion
> - To evaluate theories and ideas relating to empathy
> - To explore two distinct types of empathy

This chapter commences with definitions of empathy and compassion. While these two terms are often used interchangeably, they possess distinct differences. Empathy has been a subject of study across various disciplines, such as psychology, sociology, physiology, and neuroscience, resulting in diverse perceptions. Literature offers descriptions of different types of empathy, various stages of empathy, and the effects of empathy; however, a universally agreed-upon definition remains elusive. Psychologist Hoffman (2000, p. 30), who has spent his academic career exploring the development of empathy, captures the complexity of the subject, declaring, 'the more I study empathy, the more complex it becomes'.

The chapter then explores Carl Rogers' (1942) core conditions of empathy, congruence, and unconditional positive regard and how these principles manifest in early years practice. It begins by discussing the significance of empathy in interactions with children and families, followed by an introduction to the research participants' individual definitions of empathy.

The empathy research (Hodgkins, 2023) identified two main types of empathy in early years practice: cognitive empathy and affective empathy. These two types of empathy will be examined with examples from practitioners to illustrate each of the concepts. Subsequently, this will be related to early years practice with an examination of the features of an empathic early years setting.

 Reflective prompt - What are your own definitions of empathy and compassion? (We will revisit this later).

DOI: 10.4324/9781003464686-2

Defining empathy and compassion

The terms 'empathy' and 'compassion', although related, mean different things but are often mistakenly used interchangeably. In simple terms, empathy is the capacity to understand or share the feelings of others, whereas compassion is a desire to act, which is one of the consequences resulting from empathy (Maibom, 2017).

Empathy

Empathy is notoriously difficult to define; one of the greatest challenges is the lack of a common conclusive definition of what it is and how it relates to, or differs from, other similar experiences such as sympathy (Zahavi, 2017; in Maibom, 2017). Empathy is generally understood as the ability to see things from other people's points of view; to 'walk in another's shoes' (Smith, 2016). The work of psychologist Carl Rogers has brought the study of empathy into renown. Rogers (1942) was influential in exploring the concept of empathy as one of the 'necessary core conditions', along with 'congruence' and 'unconditional positive regard'; three attributes that Rogers deemed to be essential in establishing a productive therapeutic relationship between counsellor and client. Rogers (1980) described empathy as the 'sensitive ability and willingness to understand the client's thoughts, feelings and struggles from the client's point of view' (p. 85). Although primarily a counselling and therapy theory, Rogers believed that empathy is an interpersonal skill that is beneficial for anyone working with people. Although Rogers' principle of empathy is still a cornerstone of counselling and psychotherapy today, other interpretations have since developed. Researchers have formulated theories about types of empathy (Maibom, 2017), levels of empathy (Belzung, 2014) and stages of empathy (Cunico et al., 2012). The study of empathy is approached differently in various academic disciplines, as can be seen in Table 2.1.

In the empathy research project (Hodgkins, 2023), participants were asked to give their own definitions of empathy. The resulting definitions are diverse and support the idea from Hall et al. (2021) that empathy is very difficult to define because there are so many ways of

Table 2.1 Empathy approaches from distinct disciplines

Developmental psychology	Hoffman (2000) Eisenberg (2005)	The study of empathy development in childhood. Young children react to others' distress because of the way it affects them. As they grow and develop, their distress becomes less egocentric and develops into concern for the other person.
Neuroscience	Bernhardt and Singer (2012)	Emotions (pain, disgust, fear, anger, anxiety, pleasure, embarrassment, and sadness) can be 'contracted' from others through empathy.
Social Psychology	Mehrabian (1996)	Empathy is understood as 'perspective taking', a cognitive view. Tests are developed to measure empathy.

understanding it. One participant, Mel, expressed this difficulty: 'To be fair, when I was talking to others about it, it's a hard thing to describe'.

Figure 2.1 illustrates all of the definitions from the research participants.

Responses from all participants in the project have been incorporated in the word cloud in Figure 2.2. It is noticeable that the most used words to describe empathy were 'feeling', 'feelings', 'everything', 'relating', 'emotion', and 'understand'.

Reflective prompt - Which of the definitions and words in Figures 2.1 and 2.2 resonate with you? Can you explain why? How have you experienced empathy in your work with children and families?

Types of empathy

Two distinct types of empathy arose from the empathy research: cognitive and affective. Examples from participants in the research show instances of both types of empathy within the profession.

Cognitive empathy

Cognitive empathy can be defined as the capacity to understand someone else's state of mind from their perspective (Spaulding, 2017). It is an intentional process which involves the ability to 'put oneself in another's shoes' (Manassis, 2017, p. 9) and to do so without experiencing distress oneself. In this type of empathy, we use our own ideas and theories to infer how others are feeling, and we try to imagine how it must feel to be that person at that time, using imagination (Yarrow, 2015). This type of empathy requires the 'cognitive flexibility' (Decety and Lamm, 2006) to understand someone else's perspective. There were lots of examples of this in the research findings. Participants used phrases like 'imagining how he was feeling', 'trying to relate/understand', and 'thinking about why'. It was evident that this type of empathy involved making an effort to understand others' feelings. Participants were trying to put themselves in the position of the child and imagining how it would feel to be them. Here are some examples of cognitive empathy from the empathy research (Hodgkins, 2023).

Debbie, deputy manager of a day nursery, is faced with a member of staff who says that she may have been distracted that day as her Dad had been rushed to hospital. Debbie reflects,

> I said she must be feeling upset; I imagine I'd feel the same way if it was my Dad.

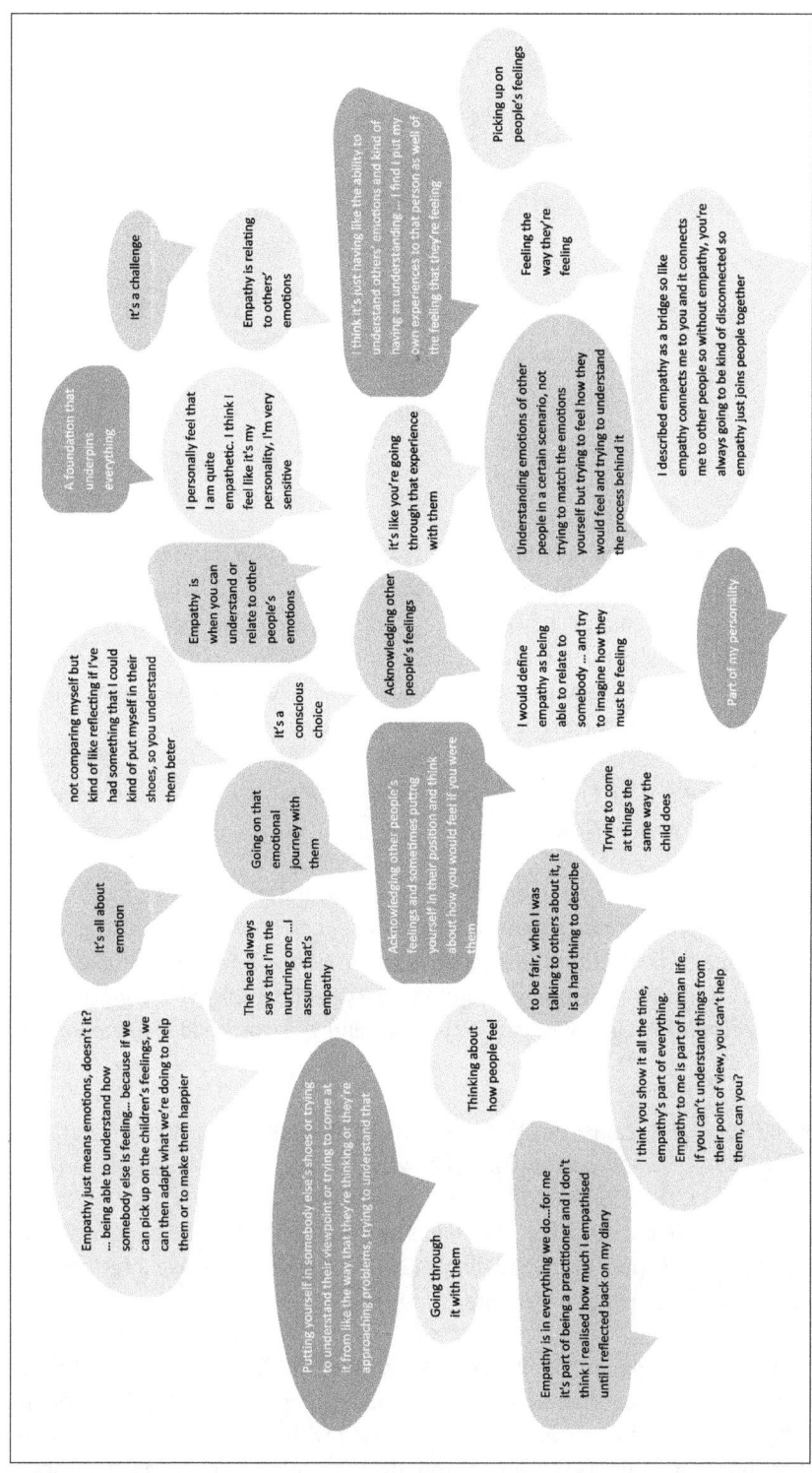

Figure 2.1 Definitions of empathy (Hodgkins, 2023)

Figure 2.2 Definitions of empathy word cloud

Here, Debbie is using her imagination to picture the situation she faces. Several reflections indicated this capability and demonstrated the creation of ideas about how other people are feeling. Some examples indicated that cognitive empathy is not always an instant understanding, and assessing and judging someone's emotion cognitively can take some time, as was seen with the use of reflective diaries. Here, George, also a deputy manager of a day nursery, describes how he reflects back on an event,

> I like to listen and get someone else's perspective, and I like to have that reflection time to think, 'Right, why are they saying this?'

Again, this describes a conscious cognitive effort to understand. The diary reflections proved to be an effective instrument in which to reflect on events and to consider the possible interpretations of others' perspectives afterwards. Another example of thinking things through after an interaction is found in Cheryl's diary. Cheryl is a learning support assistant in a reception class; after a difficult morning with the child she supports on a 1:1 basis, she says,

> I think about how confusing the world can be to them when they can't understand certain things they are being told or how to convey their emotions and feelings.

Cheryl is attempting to put herself in the child's position and to try and understand how the child must be feeling, supporting Spaulding's (2017, p. 14) view that 'we infer from another person's behaviour what his or her mental states probably are'.

Reflection appears to support cognitive empathy. Elfer (2012) researched emotion in nursery work; his research identified an emotional impact on practitioners. He recommended regular reflective conversations among staff working within early years settings, with the aim of reflecting on emotional experiences together as a team. Elfer claims that these 'work discussion groups' (p. 129) have the potential to increase empathy, as well as manage the impact of empathic interactions on practitioners.

Affective empathy

Affective empathy, in comparison, is an emotional response to another person's emotion; hence, it is often called 'emotional empathy' (Hoffman, 2000). It describes feeling the emotion with the other person, one's emotions being more akin to someone else's than one's own. Maibom (2017, p. 23) gives this example to illustrate affective empathy,

> If I am empathically sad that your cat was run over, my sadness is more appropriate to your situation – having lost a loved pet – than to my own, being a mere bystander to tragedy.

There were clear examples of affective empathy within the research. Participants described their emotional reactions in their reflective diaries and used phrases like 'going through it with them', 'you just feel it', and 'it breaks my heart'. Participants said that they were sharing the emotion of the child and feeling it themselves. Particularly at times of transition where children separate from their parent to come into the setting, practitioners feel the emotional upset of the child; several participants said that they had been very upset by this. Where cognitive empathy is a conscious decision to try to empathise, affective empathy appears to be something that is unconscious and instinctive (Belzung, 2014). In what follows, Cheryl's example of a child missing her mother is an example of affective empathy. Cheryl describes her own feeling of distress, which she portrays as having someone 'pull on her heartstrings',

> When they say, 'Oh, I miss my mom', and you just feel it . . . and it does, it pulls on your heartstrings.

George's example here demonstrates affective empathy, as George expresses that it 'breaks his heart' when a child is hurt and upset,

> Oh, bless his little heart; he hides his injuries to try and not let us see . . . . He'll show me the other limb and say, 'Look, it's absolutely fine', and we can hear it in his voice and, oh, it really breaks my heart.

According to Gallese et al. (1996), brain research suggests that the phrase 'I feel your pain' may literally be true, in affective empathy, we experience the pain of others ourselves. This explains why Cheryl and George, in the examples provided earlier, describe feeling upset with phrases like 'it pulls on my heartstrings' and 'it breaks my heart'. Affective empathy affects us personally; feeling the emotions of another person can result in 'empathic distress' (Hoffman, 2000; Grant, 2014). Researchers believe that affective empathy is important in building social relationships, but it is important to learn to manage the effects and potential personal distress. Empathic distress is discussed further in Chapter 9.

> **Individual activity**
>
> Do you think the examples in Table 2.2 describe cognitive or affective empathy or a combination of both? Complete the table, then try to add your own examples.

As explained earlier in this chapter, empathy and compassion are often confused, but compassion is an action, a result of empathy (Maibom, 2017). When we experience empathy for someone, either by imagining ourselves in their shoes (cognitive empathy) or by sharing the emotion (affective empathy), this usually motivates us to take action to help.

Compassion

Compassion underpins the building of social connections, so it is essential when building relationships with young children and for modelling compassion for others, helping children to develop compassion for each other. Lazarus (1991, p. 289) defines compassion as 'being moved by another's suffering and wanting to help'. It is a positive, active response to someone who is distressed or in need. An example of compassion is giving money to a homeless person on the street or helping someone when you can see that they are overwhelmed with too much work. Research by Lim and DeSteno (2016) suggests that we are more likely to show compassion if we have experienced adverse life experiences ourselves. The idea of the 'wounded healer' originated with Jung (1951, p. 16), who said, 'It is our own

Table 2.2 Types of empathy

Situation	Cognitive or affective?
Your friend is distraught because his girlfriend has broken up with him. While you are listening to him talk about his feelings, you feel really upset too.	
A child in your care is feeling ill and is crying. You know that when children are sick, they want to be with their parent. You try to remember what it was like when you were a sick child yourself.	
You avoid a co-worker in the staff room because she is always so negative. She brings down your mood and makes you feel miserable too.	
Your 2-year-old is scared of having his hair cut. He cried and screamed the first time you took him. Now, you feel anxious and upset every time you go too.	
A colleague has failed one of her degree assignments and is very upset. You haven't studied for many years but you know the degree is important to her, so you can imagine how she must be feeling.	

hurt that gives the measure of our power to heal'. Hence, many counsellors and therapists have experienced mental health challenges themselves, and many nurses have experienced significant illness. In a women's refuge that I recently encountered, I learned that the majority of staff and volunteers had experienced domestic abuse themselves. Going through that experience meant that they understood how women living at the refuge were feeling, and they wanted to help.

 Reflective prompt – Do you recognise the concept of the 'wounded healer' in yourself or in someone else? Do you think that by going through trauma themselves, people are in a better position to support others? Do you need to have been through something yourself to be able to truly emphasise?

The relationship between empathy and compassion

As previously discussed, compassion is the desire to help, and it develops *from* empathy. 'One must have empathy before having compassion' (Galetz, 2019, p. 453). Returning to the example of the homeless person earlier, when we feel empathy for the person, it is that empathy which results in compassion, a desire to help. Therefore, it can be said that compassion is the expression of empathy through action. Singer and Klimecki's (2014) research identified two possible reactions to empathy: compassion or empathic distress. As compassion is about taking action to help another person, it is an 'other-related emotion' leading to the motivation to help others. However, if we feel empathy and we are unable to help for some reason, this can result in emotional upset or 'empathic distress' in ourselves, which is a 'self-related emotion'. Galetz' (2019) describes the difference between empathy and compassion as the idea that empathy is about 'being one with', whereas compassion is about 'being external to'. When we empathise, we try to understand the feeling and seek common ground. When we show compassion, we feel sorry for the other person, and we try to find a solution to help them.

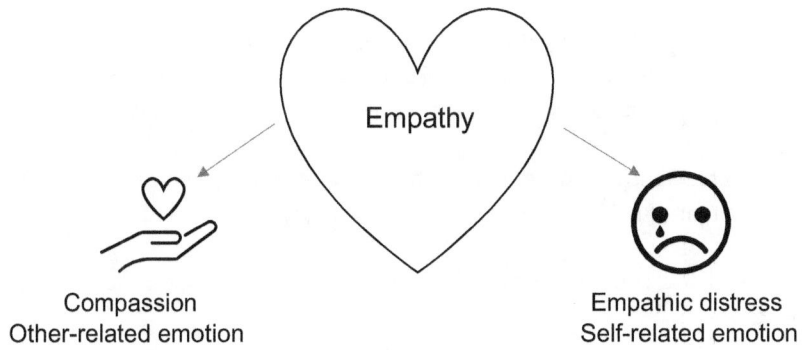

Figure 2.3 Two reactions to empathy

Empathic distress can sometimes result in acute emotional upset or even withdrawal from the situation to protect oneself from the distress. This is evidently incompatible with the empathic and compassionate care required from those working with young children. The effects of empathic distress on practitioners, and methods of managing this, are discussed in Chapter 9.

Recognising emotion in others

In order to demonstrate empathy with someone who is hurt, we first need to be able to recognise signs of hurt. Empathy requires recognition of emotion in others, active listening to the words people use, and the reading and interpretation of non-verbal signs. In early years practice, in-depth knowledge of individual children is key, so these signs are soon evident, when children have settled and built relationships with members of staff.

> **Individual activity**
>
> The following examples from the empathy research (Hodgkins, 2023) show a range of ways of recognising emotion in others. For each example, try to identify the signs that the practitioner is picking up on.

Example 1 – Aadiya describes a child coming into her pre-school class in the morning. She says,

> He'd just stand with his face against the wall because he just wanted it to swallow him up.

Example 2 – Jake describes a child displaying behaviour that is not, in itself, unusual behaviour, but which is unusual for her.

> Today I noticed F (one of the girls) had taken herself off to the mud area to sit in the trees by herself . . . . She had never done this before, and whilst she was not visibly crying or upset, this looked like a response to something.

Example 3 – Here, George is describing a child who has fallen; George had explained that this child has a fear of being given first aid. George says,

> He says, 'Look, it's absolutely fine', and we can hear it in his voice and, oh, it really breaks my heart.

In these examples, practitioners were likely to be employing their knowledge of the child and noticing both verbal and non-verbal communication.

Intuitive empathy

In the research, it became evident that some participants were sensing emotion in others without knowing how they are doing this, without any obvious verbal or non-verbal clues. In the following example, Mel appears to be able to sense how others are feeling without knowing how she is doing this, and she responds to this intuition by engaging with people to see how they are feeling and offering support. Here, she talks about interactions with her colleagues,

> I quite often know how other people are feeling, or if somebody's quieter than usual, I pick up on that really quickly. I'm always talking to people and saying, 'Are you ok? You seem a bit quiet. Is there something wrong?' . . . . If a member of staff walks in the room, I can kind of tell, and if they're having a bad day, I say 'Are you alright?' and try and talk to them and see what the problem is.

Reflective prompt: Have you ever experienced this? Have you 'sensed' emotion in someone else sub-consciously? What do you think is happening here? How can this happen?

In Mel's responses, she does not describe noticing non-verbal cues, but she does discuss having a 'sense' of what the other person is feeling. In Page and Elfer's (2013) research on emotional interactions between staff and children in a nursery, they suggest that unconscious 'ways of knowing' originate from implicit learning and sensitivity. So, it is our knowledge of the people we work with so well that allows us to pick up on subtle signs that we are not consciously aware of. In Mel's example, she makes accurate judgements based on the knowledge she has about her colleagues, and she makes subconscious decisions about how to respond. In this next example, Harriet shows that she is able to tune into a child and sense what they are feeling, which enables her to foresee what will happen next. Harriet says,

> The child knows when I'm about to leave the room, so I know they're going to be emotional.

To be able to make this statement, Harriet must have an awareness of the way the child is feeling and, consequently, how the child is likely to react when she leaves the room. This knowledge enables her to plan and prepare. Following Harriet's example, she then tries to distract the child with a toy before leaving the room, and she explains that she tries to arrange her working day so that she does not have to leave the child for longer than absolutely necessary. The anticipation of the child's emotional reaction is a very useful skill.

Claxton (2003) refers to this experience as 'intuition', which is developed over time – the idea that it is possible to 'just know' without reasoning. Intuition is the use of implicit learning and sensitivity as unconscious ways of knowing. These 'ways of knowing' include the use of knowledge that we have amassed through experience and that we use unconsciously, along with the ability to make accurate judgements and decisions without having to explain or justify them. It is evident that early years practitioners are using characteristics of intuition as in Figure 2.4. The training and qualifications that practitioners have studied produce a basis of theory and instruction that are always with us, though often not consciously. Something learned may be forgotten for a while until we experience a new situation and somehow remember what we learned. As we progress through our careers, we learn continuously through experience and through observing others. We pick up on others' practices without realising it, especially from those we see as role models. The combination of these skills and practices gives us a heightened attentiveness to the things we see and so what we understand as being a 'gut feeling' is actually based on years of implicit learning (Claxton, 2003).

Claxton refers to the perception of another person's feelings as intuition; however, Egan (2013), a counselling theorist and writer, describes the phenomenon as *advanced empathy*, 'sensing meanings of which he or she is scarcely aware' (Egan, 2013, p. 76). Egan claims that when we demonstrate advanced empathy, we have 'a conscious awareness of subtle primitive signs that serve as a way of communicating emotional states'. In the early years, this is commonplace, practitioners are tuning into children, identifying emotion, and sensing what they need without realising that what they are using is advanced empathy (Hodgkins, 2019). This is especially valuable in early years practice; it enables us to 'tune into' child and identify emotions that the child is not yet able to name.

The view in this book is that this phenomenon is an amalgamation of advanced empathy and intuition; it is *intuitive empathy* (Hodgkins, 2023). Figure 2.5 shows intuitive empathy; an amalgamation of advanced empathy and intuition which is evident in practice. The term 'intuitive empathy' encapsulates the practitioner's capacity to grasp a child's emotions through non-verbal signals, informed by their accumulated knowledge and experience, further enhanced by what is colloquially described as a 'gut feeling' (Sipman et al., 2021). This fusion of skills demonstrates a high level of intuitive empathy and emphasises practitioners' advanced understanding of a child's emotional state.

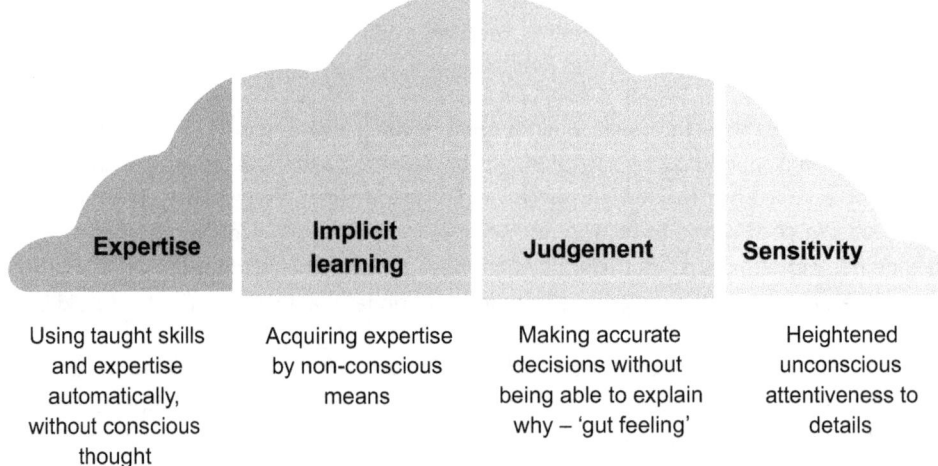

Figure 2.4 Ways of knowing, adapted from ideas by Claxton (2003)

Understanding empathy and compassion 27

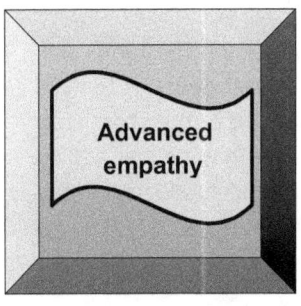
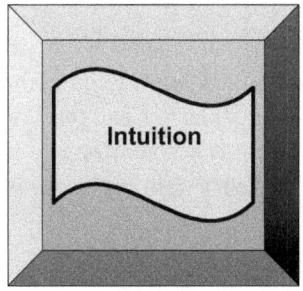
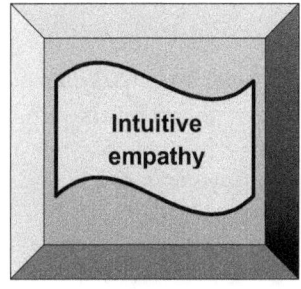

Picking up feelings recognised from body language and voice tone, sensing what is felt

(Egan, 2013)

Using knowledge and experience to unconsciously identify changes in behaviour

(Claxton, 2003; Brown, 2012)

Unconsciously using knowledge, experience and empathy to sense what is being felt, often without the other person's awareness

(Hodgkins, 2023)

Figure 2.5 Intuitive empathy (Hodgkins, 2023)

 Case study – Tony's 'gut feeling'

Tony is the manager of a wrap-around care setting which provides a breakfast club, after school club, and holiday playscheme for a large primary school. The breakfast club only has between three and six children in attendance, but the after school club caters to around 30 children. Some of the staff at the setting work at the school, but Tony has advertised for more staff. The number of applications to work at the breakfast and after school clubs has been very low; the odd hours do not suit many people's circumstances.

Tony has recently interviewed Sandy and has taken Sandy on for a month's trial. Sandy is in her 40s and she has a teaching assistant qualification, which she got ten years ago, but she only worked as a teaching assistant for a year. She has not worked for a number of years, although she has not explained why. She has good references from her old college tutor (ten years ago) and from a woman whose house she has been cleaning. Sandy is willing to work as many hours as are available.

In her first week, Sandy has worked two mornings at the breakfast club and four afternoons at the after school club. Tony has been in attendance too and has been observing Sandy's work. Sandy does everything she is asked to do; she arrives early to help set up the equipment and she follows instructions well. However, there is something that is making Tony feel uncomfortable, and he is not sure what this is. Sandy seems to be spending all of her time with the girls at the club and the girls seem very fond of her. Sandy plays with them, reads to them, and has them sitting on her lap. She doesn't seem to interact with the boys at all.

On a trip to the playground in the park opposite the school, Sandy holds hands with two of the girls. When one of the girls wants to go to the toilet, Sandy starts to head over to the toilets with her. Tony stops her and tells her that one of the other staff members will take her instead. He is not sure why he has done that; he just had an uneasy feeling and felt that he didn't want her going into the toilets alone with the child.

 Individual activity

Reflect on these points:

- Can you understand this sort of 'gut feeling'? Has it ever happened to you?
- Which of Claxton's 'ways of knowing' do you think Tony may have been using?
- Do you agree with Tony's action in the playground?
- What else do you think Tony could do?

Empathy and compassion in practice

Empathy, as we have seen, is a precursor to compassion, a skill that is essential in working with young children. Compassion is a key factor in attachment relationships. It contributes to the nurture of children into well-adjusted, compassionate adults (Taggart, 2016). Dachyshyn (2015) writes about 'heartful practice', urging the early years sector to use compassion in all interactions with children and families by always being 'heartfully present' (p. 37). Dachyshyn's description of the components of 'heartful practice' are shown in Figure 2.6.

- responding from the heart
- deep compassion and empathy
- no assumptions
- no interference or control
- allowing children to be capable and compassionate
- simple gestures and touch
- care and appreciation of self

heartful practice

Figure 2.6 Heartful practice, adapted from Dachyshyn (2015)

Table 2.3 Assessing heartful practice

Characteristic of heartful practice	Self-assessment
Responding from the heart	
Deep compassion and empathy	
No assumptions	
No interference or control	
Allowing children to be capable and compassionate	
Simple gestures and touch	
Care and appreciation of self	

 Individual activity

Look at the previous list showing the characteristics of 'heartful practice'. Try to assess how well your own practice corresponds with this list. Which are you particularly strong at? Which could you pay more attention to?

Compassionate environments

In this chapter so far, we have looked at the importance of empathy and compassion in early years practitioners. The people in the setting are the most important consideration; if your staff team is made up of empathic, compassionate people, then the children should be well cared for. However, there are other aspects of practice which can be approached with compassion, for example, the pedagogical approach and the environment. Taggart (2016) writes about 'compassionate pedagogy' which he sees as an ethical approach to practice. Taggart describes two different discourses, 'care' and 'children's rights', and suggests that compassionate pedagogy must include both. The care discourse is one that sees early years practitioners trying to replicate the parent/child relationship as much as possible and settings being made as home-like as possible. The alternative view is the 'children's rights' view, where listening to children, affording them choice, and adapting to the individual needs of each child are more important. It is clear that early years practice should include both of these components and that compassion must underpin everything. However, legislation and policy can make this challenging. In 1989, Purpel noted the influence of testing and league tables in schools and criticised schools for changing from community centres to exam factories. He called for,

> The cultivation, nourishment and development of a cultural mythos that builds on a faith in the human capacity to participate in the creation of a world of justice, compassion, caring, love and joy.
>
> (Purpel, 1989, p. 117)

Compassionate pedagogy involves the appreciation of children as capable humans who can participate in the creation of an environment based on compassion. Much of the literature about early years environments is concerned with 'enabling' children to learn, which is, of course, a vital purpose of any early years setting. Malaguzzi (1994) described three teachers of children: adults, other children, and the environment; 'the environment as the third teacher' is one of the guiding principles of the Reggio Emilia approach to early years. However, Malaguzzi also said that 'the environment should act as a kind of aquarium which reflects the ideas, ethics, attitudes and cultures of the people who live in it'. Therefore, the environment should reflect the values and attitudes of people in the setting; this creates congruence in the team.

> **Group activity**
>
> Look at some of the ideas in the previous section (Taggart, Purpel, Dachyshyn, Malaguzzi) and consider which ideas are closest to your setting's philosophy. Then organise a team discussion with the theme: *What does a compassionate early years environment look like to us?*

Bristol Early Years (2024) suggest that 'when you step into a room, your brain takes in lots of information about the physical environment'. Figure 2.7 provides some prompts for your discussion.

Brainstorm ideas and write/draw your thoughts and ideas as a group, then start creating an action plan (to be revisited in later chapters).

Chapter summary

This chapter has explored the concepts of empathy and compassion. Empathy, as we have seen, is difficult to define by writers and theorists and also by the participants in the empathy study discussed in this book. Although empathy and compassion are sometimes used interchangeably, compassion is, in fact, a result of empathy. A straightforward interpretation of empathy understood by many is one based on Rogers' writing; it is a 'sensitive ability and willingness to understand the client's thoughts, feelings and struggles from the client's point of view' (Rogers, 1980, p. 85). However, we have seen in this chapter that it is much more than that. Two distinct types of empathy have been discussed: cognitive and affective empathy, which are different but which have been observed in early years practitioners in the empathy study.

The first step in practising empathy is to recognise the emotions of others; this is something that early years practitioners are usually skilled at. We have also looked at advanced empathy and intuitive empathy, where empathic understanding is unconsciously felt. Excerpts from the empathy research have demonstrated these skills in practice.

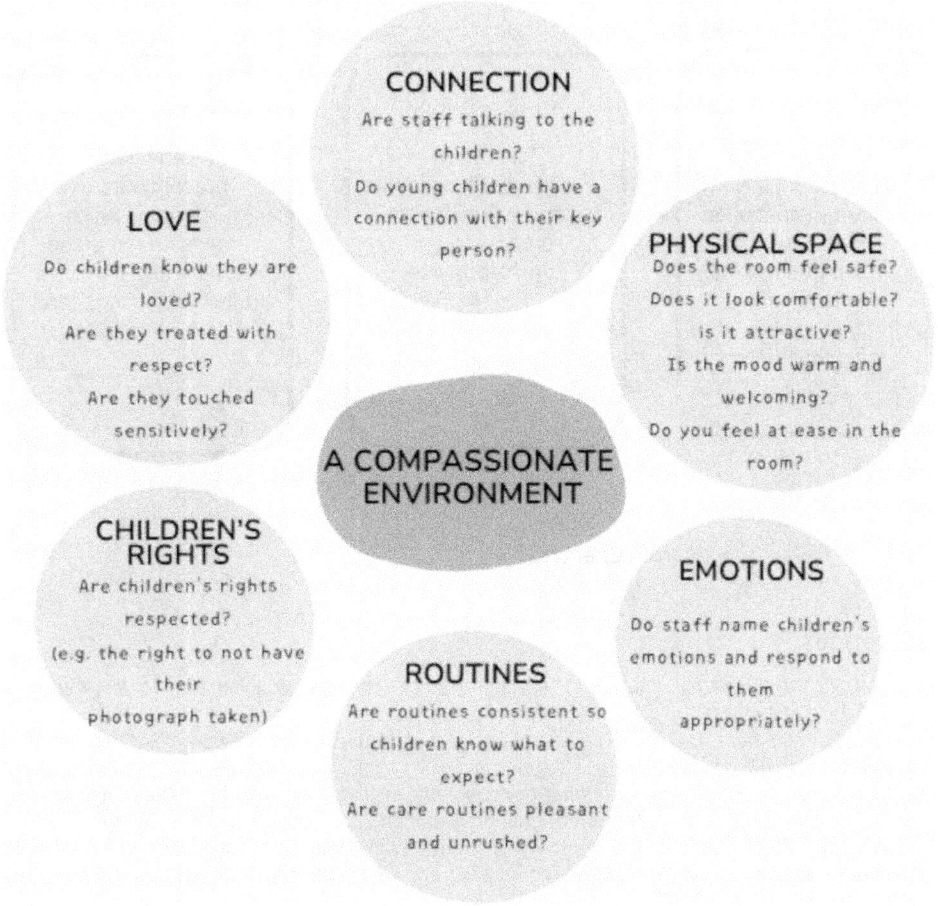

CONNECTION
Are staff talking to the children?
Do young children have a connection with their key person?

LOVE
Do children know they are loved?
Are they treated with respect?
Are they touched sensitively?

PHYSICAL SPACE
Does the room feel safe?
Does it look comfortable?
Is it attractive?
Is the mood warm and welcoming?
Do you feel at ease in the room?

A COMPASSIONATE ENVIRONMENT

CHILDREN'S RIGHTS
Are children's rights respected?
(e.g. the right to not have their photograph taken)

ROUTINES
Are routines consistent so children know what to expect?
Are care routines pleasant and unrushed?

EMOTIONS
Do staff name children's emotions and respond to them appropriately?

Figure 2.7 What does a compassionate environment look like to us?

The chapter provided some views on compassion in practice, including compassionate pedagogy, compassionate environments, and heartful practice (Dachyshyn, 2015). Practitioners who are empathic and who feel and demonstrate compassion within their practice will be aware of children's feelings and will want to act to make things better for them. When this is the underpinning ethos of an early years setting, children feel nurtured and secure.

Reflective prompt - At the beginning of this chapter, you were asked for your own definition of empathy and compassion? Can you add anything to that definition now, after reading the chapter so far?

Key messages

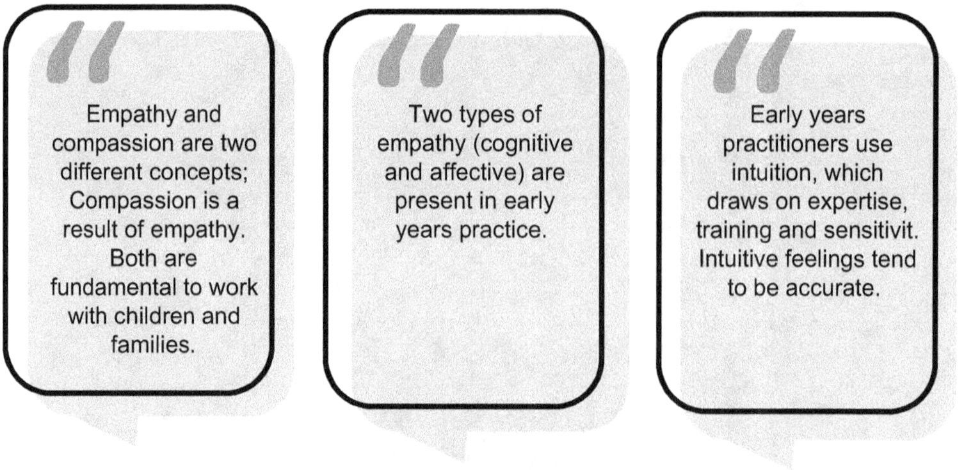

> Empathy and compassion are two different concepts; Compassion is a result of empathy. Both are fundamental to work with children and families.

> Two types of empathy (cognitive and affective) are present in early years practice.

> Early years practitioners use intuition, which draws on expertise, training and sensitivit. Intuitive feelings tend to be accurate.

Figure 2.8 Key messages from Chapter 2

References

Belzung, C. (2014) 'Empathy', *Journal for Perspectives of Economic, Political, and Social Integration*, 19(1-2), pp. 177-191.

Bernhardt, B. and Singer, T. (2012) 'The neural bases of empathy', *Annual Review of Neuroscience*, 35, pp. 1-23.

Bristol Early Years. (2024) *The emotional environment*, available at: www.bristolearlyyears.org.uk/early-learning/birth-to-three/the-emotional-environment/ (accessed 7th March 2024).

Claxton, G. (2003) 'Chapter 2: The anatomy of intuition', in Atkinson, T. and Claxton, G. (eds) *The intuitive practitioner: On the value of not always knowing what one is doing*, Maidenhead: Open University Press, pp. 32-52.

Cunico, L., Sartori, R., Marognolli, O. and Meneghini, A. (2012) 'Developing empathy in nursing students: A cohort longitudinal study', *Journal of Clinical Nursing*, 21, pp. 2016-2025.

Dachyshyn, D. M. (2015) 'Being mindful, heartful, and ecological in early years care and education', *Contemporary Issues in Early Childhood*, 16(1), pp. 32-41.

Decety, J. and Lamm, C. (2006) 'Human empathy through the lens of social neuroscience', *Scientific World Journal*, 6, pp. 1146-1163.

Egan, G. (2013) *The skilled helper: A problem-management and opportunity-development approach to helping*, 10th edn, CA: Brooks/Cole, Cengage Learning.

Eisenberg, N. (2005) 'The development of empathy-related responding', in Carlo, G. and Edwards, C. P. (eds) *Moral development through the lifespan: Theory, research, and application: The 51st Nebraska on motivation*, Lincoln, NE: University of Nebraska Press, pp. 73-117.

Elfer, P. (2012) 'Emotion in nursery work: Work discussion as a model of critical professional reflection', *Early Years*, 32(2), pp. 129-141.

Galetz, E. (2019) 'The empathy-compassion matrix: Using a comparison concept analysis to identify care components', *Nursing Forum*, 54(3), pp. 448-454.

Gallese, V., Eadiga, L., Fogassi, L. and Rizzolatti, G. (1996) 'Action recognition in the premotor cortex', *Brain*, 19, pp. 593-609.

Grant, L. (2014) 'Hearts and minds: Aspects of empathy and wellbeing in social work students', *Social Work Education*, 33(3), pp. 338-352.

Hall, J., Schwartz, R. and Duong, F. (2021) 'How do laypeople define empathy?', *Journal of Social Psychology*, 161(1), pp. 5-24.

Hodgkins, A. (2019) 'Advanced empathy in the early years – a risky strength?', *NZ International Research in Early Childhood Education Journal*, 22(1), pp. 46–58.

Hodgkins, A. (2023) *Exploring early childhood practitioners' perceptions of empathic interactions with children and families*. PhD thesis, University of Worcester, available at: https://eprints.worc.ac.uk/13525/

Hoffman, M. (2000) *Empathy and moral development*, New York: Cambridge University Press.

Jung, C. (1951) *Fundamental questions of psychotherapy*, Princeton, NJ: Princeton University Press.

Lazarus, R. S. (1991) *Emotion and adaptation*, Oxford: Oxford University Press.

Lim, D. and DeSteno, D. (2016) 'Suffering and compassion: The links among adverse life experiences, empathy, compassion, and prosocial behavior', *Emotion (Washington, D.C.)*, 16(2), pp. 175–182.

Maibom, H. (2017) *The Routledge handbook of philosophy of empathy*, New York: Routledge.

Malaguzzi, L. (1994) 'Your image of the child: Where teaching begins', *Childcare Information Exchange*, 96, pp. 52–56.

Manassis, K. (2017) *Developing empathy: A biopsychosocial approach to understanding compassion for therapists and parents*, London: Routledge.

Mehrabian, A. (1996) 'Relations among political attitudes, personality, and psychopathology assessed with new measures of libertarianism and conservatism', *Basic and Applied Social Psychology*, 18(4), pp. 469–491.

Page, J. and Elfer, P. (2013) 'The emotional complexity of attachment interactions in nursery', *European Early Childhood Education Research Journal*, 21(4), pp. 553–567.

Purpel, D. (1989) *The moral and spiritual crisis in education*, New York: Peter Lang.

Rogers, C. (1942) *Counselling and psychotherapy*, Cambridge, MA: Riverside Press.

Rogers, C. (1980) *A way of being*, Boston: Houghton Mifflin.

Singer, T. and Klimecki, O. (2014) 'Empathy and compassion', *Current Biology*, 24(18), pp. 875–878.

Sipman, G., Martens, R., Tholke, J. and McKenny, S. (2021) 'Professional development focused on intuition can enhance teacher pedagogical tact', *Teaching and Teacher Education*, 106, pp. 1–17.

Smith, F. (2016) 'Walking in another's shoes and getting blisters: A personal account of the blessing and curse of intense empathy', *Advanced Development Journal*, 15, pp. 96–107.

Spaulding, S. (2017) 'Chapter 3: Cognitive empathy', in Maibom, H. (ed) *The Routledge handbook of philosophy of empathy*, New York: Routledge, pp. 33–43.

Taggart, G. (2016) 'Compassionate pedagogy: The ethics of care in early childhood professionalism', *European Early Childhood Education Research Journal*, 24(2), pp. 173–185.

Yarrow, A. (2015) 'What we feel and what we do: Emotional capital in early childhood work', *Early Years*, 35(4), pp. 351–365.

Zahavi, D. (2017) 'Chapter 3: Phenomenology, empathy and mind reading', in Maibom, H. (ed) *The Routledge handbook of philosophy of empathy*, New York: Routledge, pp. 33–43.

3
Building empathic relationships with young children

Chapter objectives

- To analyse the skills and qualities required for working with young children
- To evaluate the importance of practitioner-child relationships
- To discuss empathy and compassion in attachment and transitions
- To debate theories of 'professional love', touch, and professional boundaries in practitioner-child relationships

This chapter begins with a discussion of the qualities and skills required to work with young children. A range of views about what constitutes the 'right kind of person' for the role are examined. In this chapter, the significance of practitioner-child relationships is emphasised, as these relationships are fundamental to the care and education of young children. In an early years setting, no factor, i.e. fabulous resources and great planning, is as important as the people working there. Human relationships which encompass empathy and compassion are of the utmost importance for young children.

Theories of attachment are outlined, and an examination of the needs of children who are not securely attached. Transitions can be difficult for children and their parents/carers; examples from the empathy research outline the challenges for practitioners working with children experiencing transitions from home to nursery.

When discussing close relationships with children, questions about touch, boundaries, and safeguarding are often debated. These issues are analysed in the chapter, culminating in an appreciation of Page's (2011, 2018) 'professional love'.

Skills and qualities

Working with children in early years, teaching, nursing, and other care occupations is perceived as 'vocational' work, the expectation being that people will enter the profession because of the sort of person they are, the sort of person who cares and wants to make a difference (Atkinson and Claxton, 2000). Colley (2006) conducted research with early years students and found that the students identified 'being kind and loving, warm and friendly, gentle and affectionate' (p. 25) as being essential qualities for the profession. Colley (2006, p. 25) suggested that the image of the 'perfectly sensitive and gentle nursery nurse' is one that has been shaped by the social conditioning of girls in the home and reinforced through training for caring roles. Early years work is of relatively low status and is poorly paid, with many qualified practitioners earning minimum wage, hence the view that people work for personal satisfaction rather than monetary reward (Erdiller and Dogan, 2015). This could be a way of justifying low-paid employment (Jovanovic, 2013). The skills that are utilised by early years practitioners are often invisible to those outside the profession, and this predominantly female profession is, therefore, a victim of gendered pay inequality (Findlay et al., 2009, p. 422). It is argued that one such unnoticed skill is likely to be empathy.

In the UK today, it appears that some skills are valued more highly than others, and some are not seen as skills at all but as part of the natural mothering instinct of the worker (Noddings, 2013; Findlay et al., 2009). There is evidence that even early years practitioners value some skills, for example, educational activities, above physical care, such as nappy changing and feeding, suggesting a belief that only the teaching/pedagogy aspect of the job is worthy. There is a fundamental assumption that 'mothering' skills are understood to be innate, as opposed to pedagogical skills, which are learnt and valuable (Findlay et al., 2009; Moyles, 2010). This echoes Solvason and Webb's (2023) assertion that practitioners have traditionally been perceived as 'less than' (p. 2) their qualified teacher colleagues. The assumption that working with young children is instinctual and only requires a caring disposition is strongly contested, as is the assumption that the play-based curriculum in early years settings only requires adults to supervise them. This is despite a wealth of research evidence to the contrary, for example, the EPPE (Effective Provision of Preschool Education) study (Sylva et al., 2010), which established a link between higher qualifications and training of staff and increased progress by children.

Since the publication of the EPPE report, a graduate-led early years workforce has been accepted as essential to improving the quality of early years provision in the UK (Henshall et al., 2018). In the study by Henshall et al. (2018), who interviewed highly qualified early years staff, practitioners saw themselves as leaders who were able to bring about change in the sector, yet they also prized the emotional qualities, including empathy, which they saw as being an important aspect of the early years practitioner role. Basford's (2019) research, which examined the views of early years graduate professionals, corresponds with this view, finding tension between the two constructs of the maternal caring practitioner and the highly trained professional.

Being the 'right kind of person' is often seen as being as important (or more important) than qualifications and skills (Colley, 2006). A study by Tietze et al. (1996), uses this description of the ideal early years worker, '*she* should display sensitivity, gentleness, enthusiasm, effort, and enjoy contact with children' (p. 452). The gendered language in this description

Figure 3.1 Conflicting constructs. Images from FreePik

substantiates the unhelpful stereotype in the literature that women are 'better biologically equipped to demonstrate altruism and self-sacrifice' (Jovanovic, 2013, p. 529).

But where does this leave men who work in the early years? These gendered beliefs create difficulties for men because being caring and nurturing are assumed to be female virtues, which is clearly incorrect. This gendered perception undervalues the profession and 'underscores the need for a more progressive and inclusive understanding of caregiving roles in society' (Hodgkins, 2023, p. 36). The subject of practitioners' sex and gender is discussed further in Chapter 5.

 Reflective prompt - Write down the skills and qualities that you believe to be important in early years practitioners. Reflect on which of these are personal qualities and which are skills which can be learned. Consider which of these are stereotypically 'female' skills and qualities. Assess your own skills and qualities against the list.

Practitioner-child relationships

Having a relationship with someone we trust and can rely on is a basic human need for everyone. As previously noted, there is evidence that relationships in early childhood affect relationships in later life. Xia et al.'s (2018) research with 10,000 participants attested that young people who were raised in a positive family climate with effective parenting are more likely to have healthy romantic relationships. There is also compelling evidence to show that adverse childhood experiences can have devastating effects on children in later life, particularly on their mental health (see, for example, Angelakis and Gooding, 2021). Research by Bussemakers and Denessen (2024) established support from adults as a protective factor for children from disadvantaged backgrounds, mitigating some of the negative outcomes of adversity. Elfer et al. (2003) stress the importance of relationships with adults outside the child's family, 'even the youngest children need special kinds of relationships when they are cared for away from their parents to "set them up" for life'. Such a relationship begins on the child's first day in a childcare setting.

Attachment and transitions

One of the foremost responsibilities of an early years practitioner is to build secure attachments with young children and to guide them through transitions. A transition for a young child is a process, a change, which can be environmental or emotional, such as the transition from home to an early years setting or from nursery to school (Seaman and Giles, 2021). Transitions from one room to another within a setting can be just as significant for a young child as transitions from one carer to another or even from one part of the day to another (Klette and Killén, 2019). Children are particularly vulnerable at times of transition, with most feeling a degree of anxiety and insecurity (Early Education, 2021); therefore, empathy and compassion are crucial in this process (Ainsworth et al., 1978). Research by Datler et al. (2010) describes the intensity of a child's emotions during this critical time. During their research, they observed,

> how hard and disturbing it is to be confronted so intimately with the primitive and often catastrophic emotions of very young children during their process of transition from home care to out-of-home care.
>
> (p. 82)

In early years settings, transitions should be managed sensitively, with a partnership between the child, the child's family, and practitioners, all working together to provide as smooth a changeover as possible. The EYFS guidance (DfE, 2023) advocates a key person system, where each child has a named worker who builds a relationship with the child and family and who is responsible for ensuring that the child's needs are met. Nevertheless, because of staff rota systems and inevitable staff changes, young children should have secure relationships with all caregivers within the setting, as their key worker is unlikely to always be there (Jarvis, 2020). The key person is a crucial link between home and the care setting and is 'vital in providing reassurance and creating close, supportive, ongoing relationships with families' (Early Education, 2021, p. 17). The birth to 5 guidance published by Early Education (2021) also stresses the importance to the child of feeling 'known'. Feeling known, and having confidence in the fact that the people around you know about who you are, your characteristics and your needs is a basic human need (Purvanova, 2013); therefore, information sharing and partnership with families is crucial during times of transition.

In some settings, children are able to choose their own key person, and staff observe the child and determine who they feel comfortable with and who they are drawn to (Rawstrone, 2009). This can be very positive and can help the attachment between child and carer develop more quickly and more effectively. In the empathy research, Andrea reflected on this,

> To build a relationship they have to be secure with you.... I think all children find their adult in one way or another in the setting. A lot of children do seem to have

a preference, and I think it's quite difficult if you know how to work with a child but someone else doesn't and they try and deal with that child.

(Andrea)

Since the seminal work by Bowlby (1969) on attachment, it has been widely accepted that a caring relationship with a consistent person who cares and is able to meet the baby or young child's needs is essential (Elfer, 2015). Research by Ainsworth et al. (1978) studied attachments and identified three types: *avoidant, resistant,* and *securely attached*. The study illustrates the way that children who are securely attached to a caregiver can explore their environment confidently, knowing that their *secure base* will be there if they need to return to it for comfort and security. Table 3.1 explains each attachment type and the likely needs of the children affected.

Table 3.1 Attachment types

Attachment type	Characteristics	Child's needs in the setting
Secure Attachment	The caregiver has been sensitive to their signals and responds sensitively to their needs. • The most prevalent attachment type. • Infants explore their environment, using their attachment figure as a safe base. • Moderate separation anxiety and stranger anxiety. • Confident that their attachment figure will meet their needs. • Easily soothed by the attachment figure when upset.	A secure attachment figure within the setting. Respond to children's needs. Soothe children in distress. Learn to read and respond to children's cues. Spend time together. Positive physical contact. Play with children.
Insecure avoidant attachment	Caused by insensitive caregivers who ignore their emotional needs. • Unconcerned with the attachment figure is not there. • Avoids contact with everyone, with no preference for a particular person. • Very independent. • Emotionally distant.	As for securely attached children PLUS: Help children to express their emotions. Nurture and reassure the child. Take care of hurt, however minor. Spend time trying to understand them. Encourage them to accept reassurance when distressed.

(Continued)

Table 3.1 (Continued)

Attachment type	Characteristics	Child's needs in the setting
Insecure ambivalent/ resistant	Caused by inconsistent responses to their emotional needs from the caregiver; sometimes sensitive, sometimes neglectful. • Clingy, unwilling to explore. • Extremely distressed when left alone by their attachment figure. • Scared of strangers. • Pleased to see their attachment figure when she/he returns but may show anger. • Difficult to soothe when distressed.	As for securely attached children PLUS: Settling-in period will need to be longer. Gentle gradual introductions to new places and people. Consistent physical and emotional soothing. Find things that feel good to the child, such as attachment objects.
Disorganised attachment (fearful avoidant)	Caused by erratic, extreme behaviour by a caregiver. Often seen in high-risk families with multiple adversities (alcohol abuse, criminal behaviour, untreated mental illness, trauma, or abuse). • Depressed and angry or completely unresponsive. • Very confused about how to have his/her needs met. • May avoid eye contact. • May scream endlessly to try to engage an adult. • Show conflicting actions, such as seeking attention and then rejecting it.	As for securely attached children PLUS: Help the child learn to self-soothe. Try to build self-confidence/ self-esteem. Create an atmosphere of safety. Try not to interrupt their space. These children need professional help.

Reflection prompt – Do you recognise any of the attachment problems in Table 3.1? Reflect on the children you work/have worked with and the support that you have provided.

Empathy and compassion are essential skills which enable interpretation of the non-verbal communication signals of the child (Eisenberg et al., 1991) and help children build secure attachments. Although the early work by Bowlby (1969) and Ainsworth et al. (1978) advocated the importance of the attachment between mother and child, later research by Gopnik et al. (1999) established that young children can form multiple attachments from birth, including with other family members and caregivers in early years settings. Two studies by Macagno and Molina (2020) examine the development between young children and their key workers in early years settings. Their results suggest a decrease in *avoidant* and *resistant* behaviours over time but no increase in *secure attachment*. However, the increase in *non-distressed* children indicates an increase in children's feelings of security over time. Macagno and Molina (2020) describe non-distressed behaviours as 'an indicator of positive adaptation' (p. 359). The research was conducted with young children between the ages of four months and three years, a crucial stage in children's emotional development.

Current research into neuroscience reinforces this view, the first 1001 days of a child's life (from conception to a child's second birthday) having been identified as a critical time for the development of emotional and mental health. The Wave Trust report (2014) reports of the first 1001 days:

> Ensuring that the brain achieves its optimal development, and nurturing during this peak period of growth, is vitally important and enables babies to have the best start in life . . . it is imperative that how children are raised is guided and influenced by this principle and evidence.
>
> (p. 5)

Several studies in the early 21st century (see, for example, Jarvis, 2020 and Conkbayir, 2021) have reported abnormally high levels of cortisol, the stress hormone, in babies and young children who spend long days in daycare settings (Jarvis, 2020). Excess stress, for babies and young children living with adversity, can result in a state of toxic stress which can impact growth, behaviour, and education and can have an impact on the school and even into adulthood (Kring, 2018). Such studies, to some extent, support Bowlby's (1969) view that young children should ideally be cared for at home for the sake of their emotional health, although this is not always possible. In most economically developed countries today, a lack of flexibility in working conditions means that if women want a career, then they cannot take extended time away from work to care for their children at home (White, 2022). Figure 3.2 illustrates levels of stress in babies.

The evidence calls for prioritising security in relationships between young children and caregivers. In most industrialised countries today, the majority of children spend some time in childcare settings; the statistics are unsurprisingly similar. In the UK, the government's estimate that 62% of children under four years of age attend early years settings (DfE, 2022). The United States also had 62.3% of children attending kindergarten or other childcare (Kolmar, 2023). In Australia, 61.5% of children attend childcare centres (Australian Government, 2023), but this does not include those in home-based childcare. The majority of these children are cared for every day by professionals, hence the necessity for attachments with young children based on 'warmth, affection and responsive care' (Conkbayir, 2021, p. 75). Research by Page and Elfer (2013) into the attachment interactions of early years practitioners and young children discusses the role of empathy in

  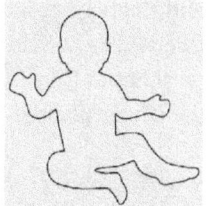

| **Positive stress** Brief increases in heart rate and levels of stress hormone. | **Tolerable stress** Serious but temporary stress response, protected by supportive relationships. | **Toxic stress** Prolonged activation of stress response systems in the absence of protective relationships. |

Figure 3.2 Effects of stress on babies (based on Kring, 2018)

building these emotional attachments, which are said to be emotionally demanding and complex for practitioners.

Participants in the empathy study saw building attachments with children and supporting them through transitions as important aspects of their role, and their diary entries often included reflections on this, as in these examples,

I reassured her that Mommy was coming back soon. (Cheryl)
She was struggling with understanding why people were going. I feel she may have felt a loss of attachment . . . being 'left'. (Harriet)
The child was more 'prepared' on Wednesday, more aware of what will happen, and that I am there to comfort her and for support. (Harriet)

Elfer and Dearnley's (2007) assertion that 'distress in children is stressful and many practitioners may feel anxious about children being separated from their families for long periods' (p. 69) seems accurate in relation to this study. There were some instances of children's distress having a significant emotional effect on practitioners. Mel's response is one example,

> If there's a child who's really struggling with separation from their parents and they're really upset, it used to get to me a lot, and I'd, you know, get really upset about it.

This reflects Datler et al.'s (2010) research in nurseries, which recognises the challenges in coping with 'the primitive and often catastrophic emotions of very young children' (p. 82). Examples from the participants describing their support for children who were upset by the transition from home to nursery or school were common, and this was clearly something that was significant and sometimes emotionally difficult, particularly for two participants,

Harriet and Cheryl. These participants gave particularly emotive examples in their diaries and interviews. They described times when they displayed empathy in their interactions with children at times of transition. Cheryl, writing in her diary about supporting a child with specific learning needs, noted,

> His needs come first, and that is my job to be there for him and to support. To him, I am that familiar and secure base that he needs when he cannot express his emotions.

Cheryl goes on to say, in a subsequent diary entry,

> He can lash out at or scream at me. I completely understand that this is due to frustration and the fact that he cannot convey his emotions.

Cheryl's example of practice corroborates Page and Elfer's (2013) assertion that practitioners prioritise the emotions of the child over their own emotions, and that this is instinctive, based on their relationship with the child. Cheryl presents as understanding the child's behaviour; she works with the child on a one-to-one basis, and the relationship they have developed means that she knows the child and his needs. Cheryl understands the child and, rather than being upset at 'being screamed at' (Cheryl's words), she prioritises his need to express his frustration over her own feelings. She understands the behaviour of the child because she knows him so well as an individual.

Individualised care

The 'unique child' (DfE, 2023) is a principle of EY practice, and it requires practitioners to demonstrate empathy and compassion. Knowing each individual child is essential; it is through this knowledge that practitioners learn to recognise emotion and pre-empt behaviour. As we have seen in the previous chapter, early years practitioners are skilled at picking up on children's non-verbal clues and using their knowledge of individual children to identify and interpret their emotions. Development of the relationship between keyworker and child is crucial here. The guidance (DfE, 2023) produced for practitioners working with children aged from birth to 5 years stresses the importance of children of feeling 'known' (Early Education, 2021). It was evident across the empathy research that practitioners know the children they work with well. Aadiya, for example, uses this phrase in her very first diary entry,

> I know this because I know my children.

Aadiya had been discussing the return of children to her reception class following the last Covid-19 lockdown, and she was able to anticipate how they would be feeling as she knew them well. Jake, who manages a preschool centre explains his view,

> The key is knowing when a child needs you and when they do not . . . . We know all the children, we see them all the time, so we can pick up when their behaviour is slightly different.

Building empathic relationships with young children 43

Cheryl gives a further example of knowing a child well,

> I was quite worried about this child as I knew that the emotion he was displaying was out of character for him.

Carl Rogers (1951, p. 17) famously once said, 'powerful is our need to be known, really known by ourselves and others, even if only for a moment'. Purvanova's (2013) contention that feeling 'known' is a basic human need supports the importance given to this in participants' comments, of which there were many examples. This knowledge of the individual child seems to be fundamental to being able to more effectively pick up on signs empathetically. Page and Elfer (2013) believe that the practitioner's relationship with, and knowledge of, the child is of the utmost importance. Their research, an intensive case study of one nursery, maintained that the consequence of this relationship is the enhanced prioritising of the child's emotions over those of the practitioners. Cheryl's descriptions of her relationship with her key child portray this view. In her diary, she describes getting to know the child she has started working with,

> I need to be mindful when he becomes overwhelmed and also sensitive to his feelings and needs. Reassurance appears to be working.

Then, in a later entry, Cheryl demonstrates her understanding of the child's needs,

> It is hard for the child to say how he is feeling . . . the child's understanding is limited. I feel, as his key person, I know when he is having a difficult day by some of the behaviours he displays.

 Individual Activity

Carry out a narrative observation of a child in your care, focussing on the child's emotions. How easy was it to 'tune into' the emotions of the child? Do you think you were using empathy? How do you know?

 Case study – Cayden

Cayden is three years old and has just started attending the preschool where you work. Cayden has a social worker and a 'child in need' plan, so you know a little about his background. Cayden's father is currently in prison for a drug offence. His mother has three other children, all older than Cayden, and she is known to be an alcoholic with mental health needs. Cayden has been cared for by many different people so far, an aunt and various friends and neighbours of his mother. When his mother is well and sober, she enjoys looking after him, and she understands how to meet his needs. However, when her depression is severe, and her drinking is in control of her life, she neglects Cayden and often passes him to someone else to look after.

In Cayden's first week at preschool, he often appears to be sad and angry. His keyworker has been working hard to try and build an attachment with him, but his behaviour is inconsistent. At times, he seems to want the keyworker's attention, sitting next to her and following her around the room. At other times, he physically pushes her away and shouts at her. The keyworker is focussing on giving consistent messages and spending as much time as possible with him so she can build this crucial relationship.

 Individual activity

Read the case study of Cayden and consider the following questions:

- Could Cayden have an attachment disorder? Why do you think this?
- How do you think Cayden may be feeling?
- Do you think the keyworker has the right ideas about what to prioritise?
- What else could the preschool staff do to help Cayden?

Professional love

The discussion of close practitioner-child relationships naturally leads us to the consideration of 'professional love', as defined by Page (2018). Early years practice is unique in that practitioners are expected to be professional educators but also loving, caring people. This has led to all sorts of issues with the professionalisation of the workforce, but the profession does require both sets of skills, 'using the word love should not diminish the early childhood education profession's identity' (Rouse and Hadley, 2018, p. 170). Fletcher (1958, p. 118, in Cousins, 2017) noted over half a century ago that,

> Nursery school teachers love children. They always have and they always will. But, for a long time we have tried . . . to keep away from using the word 'love' because it has led to a confusion of meanings.

Page's (2011) original research aimed to redress the balance between anxiety around potential allegations of abuse and expressions of love and care. The research was conducted with the mothers of young children attending a day nursery. The aim of the research was to examine the 'love' that early years practitioners have for the children in their care. The research findings indicated that parents overwhelmingly did want nursery practitioners to love their children. The subject of professional love is complex and can be controversial for several reasons.

Parents' views – Some practitioners are concerned that parents may feel threatened by the love between a practitioner and child. In fact, there have been instances of parents complaining about practitioners' use of the word 'love' with their child (Anonymous, 2011). This may be connected to parental guilt or insecure attachments (Page, 2011); however, Page's work demonstrates that the majority of parents want their children to be loved by their day carers.

Language – As the previous example (Anonymous, 2011) from an online forum, language is powerful, so choosing the right words is important. The word 'love' is a powerful one with many different meanings (the ancient Greeks identified eight main types and many others). Some early years settings discourage the word 'love' and instruct practitioners to respond to a child's 'I love you', with a lesser sentiment (for example, 'and I love being with all of you children too'). However, it is important to consider the potential impact of language on the child's perception of expressing affection and on their self-esteem.

Safeguarding – Child protection/safeguarding is, of course, of paramount importance in early years practice. Piper and Smith (2003) suggest that there is something of a 'moral panic' in the profession and that practitioners are anxious about being falsely accused of misconduct or abuse by showing physical affection towards children. This is understandable; however, showing affection is so important that it should not be denied by the children in our care. As long as safeguarding processes and policies are in place and training is updated regularly, there is no need for this worry to prevent us from showing love and affection.

Boundaries – It is useful to have agreed boundaries within a setting to make sure that practitioners are supported and confident in what is and is not acceptable. For example, a boundary might be stating that hugging a child is fine but not kissing a child on the lips. It could be that in one setting, it is decided to offer a hug first and then do so only when the child says yes. Boundaries can help to protect everyone, but they can also be fluid and adapted to meet the emotional needs of the children.

Touch

The value of touch when interacting with children is recognised by many (for example, Cousins, 2017; Svinth, 2018; Cekaite and Bergnehr, 2018). Touch is important for children's wellbeing and is one of the first experiences that help babies learn about affection. As Cousins (2017) stresses, touch is important in building self-confidence and a sense of self-worth. In Gerhardt's (2015) influential book 'why love matters', she argues that touch is crucial to learning and that 'being lovingly held is the greatest spur to development' (p. 40). Touch conveys safety and acceptance for babies and young children unable to communicate verbally. Being touched is a human right, but touching the children in our care can be a source of worry in some settings due to the anxiety surrounding abuse. Professor McGlone from the Fit and Healthy Childhood All-Party Parliamentary Group says,

> My view is that **not** touching children is a form of abuse ... touch is a necessity as much as food. What we are doing is removing an essential experience for young children.
> (cited in Goddard, 2020)

Page's later work (2018) suggested that practitioners' use of touch was mostly intuitive, as there is, then, a distinct lack of 'clarity, guidance, definitional standards' of love and affection in the early years.

> **Group activity**
>
> Discuss the ideas of professional love, language, and touch as a group. Do you all have similar views about this? If not, it would be useful to have a conversation about the issues involved in this debate. How do you share your views on professional love with parents/families? Together, devise a statement or policy which includes guidelines regarding 'love' and touch within your setting.

Chapter summary

This chapter has focussed on the relationships between practitioners and young children. It is clear that these relationships can have long-lasting effects on children as they grow to adulthood, so the quality of these relationships is crucial. The skills and qualities that practitioners need in order to create these relationships have been examined.

Secure relationships between practitioners and young children are essential. At times of transition, children are particularly vulnerable to upset; therefore, building a close attachment with a person in the setting is of the utmost importance for a child. Empathy and compassion are the keys to 'tuning into' the child and providing security; practitioners' voices taken from the empathy research show how this is exhibited in practice. The specific needs of children who have attachment difficulties are also considered in this chapter.

Love and touch are matters often debated within early years settings, but there is no doubt that young children need love and affection in order to develop. The issues of love and touch have been debated, emphasising young children's need for touch and the concept of professional love in early years practice.

Key messages

> " The skills and qualities required to work with young children have historically been grounded in gendered assumptions.

> " The relationship between practitioners and children, based on understanding, trust and empathy, is the most important aspect of practice.

> " Attachment and transitions necessitate careful planning and empathy for all involved.

> " 'Professional love', care and touch are all important aspects of a child's experience away from home.

Figure 3.3 Key messages from Chapter 3

References

Ainsworth, M. D. S., Blehar, M. C., Waters, E. and Wall, S. (1978) *Patterns of attachment: A psychological study of the strange situation*, Hillsdale, NJ: Erlbaum.

Angelakis, I. and Gooding, P. (2021) 'Adverse social relationships in childhood: Are there links with depression, obsessive-compulsive disorder and suicidality in adulthood?', *Child Psychiatry and Human Development*, 52(5), pp. 945-956.

Anonymous. (2011) *Netmums forum: Being a mum – toddlers (1-3 years)*, available at: www.netmums.com/coffeehouse/being-mum-794/toddlers-1-3-years-59/585248-my-daughter-says-her-nursery-key-worker-said-love-you.html (accessed 14th February 2024).

Atkinson, T. and Claxton, G. (2000) *The intuitive practitioner*, Buckingham: Open University Press.

Australian Government. (2023) *Department for education, early childhood, march quarter 2022 report*, available at: www.education.gov.au/early-childhood/early-childhood-data-and-reports/quarterly-reports-usage-services-fees-and-subsidies/march-quarter-2022-report#toc-child-care-usage

Basford, J. (2019) 'Being a graduate professional in the field of early years education and care: Silence, submission and subversion', *Education*, 47(7), pp. 862-875.

Bowlby, J. (1969) *Attachment and loss, Vol. 1: Attachment. Attachment and loss*, New York: Basic Books.

Bussemakers, C. and Denessen, E. (2024) 'Teacher support as a protective factor? The role of teacher support for reducing disproportionality in problematic behaviour at school', *Journal of Early Adolescence*, 44(1), pp. 5-40.

Cekaite, A. and Bergnehr, D. (2018) 'Affectionate touch and care: Embodied intimacy, compassion and control in early childhood education', *European Early Childhood Education Research Journal*, 26(6), pp. 940-955.

Colley, H. (2006) 'Learning to labour with feeling: Class, gender and emotion in childcare education and training', *Contemporary Issues in Early Childhood*, 7(1), pp. 15-29.

Conkbayir, M. (2021) *Early childhood and neuroscience – theory, research and implications for practice*, 2nd edn, London: Bloomsbury.

Cousins, S. (2017) 'Practitioners' constructions of love in early childhood education and care', *International Journal or Early Childhood Education*, 25(1), pp. 16-29.

Datler, W., Datler, M. and Funder, A. (2010) 'Struggling against a feeling of becoming lost: A young boy's painful transition to day care', *Infant Observation*, 13(1), pp. 65-87.

Department for Education (DfE). (2022) *Childcare and early years survey of parents*, available at: https://explore-education-statistics.service.gov.uk/find-statistics/childcare-and-early-years-survey-of-parents (accessed 4th March 2024).

Department for Education (DfE). (2023) *Statutory framework for the early years foundation stage*, available at: www.gov.uk/government/publications/early-years-foundation-stage-framework-2 (Accessed 3rd March 2024).

Early Education. (2021) *Birth to 5 matters: Non-statutory guidance for the early years foundation stage*, available at: www.birthto5matters.org.uk (accessed 20th December 2022).

Eisenberg, N., Shea, C. L., Carlo, G. and Knight, G. P. (1991) 'Empathy-related responding and cognition: A "chicken and the egg" dilemma', in Kurtines, W. and Gewirtz, J. (eds) *Handbook of moral behavior and development, Vol. 2: Research*, Hillsdale: Lawrence Erlbaum Associates, pp. 63-88.

Elfer, P. (2015) 'Emotional aspects of nursery policy and practice – progress and prospect', *European Early Childhood Education Research Journal*, 23(4), pp. 497-511.

Elfer, P. and Dearnley, K. (2007) 'Nurseries and emotional well-being: Evaluating an emotionally containing model of professional development', *Early Years*, 27(3), pp. 267-279.

Elfer, P., Goldschmied, E. and Selleck, D. (2003) *Key persons in the nursery: Building relationships for quality provision*, David Fulton.

Erdiller, Z. and Dogan, O. (2015) 'The examination of teacher stress among Turkish early childhood education teachers', *Early Child Development and Care*, 185(4), pp. 631-646.

Findlay, P., Findlay, J. and Stewart, R. (2009) 'The consequences of caring: Skills, regulation and reward among early childhood workers', *Work, Employment and Society*, 23(3), pp. 422-441.

Fletcher, M. (1958) in Cousins S. (2017) 'Practitioners' constructions of love in early childhood education and care', *International Journal or Early Childhood Education*, 25(1), pp. 16-29.

Gerhardt, S. (2015) *Why love matters: How affection shapes a baby's brain*, 2nd edn, London and New York: Routledge.

Goddard, C. (2020, March 16) 'EYFS best practice in schools – Be in touch', *Nursery World*, available at: www.nurseryworld.co.uk/features/article/eyfs-best-practice-in-schools-be-in-touch (accessed 3rd March 2024).

Gopnik, A., Meltzoff, A. and Kuhl, P. (1999) *How babies think*, London: Weindenfield and Nicholson.

Henshall, A., Atkins, L., Bolan, R., Harrison, J. and Munn, H. (2018) 'The motivation and perceptions of newly qualified early years teachers in England', *Journal of Vocational Education & Training*, 70(3), pp. 417–434.

Hodgkins, A. (2023) *Exploring early childhood practitioners' perceptions of empathic interactions with children and families*. PhD thesis, University of Worcester, available at: https://eprints.worc.ac.uk/13525/

Jarvis, P. (2020) 'Attachment theory, cortisol and care for the under-threes in the twenty-first century: Constructing evidence-informed policy', *Early Years*, pp. 1–15.

Jovanovic, J. (2013) 'Retaining early childcare educators', *Gender, Work and Organisation*, 20(5), pp. 528–544.

Klette, T. and Killén, K. (2019) 'Painful transitions: A study of 1-year-old toddlers' reactions to separation and reunion with their mothers after 1 month in childcare', *Early Child Development and Care*, 189(12), pp. 1970–1977.

Kolmar, C. (2023) '30+ essential U.S. childcare statistics [2023]: Availability, costs, and trends', *Zippia*, available at: www.zippia.com/advice/us-child-care-availability-statistics/ (accessed 4th March 2024).

Kring, M. (2018) 'KU researchers seek to combat 'stress hormone' in children in adverse family situations', *KUNews*, University of Kansas, available at: https://news.ku.edu/news/article/2018/02/08/ku-researchers-part-project-combat-stress-hormone-children-adverse-family-situations

Macagno, A. and Molina, P. (2020) 'The construction of child-caregiver relationships in childcare centres: Adaptation of parent attachment diary for professional caregivers', *European Early Childhood Education Research Journal*, 28(3), pp. 349–362.

Moyles, J. (2010) 'Passion, paradox and professionalism in early years education', *Early Years*, 21(2), pp. 81–95.

Noddings, N. (2013) *Caring: A relational approach to ethics and moral education*, 2nd edn, Berkeley, CA: University of California Press.

Page, J. (2011) 'Do mothers want professional carers to love their babies?' *Journal of Early Childhood Research*, 9(3), pp. 310–323.

Page, J. (2018) 'Characterising the principles of professional love in early childhood care and education', *International Journal of Early Years Education*, 26(2), pp. 125–141.

Page, J. and Elfer, P. (2013) 'The emotional complexity of attachment interactions in nursery', *European Early Years Education Research Journal*, 21(4), pp. 553–567.

Piper, H. and Smith, H. (2003) '"Touch" in educational and childcare settings: Dilemmas and responses', *British Educational Research Journal*, 29(6), pp. 879–894.

Purvanova, R. (2013) 'The role of feeling known for team member outcomes in project teams', *Small Group Research*, 44(3), pp. 298–331.

Rawstrone, A. (2009, November 3) 'Positive relationships: Key person system – Pick your own', *Nursery World*, available at: www.nurseryworld.co.uk/features/article/positive-relationships-key-person-system-pick-your-own (accessed 28th December 2023).

Rogers, C. (1951) *Client-centered therapy: Its current practice, implications and theory*, London: Constable.

Rouse, E. and Hadley, F. (2018) 'Where did love and care get lost? Educators and parents' perceptions of early childhood practice', *International Journal of Early Years Education*, 26(2), pp. 159–172.

Seaman, H. and Giles, P. (2021) 'Supporting children's social and emotional well-being in the early years: An exploration of practitioners' perceptions', *Early Child Development and Care*, 191(6), pp. 861–875.

Solvason, C. and Webb, R. (2023) *Exploring and celebrating the early childhood practitioner: An interrogation of pedagogy, professionalism and practice*, London: Routledge.

Svinth, L. (2018) 'Being touched-the transformative potential of nurturing touch practices in relation to toddlers' learning and emotional well-being', *Early Child Development and Care*, 188(7), pp. 924–936.

Sylva, K., Melhuish, E., Sammons, P., Siraj-Blatchford, I. and Taggart, B. (2010) *Early childhood matters: Evidence from the effective pre-school and primary education project*, London: Routledge.

Tietze, W., Cryer, D., Bairrao, J., Palacios, J. and Wetzel, G. (1996) 'Comparisons of observed process quality in early child care and education programmes in five countries', *Early Childhood Research Quarterly*, 4, pp. 447–475.

The Wave Trust. (2014) *1001 critical days: The importance of the conception to age two period*, available at: www.wavetrust.org/1001-critical-days-the-importance-of-the-conception-to-age-two-period (accessed 29th May 2023).

White, T. (2022, June 11) 'Women aren't choosing to be stay-at-home mothers – they're forced', *The New Statesman*, available at: www.newstatesman.com/politics/society/2022/06/childcare-flexibility-working-mothers-stay-at-home (accessed 23rd August 2024).

Xia, M., Fosco, G. M., Lippold, M. A. and Feinberg, M. E. (2018) 'A developmental perspective on young adult romantic relationships: Examining family and individual factors in adolescence', *Journal of Youth Adolescence*, 47(7), pp. 1499–1516.

4
Extending empathy and compassion to parents, carers, and families

Chapter objectives

- To emphasise the importance of the core conditions when working with families
- To critique views and assumptions of parents and families
- To discuss interactions in particular challenging circumstances
- To establish what constitutes a good partnership with families

Throughout this chapter, the term 'family members' is used for ease of reading; however, it represents a diverse range of people and family situations. The word 'parents' is commonly used to indicate those who have parental responsibility for a child, whether this is formal or informal (DfE, 2023), and it includes parents, grandparents, family members, kinship carers, legal guardians, foster carers, social workers, other professionals, and friends. Figure 4.1 shows the many family structures that exist today.

Practitioner views of parents

Vygotsky emphasised that parents are 'the child's first educator' (Smidt, 2010), and they should be appreciated and respected as such. Sadly, this is not always the case, and parents are silenced and expected to be passive, conforming and grateful (Solvason et al., 2019). There is a power imbalance between families and professionals and sometimes 'parent partnership' can be rather tokenistic. Informing families of activities, asking them for information and inviting them in for parents' evenings are sometimes the only attempts made to include them, but true partnership involves really getting to know them. We should endeavour to treat families as individuals, just as we do with children; 'It is important to remember that what teachers and other practitioners see of parents/carers is just a small part of what is going on in their lives' (Hodgkins, 2022, in Sewell, 2022). Many schools, in an effort to include parent partnership, use a home-school diary, but this only considers families' expectations as they relate to schoolwork (Hill, 2022, p. 309), it doesn't tell us anything about the lives of families.

DOI: 10.4324/9781003464686-4

Extending empathy and compassion to parents, carers, and families 51

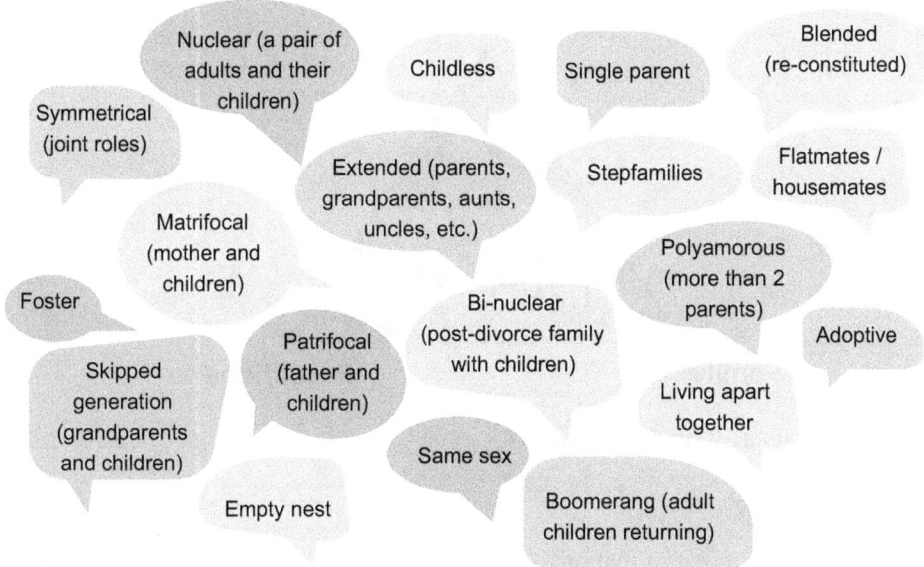

Figure 4.1 21st-century family types

As the child should always be the focus of our attention, Brooker's 'triangle of care' is the best way to provide consistent, child-focussed care and education, as the child, family and practitioners are seen as equal partners

The child has a close relationship with their family and, in early years setting, practitioners have close relationships with their key children. In order to be equal partners, there needs to be much more 'partnership' and understanding between families and practitioners. When the Covid-19 pandemic took hold in the UK and everyone had to keep their distance from others in an attempt to halt the spread of the disease, parent partnerships were very difficult. Families were no longer allowed into settings or schools, children were taken from them outside and had their hands washed with disinfectant before being allowed in. The situation was very challenging for everyone concerned, but when things were relatively 'back to normal', levels of participation and involvement did not return to the pre-Covid position.

 Reflective prompt – reflect on the ways that practices changed during the Covid pandemic. Do you think there are any residual effects relating to parent partnership? Consider the importance of re-assessing participation and involvement, in the post-Covid world.

52 *Nurturing Compassionate Connections*

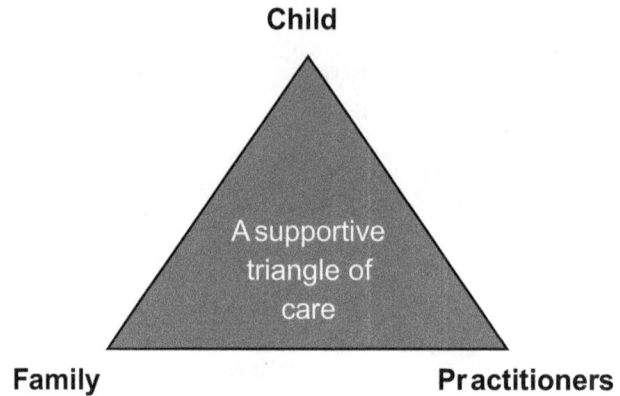

Figure 4.2 Brooker's (2010) Triangle of care

The 'ideal parent'

Solvason et al. (2019) suggest that there is a notion of 'the ideal parent', someone who conforms to the setting's practices and does not challenge them. Optimistically, this view is not universal and there are lots of early years settings who welcome participation and feedback from families. Definitions of the ideal parent, however, differ across nations and cultures. Research by Lin et al. (2010) examined views of the ideal parent across 37 countries in five continents, with 12,000 participants. Although it is unwise to make generalisations about a particular country, there were differences, but the research identified five distinct 'parenting culture zones'. For African parents, respect was particularly important; for Asian parents, family responsibility was emphasised most highly; for Western and Russian parents, being patient and loving was the main focus. In Lin et al.'s (2010) research, the words 'loving', 'responsible' and 'patient' were found in all five continents, so appear to be universal beliefs about what good parenting looks like. There are assumptions that could be made about the priorities of families, but the research ultimately showed great similarities in core beliefs.

The important thing to remember is that if we treat families as individuals, as people with their own particular ways and needs, we will be better placed to meet those needs. Solvason and Cliffe (2022, p. 22) stress the importance of remembering that, 'The traditional model of parent partnership is based upon the types of language used by, and the typical participation practices of, white and middle-class parents'. It is important to be aware of this and to make sure that all families are treated equally. By celebrating

 **Group activity**

Consider the following excerpt by Solvason and Cliffe (2022, p. 23) and discuss the implications of this for your setting.

diversity, we bring into the setting the cultures, practices and customs that can be of great benefit to all of the children.

> 'Despite the 'catch all' phrase of 'parents or carers', in reality 'mum and dad' is the audience for every registration form, every letter home, every piece of guidance. Should we really still be buying into the marketing of notions such as Mother's Day and Father's Day so wholeheartedly, when in many settings the 'nuclear family' is now the exception rather than the rule?'

A study by Chang-Kredl et al. (2021) examined views of fathers in popular culture and media and found many examples of fathers being portrayed as inept and sexist (think, for example, of the stereotypical fathers in Family Guy and The Simpsons). The myth of 'men are from Mars, women are from Venus' (Gray, 1999), a book about sex differences which, at the time, was accepted as fact, but has now been discredited, as it presented a perspective that men and women are so different that they should be regarded as members of different cultures, even from different planets (Hynan, 2005). However, there is a suggestion, according to Hynan's (2005) research with fathers and mothers, that there are some minor sex differences in communication with fathers and mothers, particularly when they are under stress. For example, women were found to be slightly more likely to self-disclose than men (45% of men as opposed to 55% of women). Men were also found to be more likely to discourage worrying and to change the subject, whilst women are more likely than men to express sympathy. However, the differences are slight and Hynan's article suggests that practitioners are more likely to show empathy and person centred support to mothers than to fathers. Clearly, the message we should take from this is to treat all parents with the core conditions, with empathy, congruence and unconditional positive regard, whilst acknowledging that people are different and what works with one individual may not work with another.

 Case study – Kaspar

"My name is and Kaspar* and I am a stay-at-home Dad. I took my 18-month-old son, Alek*, to a playgroup for the first time yesterday, but I won't be returning, as I felt intimidated and uncomfortable.

This is what happened: Everyone turned to stare at me when I walked in, there were a few smiles, but no one spoke to me. I sat near a group of Mums as they chatted; no one spoke to me the whole time I was there. I tried to speak to a young mother sitting near me, but she answered me quickly and then moved across the room. I noticed her friend laughing. The person running the group spoke to me once, as I was leaving. She said: 'your turn to babysit the kid today, was it?' "(*names changed)

> **Reflective prompt** - reflect on Kaspar's experience. What went wrong? Why was his experience so poor? What was the laughter about? Who was at fault? What needs to change?

Sex and gender

The terms 'sex' and 'gender' are often confused; here are some definitions:

Table 4.1 Definitions of sex and gender

Sex	From a traditional medical perspective two separate sexes have been identified. These are male and female. Children are assigned their sex (male or female) from birth based on visual anatomy (Kennett et al., 2022, in Sewell, 2022).
Gender	An achieved status that which is constructed through psychological, cultural, and social means. 'Gender as a process of *doing* which can be considered a *performance* of specific acts concerning the social ideas of gender' (Butler, 1988).

Kennett et al.'s (2022, in Sewell, 2022) view is that the idea of the two male and female sexes is too simplistic, as the labelling of a child's anatomical sex is derived from visual anatomy rather than any other determining factor. They suggest the idea of 'a spectrum of anatomical and biological sex' (p. 133) is more accurate. The terms 'trans' and 'gender diverse' are umbrella terms which relate to anyone whose gender does not sit comfortably with the sex they were assigned at birth (Amnesty International, 2020). Figure 4.3 illustrates ways of supporting people who identify as trans or non-binary.

Now that there are more single fathers, families with two fathers, fathers as full time carers, and trans parents, it is important to recognise the needs of all people and to ensure equality and anti-discriminatory practice. The subject of sex and gender in the early years is multifaceted. On one hand, gender is increasingly recognised as fluid, with blurred distinctions that underscore the importance of treating all parents and carers equally, irrespective of gender. However, it is equally imperative to acknowledge instances where one gender is treated less favourably. In such cases, it becomes crucial to address these disparities and strive for equality by offering tailored support. Chapter 5 will revisit this topic, delving into a discourse on male childcare workers. We will return to this subject in Chapter 5, with a discussion on male childcare workers.

Using the core conditions with families

As shown in Figure 4.1, many family structures can be seen today, with more diversity than ever before, so it is important to embrace such diversity and to treat families with the

Extending empathy and compassion to parents, carers, and families 55

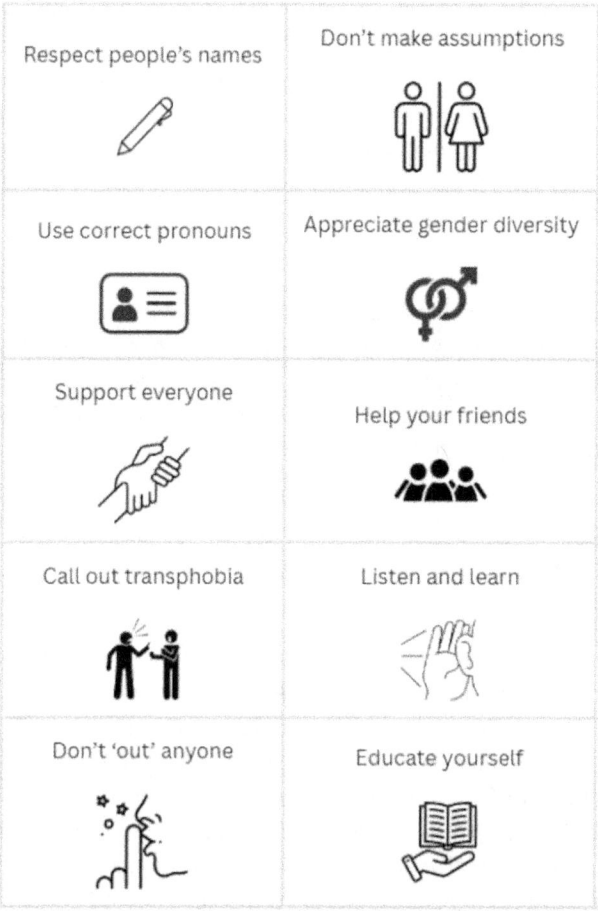

Figure 4.3 How to support trans people (adapted from Amnesty International, 2020)

core conditions of empathy, congruence and unconditional positive regard. Empathy is the overriding principle of this book, essential as it is for building relationships and promoting compassionate interactions. As we have seen in Chapter 2, empathy is about putting oneself in the position of the other person and trying to imagine what it must be like to be them, to 'walk in their shoes' (Smith, 2016). Empathy usually results in compassion (Galetz, 2019), as we want to take action to improve things for the other person. The second core condition is congruence, meaning genuineness or authenticity. Being congruent is being true to your own beliefs and values so in interactions with families, people should see honesty and consistency. An example of this might be when a parent/carer asks you something that you do not know, and you admit to them that you don't know; honesty builds trust in relationships. The final core condition is unconditional positive regard (UPR). This describes an attitude of acceptance without assumptions or stereotyping, it means valuing everyone without judgement. An example of this might be talking to a parent/carer who evidently practices self-harm. In this instance, you would not show any judgement or any focus on the social or moral aspects of the situation, but you would demonstrate acceptance of the person. Although it can be challenging, sometimes, to focus on positives and to ensure that you are not showing any judgement or prejudice, it is an important skill to develop; families should always feel accepted and valued as people. The Parental Engagement Network (2023) appeal to early years settings to be 'an 'open-door' setting with 'open-heart' staff.'

 Reflective prompt - reflect on the three core conditions. Do you follow these in your interactions with families? Are any of them a challenge for you? Can you think of a time when you have had to consciously make an effort to not judge a parent/carer? How did you manage the situation and why was it important to show UPR?

Supporting families

In the UK, poverty has risen sharply since the return to normal life after the Covid-19 pandemic, when temporary support ended in 2021 (JRF, 2024). Currently, 4.3 million children in the UK are living in poverty, 30% of children in an average classroom (CPAG, 2024a). Research by the Joseph Rowntree Foundation concluded that the UK is now in a state of 'deep poverty and destitution', causing a 'mounting catastrophe' of health problems throughout the nation (JRF, 2024). The effects of poverty are wide-ranging and can last a lifetime. The Child Poverty Action Group (CPAG, 2022) explains that children living in constant poverty have cognitive development scores on average 20% below those of children who have never experienced poverty. Similarly, the Millennium Cohort Study (UCL, 2023) shows that they are four times more likely to suffer a mental health problem before the age of 11. The effects of poverty on children are multidimensional; multidimensional child poverty is a concept that describes children lacking in basic necessities, such as nutritious food, clean water, shelter, sanitation, healthcare, and education, to survive and thrive. It is a way of measuring poverty that goes beyond absolute poverty by considering deprivations in key areas, such as living conditions, health, and education. This situation does not only affect the UK. According to UNICEF (2024a), 333 million children around the world currently live in extreme poverty. Sustainable Development Goals (the world's 17-point plan to radically improve the lives of people and the planet by 2030) call for child poverty to be halved by 2030 (UNICEF, 2024b). However, this does not now seem achievable due to climate change, conflict, Covid-19, and economic crises (UNICEF, 2024b).

Many families can no longer afford to pay for childcare, as shown for example in Garvis et al.'s (2012) Australian research entitled, 'Get real – we can't afford kindergarten'. Those who do bring their children to an early years setting may well be in need of support, which practitioners can provide. Some settings have set up food banks or community cupboards, which families can donate to or take things from if they need to. In some settings, it may

Extending empathy and compassion to parents, carers, and families 57

Community cupboard for families
(Hodgkins & Boddey, 2023)

A flexible approach to charging fees
(Hodgkins & Boddey, 2023)

Signposting families to support services
(Hodgkins & Boddey, 2023)

Exploring funding/fundraising for trips and events, rather than asking parents to pay
(CPAG, 2022)

Taking time to talk to parents/carers
(CPAG, 2022)

School uniform banks
(CPAG, 2024)

Figure 4.4 Helping families in poverty

be possible to only charge fees for the hours a child attends rather than for full days or weeks (see Hodgkins and Boddey, 2023, for an example case study). As always, welcoming parents/carers into your setting and getting to know them is the key to understanding families' circumstances and needs. The list in Figure 4.4 illustrates some of the ways that some settings are helping families during the current cost of living crisis.

> **Group activity**
>
> Look at Figure 4.4. Is there anything here that your setting could adopt in order to help families living in poverty? As a group, brainstorm ideas; can you add more ideas to the list? Make a pledge to help the families you work with who may be living in poverty. Take action to make a difference.

Challenging partnerships

Partnership with families is not always easy; there are many reasons why family members may not be involved with their child's nursery or school (see Figure 4.4). You may be able to add more to the list. We still hear terms like 'problem' families, which supposes that families are at fault for such disinvolvement. 'Hard to reach' families, a term still widely used, assumes that there is a level of engagement that is expected (see Solvason et al.'s 'ideal parent' earlier in this chapter). Research with early years practitioners by Sims-Schouten (2016) highlighted some negative views of parents/carers viewed by practitioners as 'deficient' or 'lacking . . . in their willingness to engage' (p. 1402).

Faulkner et al. (2016) suggest that interactions with families and the public concerning the perception of their role as merely babysitters were the most prominent stressors. Chang-Kredl et al. (2021) quote a parent used when talking to an early years educator, 'you're all so good with poo here', which the authors claim to belittle the role of educators. Stereotypical

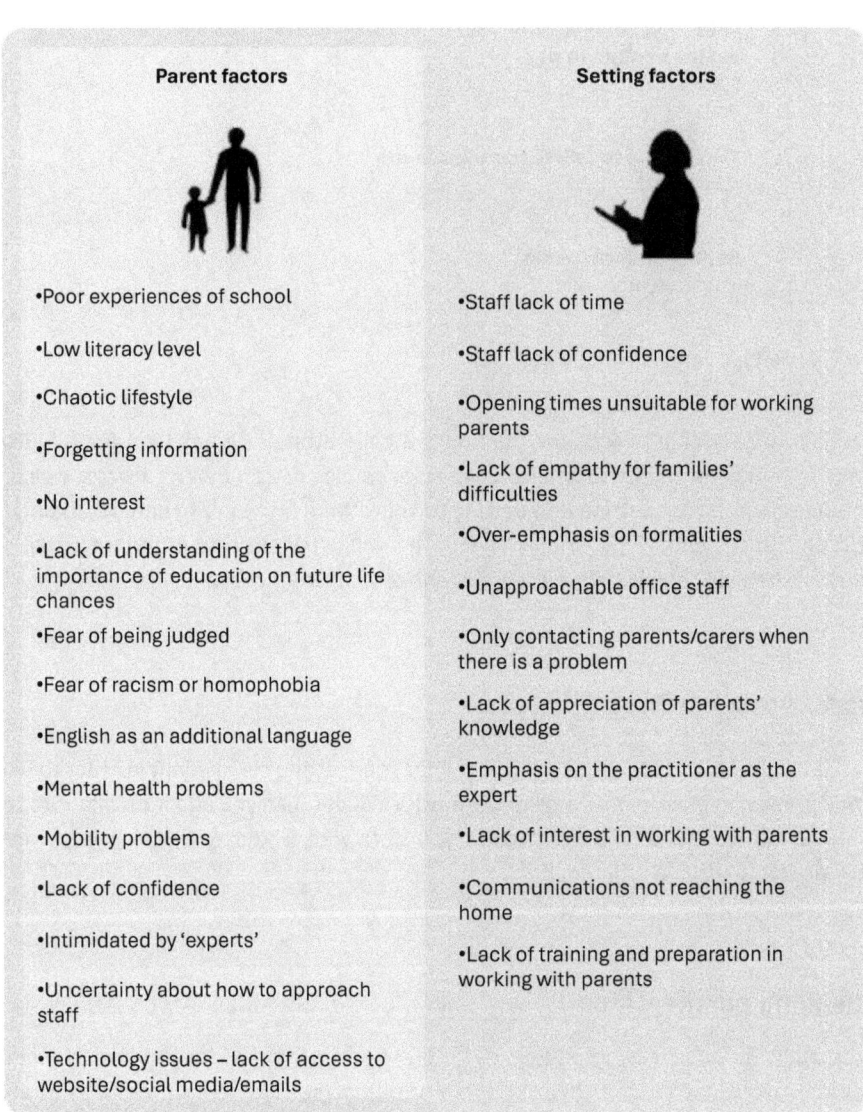

Figure 4.5 Factors affecting parent engagement

views of early years work are still rife, according to Gaunt (2022), who says educators are told that they are 'just babysitting', 'playing with toys all day', and that 'there's no skill in the job'. A preschool educator, quoted in the report, says, 'I think we're an invisible workforce. Everyone knows we are there but don't fully understand what goes into being a quality educator' (Famly, 2022). This is very frustrating for practitioners who have undergone rigorous professional training for the role. In the empathy research, George contemplates this,

> If the parents came in for just an hour, they'd be like, 'Wow, you do so much more', and that recognition really would make it feel just that little bit more worthwhile.
>
> (George)

During the Covid-19 pandemic, there was an increase in recognition of early years practitioners following the lockdowns when childcare facilities were closed to prevent the spread of the disease. A good example of this gratitude comes from Wales. Julie Morgan, Deputy Minister for Health and Social Services in Wales, said,

> Childcare practitioners are absolutely key in our ability to respond to Covid-19, and you've truly risen to the challenge with great commitment and drive. As a nation we are incredibly grateful for all you have done and continue to do. Thank you.
>
> (We care Wales, 2020)

However, this appreciation (much like the clapping for NHS staff) seems not to have been accompanied by an increase in pay or conditions. A study by Nelinger et al. (2021) showed that early years practitioners struggled when having to provide additional mental health support to children and their parents during the pandemic, with no additional training. When asked how often they encountered parents or carers who they felt were struggling to manage the emotional, social, or mental health needs of their children, 53% said 'sometimes', 20% said 'often', and 5% said 'very often' (Nelinger et al., 2021, p. 5).

According to research carried out for the Royal Foundation in 2023, with the aim of understanding public attitudes towards early childhood, 'three in five (60%) [parents] said they knew how children develop; roughly a third still knew just a little or nothing.' (Ipsos, 2023, p. 19). This adds to the poor perception of early years practitioners' expertise.

Working with parents/carers can be challenging; in fact, Faulkner et al. (2016) believe that it is the biggest stressor in the profession. Despite practitioner/parent relationships being complex, supporting parents is an integral aspect of the practice (Vollans, 2023). In the empathy research (Hodgkins, 2023), there were some examples of stressful interactions between practitioners and parents/carers. The following three examples involve practitioners managing interactions involving emotion. In the first example, Joel, a nursery manager, describes talking to a child's mother about his belief that her child's development was delayed and that he may have some special educational needs. Joel described his emotions before the interaction and said he felt both sad and nervous about the upcoming conversation. Joel said,

> I felt a sense of responsibility to convey accurate information and was worried about how the parent may respond to hearing their child has a developmental delay. I felt sorry for the parent as they tried to make sense of this interaction.
>
> (Joel)

Joel felt empathy for the parent; the fact that he was feeling sad and worried probably indicates affective empathy. Joel was 'feeling with' the parent, understanding their point of view, even when the parent became defensive during the interaction. According to Solvason and Proctor (2021), who write about working with the parents of children with additional needs, 'parents could 'be very, very defensive, quite angry sometimes, very frustrated. You just have to remember all that rubbish that they've been through; and be kind to them' (p. 479). Joel's empathy for the parent ensures that this is what he does; he listens, and he carefully considers the way that he communicates.

In the second example, George, who is the deputy manager of a nursery, has to handle a difficult situation with a parent who has made a sexist remark aimed at George. The parent had brought her child into nursery in the morning, and the child had been very upset. The parent had made the comment, 'It must be because there's a man here; she must be scared'. George reflects on this,

> I understand that the family is looking for reasons why their child won't settle, but I am gentle and try to develop a relationship with them. However, when they aren't around, my emotions differ, and I'm sad and angry as I wonder why they blame me? I know it probably wasn't personal, but I couldn't help but take it personally.
>
> (George)

In this example, George is trying to show the parents that he is a gentle and caring practitioner, but the sex discrimination by the parents has clearly upset him.

Reflective prompt - George is clearly upset by the incident with this parent. Why do you think George is so upset? What do you think is the right way to handle a situation like this?

In this third example, Aadiya, a reception class teacher, is reflecting on the parent of a child in her class. The child displays challenging behaviour and has been doing so since starting the school nursery. Aadiya arranges for the parents to come into school and talk to her about the child at the start of the school year, and she welcomes them to come in and talk to her whenever they want to. Aadiya was very aware of the challenges that the child would bring to the class, and by listening to the child's parents, she was able to learn as much as she could about the child and family. Aadiya says,

> I validated her feelings and listened ... we built up a really good relationship with the family.
>
> (Aadiya)

Aadiya realised that the child's parents had consistently been told how difficult their daughter was with the preschool staff and how they were greeted at the end of the day with a list of problems there had been. This made the parents feel despondent. Aadiya said,

> They said they felt down every day when they went to preschool to pick her up; they didn't know what they were going to be greeted with, so I squashed it. As soon as she joined my reception class, every time the parents came, I said something lovely she had done. That doesn't mean I don't share problems when I need to, but I know they need to hear something positive as well.
>
> (Aadiya)

Aadiya's reflection is a great example of empathy with parents and the importance of spending time getting to know them, which ultimately benefits the parents, child, and practitioners.

 Reflective prompt - Reflect on a good relationship with a parent; why was it good? Reflect on a difficult situation; why was it difficult? What did you learn from it?

Sometimes, in the early years profession, it is necessary to have a difficult conversation with a parent/carer. These 'courageous conversations' may be about a child's developmental progress, a child's behaviour, or a safeguarding concern. If there is a clear safeguarding concern or a clear case of discrimination, then the position should be clear, and we need to stand up for what is right and ethical. However, at other times it can be difficult to know what is the right thing to do. The case study that follows is about Mel, a participant in the empathy research (Hodgkins, 2023). Here in her reflective diary, Mel struggles with tension between her own emotions, her empathy for a parent, and the conflict between her own values and what is expected of her in her role. Courageous conversations are revisited in Chapter 7.

 Individual activity

Look at the following scenarios they describe the sorts of situations you may have found yourself in. For each example, identify a compassionate response that includes the core conditions whilst remaining professional and keeping the welfare of the child as paramount.

- A parent/carer asks you not to let her toddler sleep during the day. The child will be with you from 8.30am till 4pm.
- When a parent/carer brings their child in the morning, you notice a strong smell of alcohol and the parent's slurred speech.
- A parent is angry with you for letting her child's designer dress get dirty whilst playing outside.
- A parent/carer requests that her child is not cared for by a male practitioner.
- A child's parents/carers do not agree that their child needs a speech and language referral.
- In your reception class nativity, a parent/carer whose child has been cast as a sheep keeps pestering you to let her play the part of Mary. She even brings in a costume for her to wear.
- A parent/carer asks you not to let her child play with or sit next to a particular child in the group.

Some of these examples are easier to respond to than others. The following case study, taken from the empathy research project, details a complex ethical situation and its effect on practitioner Mel.

 Case study – Mel

Mel had been working with a baby who had recently started at the nursery and who was struggling to settle. The baby was distressed for a large portion of the day and his mother was also very upset. The baby's mother asked how the baby had been one day, and Mel had to follow the nursery's policy of not telling parents if their baby had been upset all day. The reason for this rule, according to the nursery management, is that babies often take a while to settle, but they always do settle in the end, so staff are instructed to tell parents only about positive aspects of the child's day to prevent unnecessary upset. Mel followed this instruction, but the tension is clear in her description,

> I was feeling good at not adding to the guilt, seeing Mom's relief at not being told her son had struggled again . . . . I chose to tell Mom about the positives to spare her feelings. I had mixed emotions, feeling glad at sparing Mom's feelings, feeling guilty about omitting the truth and not sure whether it was the right thing to do!
>
> (Mel)

Extending empathy and compassion to parents, carers, and families 63

 Individual activity

Read Mel's case study; what are the ethical issues here? In Chapter 1, we discussed congruence, one of Rogers' (1961) core conditions. Congruence is about being genuine and authentic; being true to our own values when interacting with people. Mel's reflection shows that she is feeling conflicted about doing something that goes against her personal values. What are the possible outcomes? Consider the viewpoints of the practitioner, child, parent, and manager (Table 4.2), then reflect on your learning.

Table 4.2 Mel's ethical dilemma

	How are they likely to be feeling?	What are their responsibilities?	What is the possible impact/outcome?
Practitioner (Mel)	Sorry for the parent	To follow the rules/policy of the nursery	Emotional reaction – guilt, uncertainty
	Sad for the baby Guilty and confused	To support the parent and child through the transition	Possible empathic distress
			Worrying about it outside work
		To safeguard the child	Unhappy in the role
Manager			
Parent			
Child			

When considering difficult conversations, it is important to remember that the welfare of the child is paramount (The Children Act, 1989) and also that these conversations are always about the parents'/carers' most treasured possession. As Cliffe (2022, in Solvason and Cliffe, 2022, p. 101) says, 'That is what we need to keep holding first and foremost when things get tough'.

Partnership models

Figure 4.5 illustrates three models of parent partnership, as defined by the now-disbanded CWDC (2010). It shows very different ways of working. In the expert model, practitioners and teachers are assumed to be the experts, and parents/carers are expected to accept their views and to be compliant. In schools throughout the world, this is the most prevalent model. Parents/carers are expected to stay out of the classroom unless invited in for a specific purpose (e.g. parents' evening) and to listen as teachers judge children's progress and needs. This model is in direct opposition to the befriending model, where parents/carers are welcome, but there is no real structure to the partnership. This may be seen in an informal 'parent and baby' or playgroup setting. The ideal relationship is the partnership model

Partnership model	Expert model	Befriending model
Parents and practitioners actively working together	Practitioner is the expert and has superior knowledge	Warm and friendly engagement with parents
Valuing each others' strengths and knowledge	Practitioner leads and controls interactions	No clear expectations or boundaries
Resolving disagreements by careful negotiation	Parent is assumed to have less knowledge	No clear model for working through a problem
Both reach agreement on what to achieve and how	Practitioners provide diagnoses and outcomes for problems	Parent may not think the practitioner has any expertise
Mutual respect	Parent is expected to accept what is offered and to be compliant	Parent may sort through own problems
Open, honest communication		

Figure 4.6 Three parent partnership models (adapted from CWDC, 2010)

(see Figure 4.6), which describes a mutually respectful relationship with respect for each other's individual skills and with clear communication. This model describes the authentic relationships recommended by (Solvason et al., 2019)

>  **Group activity**
>
> how well do you know the families you work with? What are the benefits of increased parent involvement? How can you gather feedback on ways that partnership could be improved? How close do you think your setting's parent partnership is to the partnership model (Figure 4.5)? Are there elements of the expert model? Or the befriending model? Reflect on the possibility of developing a more equal partnership.

Chapter summary

This chapter began by discussing the diverse range of family structures that practitioners are likely to encounter. Recognising that parents and carers are a child's first educators emphasises the need to respect and appreciate their role. The chapter explores methods for collaborating with parents and carers as part of a supportive 'triangle of care' for children, with a focus on valuing individual differences. It examines the impact of cultural

Extending empathy and compassion to parents, carers, and families 65

assumptions, gender stereotypes, and professionals' expectations of the 'ideal parent.' Additionally, it analyses expectations of parental engagement and public perceptions of early years practice.

Examples from the empathy research are used to highlight some of the challenges involved in building partnerships with parents and carers. The importance of the core conditions – empathy, respect, and genuineness – is underscored, particularly in challenging situations. Strategies for supporting families living in poverty are also presented. The concept of courageous conversations is examined, with a focus on the role of core conditions when addressing differing opinions and concerns about children. Ethical practice is discussed, including a research-based scenario used to prompt ethical decision-making. Partnerships with parents, carers, and families are fundamental to early years practice and should be grounded in empathy and compassion.

Key messages

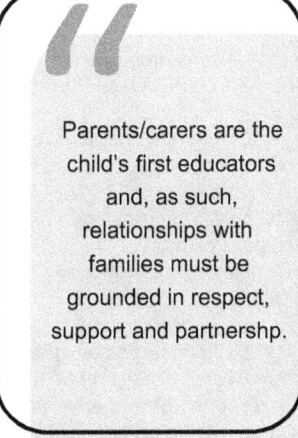
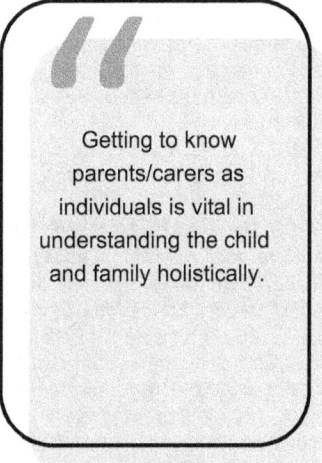

Figure 4.7 Key messages from Chapter 4

References

Amnesty International. (2020) *Gender identity for beginners: A guide to being a great trans ally*, available at: www.amnesty.org.uk/LGBTQ-equality/gender-identity-beginners-guide-trans-allies (accessed 30th March 2024).

Brooker, L. (2010) 'Constructing the triangle of care: Power and professionalism in practitioner/parent relationships', *British Journal of Educational Studies*, 58(2), pp. 181-196. https://doi.org/10.1080/00071001003752203

Chang-Kredl, S., Pauls, K. and Foster, K. (2021) '"You're all so good with poo here": Mainstream media representations of the early years educator', *Gender and Education*, 33(1), pp. 103-118.

Child Poverty Action Group (CPAG). (2022) *Supporting families in times of financial hardship*, available at: https://cpag.org.uk/news/supporting-families-times-financial-hardship-guide-schools (accessed 7th April 2024).

Child Poverty Action Group (CPAG). (2024a) *Poverty: Facts and figures*, available at: https://cpag.org.uk/child-poverty/poverty-facts-and-figures (accessed 7th April 2024).

Child Poverty Action Group (CPAG). (2024b) *Cluster-wide uniform bank*, available at: https://cpag.org.uk/what-we-do/project-work/cost-school-day/resources/ideas-bank/uniform/uniform-bank (accessed 7th April 2024).

Cliffe, J. (2022) 'Chapter 5: Tackling difficult conversations', in Solvason, C. and Cliffe, J. (eds) *Creating authentic relationships with parents of young children*, London: Speechmark, Routledge, pp. 87–104.

CWDC. (2010) *Reaching out to families*, available at: https://assets.publishing.service.gov.uk/media/5a7a0c00e5274a34770e3dd0/SP211-0311.pdf (accessed 13th March 2025).

Department for Education (DfE). (2023) *Understanding and dealing with issues relating to parental responsibility*, available at: https://www.gov.uk/government/publications/dealing-with-issues-relating-to-parental-responsibility/understanding-and-dealing-with-issues-relating-to-parental-responsibility (accessed 13th March 2025).

Famly. (2022) *Respect the sector: The early years reputation report 2022*, available at: www.famly.co/blog-resources/guides/respect-the-sector#:~:text=Worries%20about%20staffing%20(86%25),don't%20feel%20connected%20enough (accessed 30th March 2024).

Faulkner, M., et al. (2016) 'Childcare providers: Work stress and personal well-being', *Journal of Early Childhood Research*, 14(3), pp. 280–293.

Galetz, E. (2019) 'The empathy-compassion matrix: Using a comparison concept analysis to identify care components', *Nursing Forum*, 54(3), pp. 448–454.

Garvis, S., Pendergast, D. and Kanasa, H. (2012) '"Get real – we can't afford kindergarten": A study of parental perceptions of early years services', *International Journal of Early Years Education*, 20(2), pp. 202–211.

Gaunt, C. (2022, July 5) 'Early years is "an invisible workforce" – report', *Nursery World*, available at: www.nurseryworld.co.uk/news/article/early-years-is-an-invisible-workforce-report (accessed 30th March 2024).

Gray, J. (1999) *Men are from Mars, women are from Venus: A practical guide to improving communication and getting what you want in your relationships*, New York: Harper Collins.

Hill, N. (2022) 'Parental involvement in education: Toward a more inclusive understanding of parents' role construction', *Educational Psychologist*, 57(4), pp. 309–314.

Hodgkins, A. (2022) 'Chapter 3: Parent and carer voice: Listening to, understanding, and acting on parental and carer perceptions and opinions', in Sewell, A. (ed) *Diverse voices in educational practice: A workbook for promoting pupil, parent and professional voice*, Speechmark, Routledge.

Hodgkins, A. (2023) *Exploring early childhood practitioners' perceptions of empathic interactions with children and families*. PhD thesis, University of Worcester, available at: https://eprints.worc.ac.uk/13525/

Hodgkins, A. and Boddey, J. (2023) 'Supporting parents with empathy and compassion', *International Journal of Birth and Parenting Education*, 10(2), pp. 29–33.

Hynan, M. (2005) 'Supporting fathers during stressful times in the nursery: An evidence-based review', *Newborn and Infant Nursing Reviews*, 5(2), pp. 87–92.

Ipsos, on Behalf of the Royal Foundation Centre for Early Childhood. (2023) *Understanding public attitudes towards early childhood*, available at: www.shapingus.centreforearlychildhood.org/wp-content/uploads/2023/06/The-Royal-Foundation-Centre-for-Early-Childhood_Public_Perceptions_Survey_first_release_June_2023.pdf (accessed 30th March 2024).

Joseph Rowntree Foundation (JRF). (2024, March 21) *Poverty's toll on the nation's health a "mounting catastrophe" in need of political attention*, available at: www.jrf.org.uk/news/povertys-toll-on-the-nations-health-a-mounting-catastrophe-in-need-of-political-attention (accessed 7th April 2024).

Lin, G. X., et al. (2010) 'Parenting culture(s): Ideal-parent beliefs across 37 countries', *Journal of Cross-Cultural Psychology*, 54(1), pp. 4–24.

Nelinger, A., Album, J., Haynes, A. and Rosan, C. (2021) *Their challenges are our challenges – a summary report of the experiences facing nursery workers in the U.K. in 2020*, available at: www.annafreud.org/media/13013/their-challenges-are-our-challenges-survey-report.pdf (accessed 30th March 2024).

Parental Engagement Network. (2023) *What are the parental engagement challenges faced by early years practitioners?* available at: www.linkedin.com/pulse/what-parental-engagement-challenges-faced-early-years-practitioners/ (accessed 6th April 2024).

Sewell, A. (ed). (2022) *Diverse voices*, Speechmark, Routledge.

Sims-Schouten, W. (2016) 'Positioning in relationships between parents and early years practitioners', *Early Child Development and Care*, 186(9), pp. 1392-1405.

Smidt, S. (2010) *Playing to learn: The role of play in the early years*, London: Routledge.

Smith, F. (2016) 'Walking in another's shoes and getting blisters: A personal account of the blessing and curse of intense empathy', *Advanced Development Journal*, 15, pp. 96-107.

Solvason, C. and Cliffe, J. (2022) *Creating authentic relationships with parents of young children*, London: Speechmark, Routledge.

Solvason, C., Cliffe, J. and Bailey, E. (2019) 'Breaking the silence: Providing authentic opportunities for parents to be heard', *Power and Education*, 11(2), pp. 191-203.

Solvason, C. and Proctor, S. (2021) 'You have to find the right words to be honest': Nurturing relationships between teachers and parents of children with Special Educational Needs', *Support for Learning*, 36(3), pp. 470-485.

UNICEF. (2024a) *Child poverty*, available at: www.unicef.org/social-policy/child-poverty (accessed 7th April 2024).

UNICEF. (2024b) *UNICEF and the sustainable development goals*, available at: www.unicef.org/sustainable-development-goals#17-goals (accessed 7th April 2024).

University College London (UCL). (2023) *Millennium cohort study*, available at: https://cls.ucl.ac.uk/cls-studies/millennium-cohort-study/ (accessed 13th March 2025).

Vollans, C. (2023, November 21) 'Making relationships with parents key to positive behaviour', *Nursery World*, available at: www.nurseryworld.co.uk/features/article/social-interactions-part-4-making-relationships-with-parents-key-to-positive-behaviour (accessed 6th April 2024).

We Care Wales. (2020) *Children and parents show gratitude to childcare workers during lockdown*, available at: https://wecare.wales/news/children-and-parents-show-gratitude-to-childcare-workers-during-lockdown (accessed 30th March 2024).

5
Fostering empathic and supportive teams

Chapter objectives

- To examine teamwork and effective team skills in early years settings
- To investigate the benefits of diverse teams
- To explore empathic and compassionate leadership
- To evaluate aspects of motivation and wellbeing in the early years profession

This chapter examines the dynamics of teamwork by analysing theories related to effective teams. This explores a range of team theories through the lens of empathy and compassion. The application of Rogers' (1942) core conditions in interactions with colleagues is illustrated with examples from the research. The merits of diverse teams are explored, highlighting the value of embracing differing values and beliefs. Respect for the views of others is an essential facet of integrated working.

Motivation theories are explored, interwoven with job satisfaction and the underlying motives driving individuals towards working with children. Within a management and leadership context, the significance of fostering support for staff will be underscored.

Working in a team

Working within the early years profession usually involves collaborating with others within a team. Exceptions to this may be home-based practitioners, such as nannies or childminders, although most of these practitioners belong to networks, enabling them to socialise with others and team up for child-centred activities on a regular basis. Whatever the situation, early years practitioners interact with other adults; parents and families are often included in the 'team', depending on the setting. The very nature of early years is concerned with people, relationships, feelings, and interactions with others. Working with others has many advantages, some of which are detailed in Figure 5.1. Working with other people enables us to learn from others who have different skills and who have had different experiences. A supportive team can make us feel secure and able to suggest ideas, take risks, and be creative, knowing that the others around us are there for us. Empathy and compassion are crucial in any relationship, but in a work team, creating a culture of empathy and compassion will ensure that we are aware of and understand each other's needs. Cook et al.'s (2020) suggestion that a team can be a secure base for us is an interesting one. Just as a toddler explores his/her surroundings in the knowledge that their parent is there if needed, we can explore new ways of doing things, safe in the knowledge that we have our team to help us if we need them.

The image of a supportive, respectful team with positive relationships and a common goal may be an idealistic one. The ultimate aim of a team is 'to fulfil different roles but work together to defend the same goal' (Wei, 2020, p. 326), but individuals have their own values and beliefs based on their particular experiences, so what happens when the individuals within a team have conflicting values? For example, there could be different views on the amount of formal preparation for school children should have or about how early children should be given a diagnosis of a special educational need.

 Reflective prompt - Reflect on your experience of practitioner values clashing in an EY setting. How do you think this could/should be managed?

Recognising and addressing negativity

Even in the most supportive, positive teams, there is a potential for negativity, which can take a huge amount of emotional energy to manage and can destroy working relationships. The Equality Act (2010) legally protects people from discrimination in the workplace,

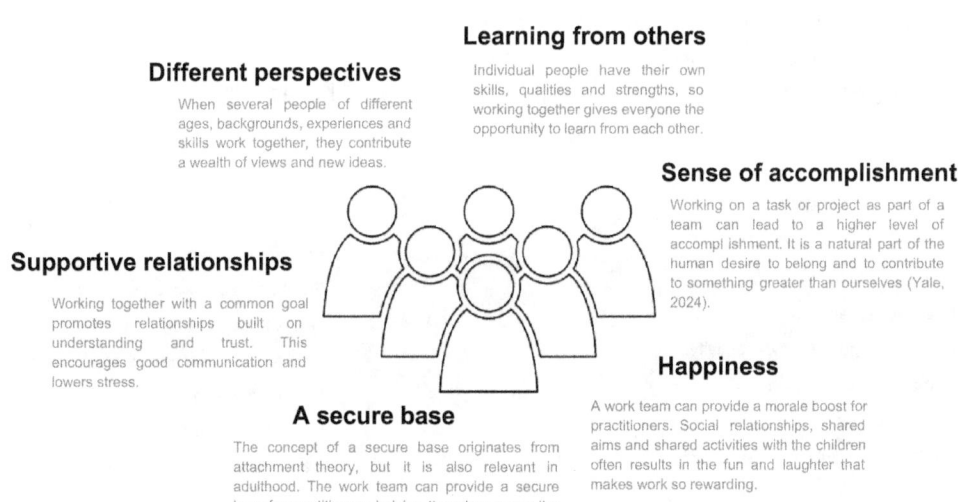

Figure 5.1 Benefits of working in a team

demonstrating that every individual has the right to feel safe in their workplace. Gossip, complaining, and workplace bullying can have a huge negative impact on the morale of the person experiencing it, which can, in turn, impact negatively on their practice and, therefore, can impact on the children and families attending the setting.

It is important to acknowledge that everyone experiences a whole spectrum of emotions every day and that it is ok to feel upset, angry, worried, or sad sometimes. Accepting this fact can help us to be compassionate towards ourselves and others. Many people have negative thought patterns which affect the way they react to situations, so some may always focus on the negatives, whilst others may become defensive. These thought patterns may result from experiences in childhood, past trauma, or mental health problems. Using empathy to get to know people and understand what life is like for them helps us to recognise what might be difficult or challenging for them. As Sutton-Tsang (2022, cited in Richards and Malomo, 2022, p. 146) explains, 'as an individual, you have the power to make positive changes'. Figure 5.2 lists some common negative thought processes and some ways of managing negativity within the team.

One of the best ways to manage negativity is by developing a positive or growth mindset. People who have a growth mindset believe that their abilities can be developed through dedication and hard work. One of the examples (Figure 5.2) is of a person who believes that they are not good at maths; this shows a fixed mindset; it is a fact that is fixed. However, if the person can develop a growth mindset, they will understand that this can change that, with time and effort, they can improve in this area. This view creates a love of learning and a resilience that is essential for great accomplishment (Dweck, 2006).

Social pedagogy

Social pedagogy describes a relationship-centred way of working with people. It is based on humanistic values and is primarily concerned with well-being, learning, and growth, seeking to recognise and promote individuals' potential. The social pedagogy approach is rooted

Figure 5.2 Managing negativity within the team

in Rogers' core conditions (1942); and the belief that 'each person deserves to be treated with human dignity and possesses unique inner resources and potential, which we can help them unfold' (Thempra, 2024). Social pedagogy incorporates many different concepts; one of these is *'The Relational Universe'*, a metaphor to illustrate relationship-centred practice. Thempra (2024), the organisation pioneering the social pedagogy approach, describe the relational universe:

> *It emphasises that human beings are interdependent. We are all part of other people's relational universes, just as others are part of ours. They might be close to us or be farther in the distance. Their presence might have a strong gravitational pull on us or less of an effect. They might be looming large or play a smaller role, perhaps like distant stars guiding us . . . each of these relationships has meaning, albeit in a multitude of different ways, with a wide variety of emotions and needs connected to every single relationship. Some might be toxic or laden with trauma, whilst others are characterised by love and a strong bond of trust – there's a story to each and every relationship* (Thempra, 2024).

 Individual activity

Draw a diagram of the team that you work with (or have worked with in the past) and place yourself within that team. You may want to use the image of a universe as shown previously, but be as creative as you like. Include the core and wider team. Now choose three individuals from your diagram, and for each person, answer these questions:

- How would you describe your working relationship with this person?
- How do you communicate with them in a manner likely to promote trust and confidence?
- How do you share information and skills with them?
- How do you demonstrate empathy and compassion with them?

Reflect on what you have learned from this exercise.

Embracing diversity

Just as an early years setting benefits from a diverse community of children, staff teams, too, are enriched by diversity within the team. There is evidence which suggests that teams made up of people with different characteristics and backgrounds can be more creative and innovative. Gómez-Zará et al.'s (2022) research shows that demographic diversity – team members of different genders, cultures, races, etc., can boost team performance. Rock and Grant (2016) suggest that 'working with people who are different from you may challenge your brain to overcome its stale ways of thinking and sharpen its performance'. This makes perfect sense; for example, working with someone from a particular religious group enables us to learn about that religion. Working with someone who is neurodivergent helps us understand the abilities and needs that they have.

Sex and gender

It should not be necessary to discuss the particular difficulties around sex and gender in the 21st century. Unfortunately, there still appear to be instances of sex discrimination towards males working in early years. Within the domain of early childhood practice, there is a prevailing perception that it is inherently 'women's work', perpetuating stereotypes that associate emotion and sensitivity with femininity, as outlined by Richards (2013). The comedy film *Daddy Daycare* revolves around the idea of successful businessmen suddenly finding themselves running a childcare setting. In the film, these fathers succeed by using a business model, and 'they provide the children with childcare that the audience accepts as superior to what women educators can provide' (Chang-Kredl et al., 2021, p. 110). The idea that men and women have such different strengths and behaviours is outdated, but this view that the neoliberal (and masculine) model of business and objectivity is the superior system (Osgood, 2010) prevails. Even in 2019, research by Hedlin, Åberg, and Johansson saw male early years practitioners feeling under pressure to live up to the image of the 'fun guy' whilst also striving to be seen as a physically cautious 'safe' man (p. 111). Men should not have to feel pressured to be anything other than caring childcare workers; sex discrimination and stereotyping should always be challenged.

In the empathy research (Hodgkins, 2023), manager Joel talked about discussing sex discrimination with a young man being interviewed for an early years educator position at Joel's nursery. The man had been treated differently from his female colleagues in a previous job and had felt bullied and belittled. Joel explained,

> The man discussed previous discrimination he faced in his previous workplace. I asked him how this made him feel and reassured him of the policies and procedures we have in place to avoid this behaviour happening in the future.
>
> (Joel)

 Reflective prompt – It is interesting to see that, at Joel's nursery, there is seen to be a need for policies and procedures which protect men in the workplace. Reflect on your own view of policies and procedures to protect people with particular, or protected, characteristics.

Fostering empathic and supportive teams 73

Sex relates to characteristics that are biologically defined, whereas gender is based on socially constructed features. The World Health Organization (2024) recognise that there are variations in how people experience gender based upon self-perception and expression and how they behave. Essentially, nearly all people are born with physical characteristics that are labelled male or female. However, through learned behaviour people become boys and girls, then men and women, or have a non-binary gender. Children are encouraged, either through explicit teaching, modelling, or subtle encouragement of certain behaviours, to adopt gender-consistent behaviours. However, gender is increasingly understood as a spectrum and people are increasingly referring to themselves using their own terminology. However, the LGBTQIA+ community experiences repeated injustice, prejudice, and exclusion. Kirk (2022) advises that the most important thing is to be open and honest with people, to include them, involve them, and treat them like the adults they are. This is good advice to follow with everyone, as it mirrors Rogers' (1942) core conditions.

 Individual activity

What follows are some examples of people in the early years being treated differently. Consider the options and choose the empathic and compassionate response to these scenarios.

Table 5.1 Diversity scenarios

Scenario	Responses
1. A new parent comes into a nursery with her baby daughter. She asks for the male practitioner not to be involved in her daughter's personal care (i.e. nappy changing).	Assure the parent that you will do as she asks and ensure that only female members of staff change her baby's nappy.
	Tell the parent that all staff are equally capable and trustworthy and refuse to follow their demand. Suggest that they take the baby to a different setting if they do not accept this.
	Something different –
2. You are told that the young early years student about to start their placement at your setting is a trans woman.	Arrange a staff meeting with all of your staff to discuss the new student and discuss what special steps need to be taken when they start.
	Do nothing; being trans is not a problem, so there is no need to do anything different.
	Something different –
3. Two members of your staff come from Romania and have been in the UK for five years. They sometimes speak to each other in their home language.	Ask them politely to only speak English at work.
	Do nothing; it is natural to speak in your own language to a fellow countryman.
	Something different –

(Continued)

74 Nurturing Compassionate Connections

Table 5.1 (Continued)

Scenario	Responses
4. You are setting up a summer playscheme for children with SEND. You are interviewing for both qualified and unqualified staff. A young man who has moderate learning difficulties has applied for a job at the scheme.	Let the young man work as a volunteer with expenses but as a supernumerary staff member under supervision. Welcome the young man to the team. He is likely to be a great role model for the children in the scheme, as he has similar needs. Something different –

Empathic and compassionate leadership

Management and leadership are usually understood to be different concepts; managers plan and manage an organisation's systems, and leaders focus on change and leading people by motivating and inspiring. Thus, anyone can be a leader, not just the manager of a setting, and any member of staff can instigate change and influence quality improvement. Wajdi (2017) suggests that the two roles are not completely unconnected, as 'good managers should strive to be good leaders and good leaders need management skills to be effective' (Wadji, 2017, p. 75).

Empathy in leadership involves prioritising listening, supporting staff through challenges, and maintaining strength-based interactions. Brower (2021) suggests that empathic leadership is more important than ever now, as there has been a global decline in mental health and an increase in stress, anxiety, and exhaustion. Empathy, seen in the past as a 'soft skill', is now accepted as a skill that can impact engagement, happiness, performance, and retention of staff. Sinek (2023) believes that empathetic leaders inspire trust and loyalty in their teams. This appears to have been the case in the empathy research (Hodgkins, 2023), with examples of empathy from managers Jake and Joel. Jake's reflections on empathy focussed on prioritising listening to staff. He wrote,

> It is difficult as we are all busy, but it is important to listen to the staff team and be there for them.
>
> (Jake)

Jake's comment supports Elfer's (2012) claim that nursery managers often feel responsibility akin to parental concern for their staff. For managers working in the early years sector, managing relationships with adults as well as children adds another tier of interpersonal relationships. Whalley (2019, p. 406) asserts that in the early years managers and leaders 'seek to act *with* others rather than assert power *over* others'. There were many examples in the empathy research of the significance of this relationship *with* the team; the following examples are all from Joel, who manages a large private nursery.

> A member of the team was able to discuss their worries/anxieties . . . . I listened to the professional and provided her with more support.
>
> (Joel)

> I feel as though I have shown empathy to the staff team by offering support with their increased workload, and where staff members have shown increased worries and concerns – we have worked together to create a practical plan.
>
> (Joel)

> Trying to dig to find the root cause of the problem with that member of staff and every individual is slightly different so it's understanding their point of view.
>
> (Joel)

The role of the manager in an early childhood setting can be very challenging and demanding, often with no system of support for managers (Elfer, 2012). For Joel, the role had many challenges, and he took great care during interactions with staff, ensuring that he was aware of how the other person was feeling and of the potential impact of his words. Joel's organisation operated a strength-based approach to management, which Joel evidently found demanding on an everyday basis; he said,

> Sometimes it's mentally tiring because every conversation that you have has always got to be strength-based, so you're always thinking, how am I going to word this?
>
> (Joel)

However tiring this may be, Joel prioritises his team's wellbeing. In one of his diary entries, Joel describes a meeting with a practitioner who was upset about the lack of progress made by a child. Joel responded,

> They said they felt they weren't doing enough; that was the emotion they felt and were showing me. So, I said, 'Well, let's look at what you've actually done for that child over the last few months, and you'll see just how much effort you've made to help him'.
>
> (Joel)

In these examples, managers demonstrate empathy and compassion for their teams, and it is clear that they have made time to get to know them as people. This is a good example of the relational universe described earlier in the chapter.

Compassionate teams need compassionate leaders who lead by example and set the tone for the organisation. A good example of compassionate leadership comes from the prime minister of New Zealand, Jacinda Ardern, who famously said,

> One of the criticisms I've faced over the years is that I'm not aggressive enough or assertive enough, or maybe somehow, because I'm empathetic, it means I'm weak. I totally rebel against that. I refuse to believe that you cannot be both compassionate and strong.
>
> (Van Wart et al., 2022)

Ardern's leadership has been praised worldwide by leaders and by her own team. However, as she says, leadership is hard. There are many difficult decisions to be made as a leader and tough feedback to give, so strength and compassion need to go hand in hand, which is no easy task.

Individual or 👥 **group activity**

Look at the leadership types in Table 5.2. Consider them and identify which best aligns with your leadership style. Are you happy with your leadership style? Are you interested in trying any aspects of the other types here? What are your reasons? Which do you think best aligns with empathy and compassion for others?

(If you do not have leadership responsibility, reflect on a leader you have known or on how you would lead in the future).

Table 5.2 Leadership types

Leadership type	Characteristics	Reflection
Democratic leadership	Allowing other members of the team to participate in the decision-making process.	
Transformational leadership	Engaging with and influencing others by paying attention to their needs, motivating employees, and inspiring them to strive beyond required expectations to work toward a shared vision.	
Servant leadership	Focussing on the needs of others before you consider your own needs and ambitions.	
Collaborative leadership	Regularly seeking out diverse opinions and ideas among the team to build strategies and solve problems.	
Distributed leadership	Sharing leadership responsibilities among various individuals rather than being centralised with one person.	
Situational leadership	Paying close attention to the changing needs of the team, task, and organisation. Adjusting their leadership style as needed to bring out the best in team members and ensure success.	

Motivation and empowerment

Understanding what motivates people is important in getting the best out of people and encouraging them to self-actualise and be the best they can be. In the empathy research (Hodgkins, 2023), Joel expresses this well,

> As an Early Years leader, I have realised how I spend the large part of each day thinking about how the team members feel – what motivates and demotivates, their strengths and interests – how they might act in different scenarios.
>
> (Joel)

One of the first theories about motivation that was published was Maslow's (1943) hierarchy of needs. This renowned theory places the needs of humans in a hierarchy, the idea being that the needs at the lower levels must be met before one can progress to higher levels (see Figure 5.3). The model was first applied to the industry to identify the needs to be met before people can do purposeful work. For example, if workers in a factory do not have enough warmth, fresh air, food and rest, they will not be able to do their best work. This makes perfect sense, and the model has since been applied to education, counselling, nursing, and early years practice.

However, the theory has its downfalls and has been criticised since publication. King-Hill (2015, p. 55), for example, has criticised Maslow's inclusion of 'sex' as a basic physiological need, suggesting that 'this does not acknowledge the emotional and psychological impacts that this has upon an individual'. Others have identified the theory as being ethnocentric, assuming that all people have the same needs, regardless of culture, nationality, gender, etc. An important thing to acknowledge is that what is more important for one person is less important for another. Whilst one person may focus on job security and sufficient pay to meet their needs, another might focus on the opportunity to progress to management. In Maslow's hierarchy, empathy and compassion would appear to be situated in the social and emotional needs, but I would suggest that they are applicable to all levels, particularly when working with young children. A young baby who needs to be fed will only have this need met when a caring adult notices and meets this need. Emotional security is of the utmost importance to a child in an early years setting; feeling known, feeling cared for, and loved by an attachment figure is crucial to children.

The principles can easily be related to workers within an early years team. Workers need their physical needs to be met; they need food and drink, appropriate warmth and fresh air, rest breaks, and lunch breaks. Their safety needs need to be met through appropriate health and safety and job security in a setting that feels emotionally safe and free from conflict. Social and

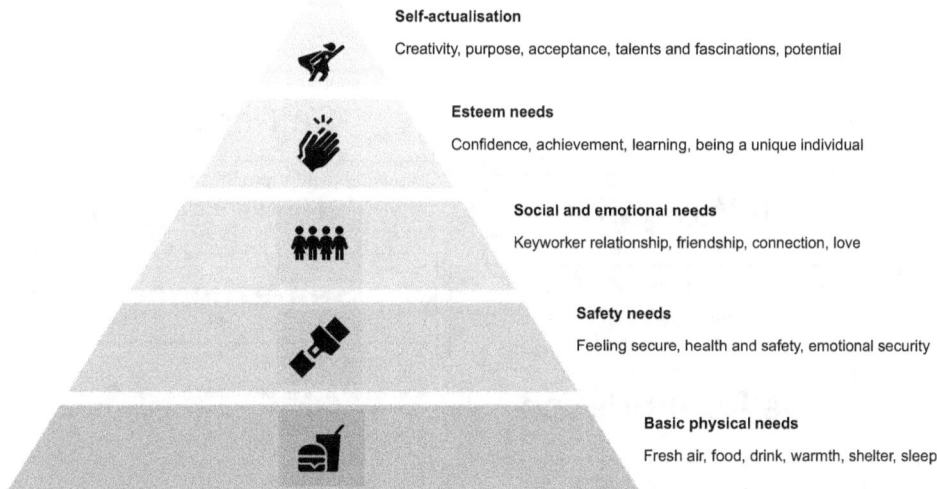

Figure 5.3 Maslow's hierarchy of needs

emotional needs are the essence of what keeps us happy to go to work. Feeling a valued member of the team and having friendships at work is important as we spend a large proportion of our day at work. When things inevitably get tough at work, staff need attachment figures to give support just as much as the children. In the empathy research, one of the nurseries taking part was in financial difficulty and in danger of closing. This was also at the time of the Covid-19 pandemic, so stress levels were high. Debbie, the deputy manager of the nursery, talked about,

> crying together daily and supporting each other.
>
> (Debbie)

Although we would rather practitioners didn't have to cry together every day, the example shows the importance of support and friendship at work. Research by Gallup (Patel and Plowman, 2022) identified the fact that having a best friend at work has become more important to people since the pandemic, as social and emotional support became more important through shared trauma.

Self-esteem and associated concepts can be complex to define (see Figure 5.4), with some interrelating ideas, for example, self-efficacy and self-esteem.

According to Maslow (1943), self-esteem needs should be met before a person can achieve self-actualisation, the ultimate goal. Research suggests that if workers have job security, autonomy, and feedback, their self-confidence in their abilities will improve, resulting in organisation-based self-esteem, which acts as a personal resource at work (Kim and Beehr, 2021, p. 2). Kim and Beehr's (2021) research suggests that the higher employees' self-esteem, the

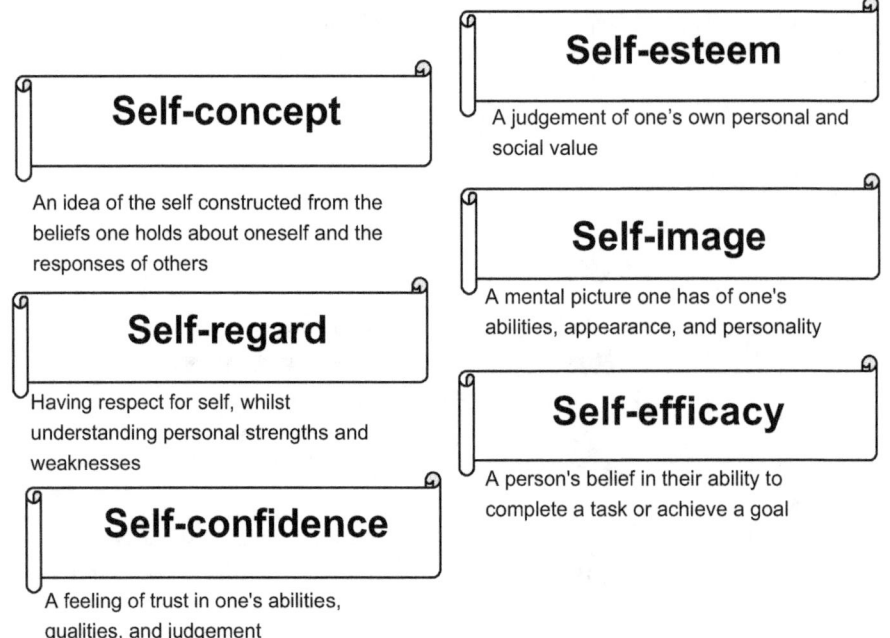

Figure 5.4 Self-beliefs

more likely they are to create their own perfect job role which uses their talents effectively; this is 'job crafting' and resonates with self-actualisation; 'the complete realization of one's potential, and the full development of one's abilities and appreciation for life' (Perera, 2024). Pierce et al. (1989, p. 634) devised a measure of organisation-based self-esteem, devising a Likert-scale test (agree, disagree, strongly disagree, etc.) with the following ten statements,

1. I count in this organisation
2. There is faith in me in this organisation
3. I am valuable in this organisation
4. I am trusted in this organisation
5. I can make a difference
6. I am taken seriously in this organisation
7. I am important around here
8. I am cooperative in this organisation
9. I am efficient in this organisation
10. I am helpful in this organisation

> **Individual activity**
>
> Try carrying out an audit of how well your needs are met within your workplace by asking yourself the following questions based on Maslow's hierarchy.

Table 5.3 Reflecting on your own needs

Need	Reflection	Could things be improved?
Physical needs	Do you have sufficient opportunities to eat, drink, rest, and use the bathroom?	
	Is your workplace an appropriate temperature to work in, with fresh air?	
Safety needs	Do you always feel safe and protected from danger/hazards at work?	
	Is your working day free from conflict, harassment, and bullying?	
Social and emotional needs	Do you have good working relationships with your colleagues?	
	Do you have friendships at work?	
	Do you have good, close relationships with children and their families?	
Self-esteem	Do you feel confident and capable?	
	Are you appreciated and thanked for your work?	
	Do you have opportunities to learn and develop new skills?	

(Continued)

Table 5.3 (Continued)

Need	Reflection	Could things be improved?
Self-actualisation	Do you have opportunities for creativity?	
	Are you able to pursue your own individual interests and passions?	
	Do you feel that you have the potential to grow and achieve more?	

Empowering the workforce

Empathetic leaders want to understand why people are the way they are, and this desire helps them become leaders who are able to connect with many types of people and adapt their style depending on who they are interacting with. They take a genuine interest in the people around them – what *makes them tick*, what inspires them, the way they feel, and what they need.

No two people are the same, so what is appropriate for one person will not be for another. One member of staff may thrive on routine, knowing they are doing a good job every day; others may only feel content if they have opportunities to develop things themselves. Empowering employees often bolsters well-being, as does 'tuning into' people, using empathy to identify what people want and need.

In the empathy research, deputy manager George described a situation he had with a member of staff who was struggling with mental health since returning to work after the Covid-19 lockdown. The staff member was clearly unhappy and was becoming upset when carrying out physical care. The staff member had been off work on maternity leave, then Covid-19 pandemic hit, so she had been away from the nursery for a long time. George said,

> Post-Covid, coming back to work ... she found that very difficult ... when she came back, she was really upset, inconsolable, so I took her outside and I said, 'What is it that you're stressed about?'

(George)

The staff member talked about missing her baby and about her fears of getting physically close to people after so many months of isolation and confinement due to the pandemic. George responded with,

> I told how we dealt with those scenarios while she's been gone, and I said you're not going to have to deal with things you don't feel comfortable with yet. She was really worried about getting so close to the children when changing nappies, so I said, 'Well, in the meantime, why don't I do the majority and you do just one

or two when you're ready, and then overtime we can build it up?' And now she's fine with it all; she gets involved with everything; she's happy to hold the children again; she changes the nappies, and she wipes the noses!

(George)

George's example demonstrates emotionally intelligent leadership and a real commitment to understanding how other staff members feel. The following case study details a nursery with some negativity and conflict.

Case study – a new start for Butterflies Day Nursery

Butterflies is a small private day nursery on the outskirts of a town. It has three rooms for three different age groups and employs a team of qualified early years educators and a young apprentice. Each room has a room leader; the preschool room leader is also the deputy manager. The nursery's Ofsted rating is 'good', and they have the maximum number of children attending.

You have just been appointed as the manager, having worked as a manager in a different setting for three years. You have spent the first few days at Butterflies observing practice and talking to members of staff, and you quickly become aware of some negativity within the team. You hear two members of staff (A and B) complaining about another member of staff (C) in an extremely derogatory way. You also hear some negative, culturally inappropriate comments about one of the parents from staff member A. You arrange a quick meeting with the apprentice to see how he is getting on, and he tells you that he has considered not continuing in the early years profession because he gets fed up with what he calls the 'bitchiness' within the team.

 Individual activity

Consider the following:
- What do you think the main problem might be?
- How would you respond to the apprentice?
- How might you approach the situation as a new manager?

OR
- As another member of staff working in this team, how might this environment affect your own work?

Appreciation of staff

Public perception often undervalues early years work. Overcoming stereotypes and appreciating the complexity and importance of the role is crucial for self-actualisation. It is difficult to feel valuable and important when the role has been subject to the stereotype of unskilled workers who are 'just babysitting', or 'playing with toys all day' (Gaunt, 2022). A study by Faulkner et al. (2016) found that the public perception of their role as mere babysitters was one of the most prominent stressors for practitioners. This feeling was evident in the empathy research in the following examples,

> *If the parents came in for just an hour, they'd be like, 'Wow, you do so much more', and that recognition really would make it feel just that little bit more worthwhile.*
>
> (George)

> *I've worked in early years now since I was 18, and yes, it's challenging, and it's hard work, and I do feel underpaid, and I do feel that as a sector, we are underappreciated, so I think if you didn't do it for the love of the job you'd never do it would you? We've got our work cut out, definitely, and we're not acknowledged enough for it. I don't think we're going to get a pay rise any time soon, but we deserve more money and better conditions.*
>
> (Cheryl)

> **Group activity**
>
> Showing appreciation for staff is vital for meeting self-esteem needs, improving morale, and reducing stress. Many settings have developed strategies to support this; in a group, brainstorm as many ideas as you can to show appreciation for staff. As a group, discuss which ideas would work for you. Here are some ideas to start you off (Figure 5.5).

It is important to think about all staff in the activity. Often, the manager is responsible for showing appreciation and supporting staff. In the empathy research, there was evidence that managers felt responsibility for their staff's wellbeing; often, this responsibility was similar to parental concern, echoing the findings of Elfer's (2012) research with nursery managers. Elfer (2012) found that managers of early childhood settings experienced many challenges and demands within the role and that a lack of support for them meant they often felt lonely. In an interview response to the empathy research, Joel says exactly that,

> *management is quite a lonely place to be.*
>
> (Joel)

For managers, there is an additional tier of empathy; they show empathy with the children in their care, and to parents and families, and also to their staff teams who, as previously

Figure 5.5 Showing appreciation for staff

discussed, are often experiencing significant stress and emotion themselves. The role of a manager in the early years is often associated with a sense of 'overwhelming responsibility ... a professional who is many things; to many people' (Preston, 2013). Bethan Rose (2023) paints a realistic image of the role of a nursery manager by outlining some of the key pressures in the role, such as 'there's a show around arriving in a few hours, invoices need to go out, lunch cover is off sick, a parent is ringing, a member of staff has handed in their notice, and there is an awkward issue to address with an apprentice'. An Early Years manager is required to bend to meet the demands of everyone and to develop the skills of others.

> **Reflective prompt** – Who looks after the manager's mental health in the workplace?

Chapter summary

This chapter has explored the strengths, benefits, and dynamics of teamwork, emphasising the effectiveness of a supportive and respectful group working toward a common goal. Social pedagogy provides a strong example of a team grounded in relationships and core conditions, incorporating concepts such as the 'relational universe'. The chapter reflects on relationships within teams and identifies strategies for leading with compassion and managing negativity. Celebrating the diversity within a team is highlighted as a powerful way to learn about the lives of others, thereby increasing understanding and compassion.

Empathic and compassionate leadership focuses on placing people at the centre of the organisation. Real-life examples from the empathy research illustrate how empathy and compassion can be integrated within teams, management, and leadership. The chapter also evaluates different leadership styles and discusses motivation theories that offer insights into how to motivate and empower team members. It underscores the responsibility of managers and leaders to meet the needs of their staff and show appreciation for their work. For early years managers, this responsibility extends to addressing the needs of children and families as well. The specific needs of managers themselves have been identified as an important area for reflection.

Creating empathic and supportive teams in early years settings involves understanding team dynamics, effectively managing negativity, embracing diversity, and leading with empathy. By fostering such a supportive environment, practitioners can thrive, ultimately benefiting the children and families they serve.

Key messages

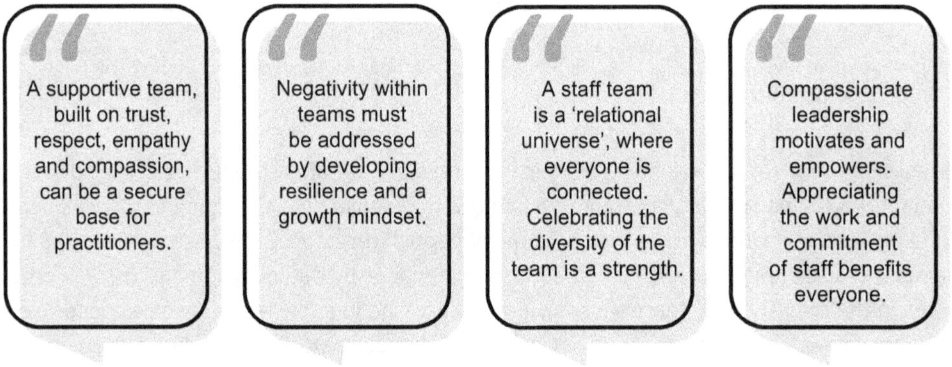

> A supportive team, built on trust, respect, empathy and compassion, can be a secure base for practitioners.

> Negativity within teams must be addressed by developing resilience and a growth mindset.

> A staff team is a 'relational universe', where everyone is connected. Celebrating the diversity of the team is a strength.

> Compassionate leadership motivates and empowers. Appreciating the work and commitment of staff benefits everyone.

Figure 5.6 Key messages from Chapter 5

References

Bethan-Rose, J. (2023) 'Early years voices: Releasing the pressures on early years managers', *Famly*, available at: www.famly.co/blog/early-years-voices-supporting-early-years-managers (accessed 1st March 2024).

Brower, T. (2021) 'Empathy is the most important leadership skill according to research', *Forbes*, available at: www.forbes.com/sites/tracybrower/2021/09/19/empathy-is-the-most-important-leadership-skill-according-to-research/?sh=3e38a8553dc5 (accessed 12th May 2024).

Chang-Kredl, S., Pauls, K. and Foster, K. (2021) '"You're all so good with poo here": Mainstream media representations of the early years educator', *Gender and Education*, 33(1), pp. 103–118.

Cook, L., Zschomler, D., Biggart, L and Carder, S. (2020) 'The team as a secure base revisited: Remote working and resilience among child and family social workers during COVID-19', *Journal of Children's Services*, 15(4), pp. 259–266.

Dweck, C. (2006) *Mindset: The new psychology of success*, London: Random House.

Elfer, P. (2012) 'Emotion in nursery work: Work discussion as a model of critical professional reflection', *Early Years*, 32(2), pp. 129–141.

Equality Act. (2010) [online]. Chapter 15. *Legislation.gov.uk*, available at: legislation.gov.uk/ukpga/2010/15/contents (accessed 13th March 2025).

Faulkner, M., Gerstenblatt, P., Lee, A., Vallejo, V. and Travis, D. (2016) 'Childcare providers: Work stress and personal well-being', *Journal of Early Childhood Research*, 14(3), pp. 280-293.

Gaunt, C. (2022, July 5) 'Early years is "an invisible workforce" - report', *Nursery World*, available at: www.nurseryworld.co.uk/news/article/early-years-is-an-invisible-workforce-report (accessed 26th May 2024).

Gómez-Zará, D., Das, A., Pawlow, B. and Contractor, N. (2022) 'In search of diverse and connected teams: A computational approach to assemble diverse teams based on members' social networks', *PLoS ONE*, 17(11).

Hodgkins, A. (2023) *Exploring early childhood practitioners' perceptions of empathic interactions with children and families*. PhD thesis, University of Worcester, available at: https://eprints.worc.ac.uk/13525/

Kim, M. and Beehr, T. (2021) 'The role of organization-based self-esteem and job resources in promoting employees' job crafting behaviors', *The International Journal of Human Resource Management*, available at: https://doi.org/10.1080/09585192.2021.1934711 (accessed 26th May 2024).

King-Hill, S. (2015) 'Critical analysis of Maslow's hierarchy of need', *The STeP Journal (Student Teacher Perspectives)*, 2(4), pp. 54-57.

Kirk, M. (2022) 'Chapter 8: Voice practices to support LGBTQIA+ educators and pupils', in Sewell, A. (ed) *Diverse voices in educational practice*, London: Speechmark, Routledge.

Maslow, A. H. (1943) 'A theory of human motivation', *Psychological Review*, 50(4), pp. 370-396.

Osgood, J. (2010) 'Reconstructing professionalism in ECEC: The case for the "critically reflective emotional professional"', *Early Years*, 30(2), pp. 119-133.

Patel, A. and Plowman, S. (2022) 'The increasing importance of a best friend at work', *Gallup*, available at: www.gallup.com/workplace/397058/increasing-importance-best-friend-work.aspx (accessed 25th May 2024).

Perera, A. (2024) 'Self-actualization in psychology: Theory, examples & characteristics', *Simply Psychology*, available at: www.simplypsychology.org/self-actualization.html#:~:text=Self%2Dactualization%20is%20the%20complete,every%20human%20being%20reaches%20it (accessed 26th May 2024).

Pierce, J. L., Gardner, D. G., Cummings, L. L. and Dunham, R. B. (1989) 'Organization-based self-esteem: Construct definition, measurement, and validation', *Academy of Management Journal*, 32, pp. 622-648.

Preston, D. (2013) 'Being a manager in an English nursery', *European Early Childhood Education Research Journal*, 21(3), pp. 326-338.

Richards, A. (2013) 'Overly sensitive, highly emotional, and other "feminine flaws"', *Everyday Feminism*, available at: https://everydayfeminism.com/2013/09/over-sensitive-and-other-feminine-flaws/ (accessed 13th March 2025).

Rock, D. and Grant, H. (2016) 'Why diverse teams are smarter', *Harvard Business Review*, available at: https:// hbr.org/2016/ 11/why-diverse-teams-are-smarter (accessed 25th May 2024).

Rogers, C. (1942) *Counselling and psychotherapy*, Cambridge, MA: Riverside Press.

Sinek, S. (2023) *Inspiring leadership through vision and purpose*, available at: www.linkedin.com/in/simonsinek/ (accessed 12th May 2024).

Sutton-Tsang, S. (2022) 'Chapter 8: Workplace relationships and power struggles', in Richards, H. and Malomo, M. (eds) *Developing your professional identity: A guide for working with children and families*, St. Albans: Critical Publishing.

Van Wart, M., Macaulay, M. and Haberstroh, K. (2022) 'Jacinda Ardern's compassionate leadership: A case of social change leadership in action', *International Journal of Public Sector Management*, 35(6), pp. 641-658.

Wajdi, M. (2017) 'The differences between management and leadership', *Synergy: Scientific Journal of Management Science*, 7(2), pp. 75-84.

Wei, H., et al. (2020) 'A culture of caring: The essence of healthcare interprofessional collaboration', *Journal of Interprofessional Care*, 34(3), pp. 324-331.

Whalley, M. E. (2019) 'Leading quality practice', in Fitzgerald, D. and Maconochie, H. (eds) *Early childhood studies*, London: Sage.

World Health Organization. (2024) *Gender and health*, available at: www.who.int/health-topics/gender (accessed 12th May 2024).

6
Supporting and promoting positive behaviour

> **Chapter objectives**
>
> - To investigate the role of empathy in understanding and interpreting children's behaviour
> - To identify and examine various factors influencing a child's behaviour
> - To analyse strategies for providing positive, individualised behaviour support for young children
> - To explore the principles and practices of emotion coaching for young children

In this chapter, we investigate empathy and compassion in relation to children's behaviour. Factors affecting children's behaviour are examined using a bio-ecological systems theory approach (Bronfenbrenner, 1979). Rather than managing children's behaviour, the chapter takes the approach of attempting to understand behaviour and help the child to acknowledge and learn to cope with it themselves. The principles of emotion coaching are analysed with examples from empathy research. Traditional methods of 'managing behaviour' are critiqued from the child's perspective, and more positive caring ways of approaching conflict are suggested.

Empathy in understanding and interpreting behaviour

Watzlawick et al. (1967) first coined the phrase 'every behaviour is a form of communication' to describe relationships within families. They highlighted the fact that communication is constant and suggested that it is impossible *not* to communicate; even avoiding communication with others is a form of communication in itself. The phrase 'all behaviour is communication' is often used by those working with children today as a positive response to a child's actions. When presented with a behaviour response which is unwanted, we should ask, 'What is this telling me? What is the child trying to communicate?' This involves taking a step back from the behaviour, depersonalising it and analysing the message, thinking about what is at the 'heart of the intended communication' (Moore, in Robinson, 2010, p. 3).

> **Reflective prompt** - Imagine the everyday scenario of a toddler in a supermarket, lying on the floor, kicking and crying. The child's parent is struggling to get the child to stop, and she is very conscious of the judgemental expressions on the faces of fellow shoppers as the child 'has a tantrum'.¹ This situation is very familiar; most of us have experienced it as a passer-by or as a parent. In this situation, think about what the child might be trying to communicate. Why might the child's parent not be listening?

Using empathy to 'tune into' children's feelings

There is ample evidence in the empathy research data of their ability to recognise emotion in the children they work with. Rogers' (1980) description of empathy as 'the sensitive ability and willingness to understand the client's thoughts, feelings and struggles' (p. 85) seems to be widespread within early years practice. See Chapter 2 for more about recognising emotion in others.

Practitioners use their knowledge of individual children to predict or pre-empt how a child will react. They pay attention to children's body language, facial expression, and voice tone, often without realising this is what they are doing. Reading signs of emotion in a child you know well becomes intuitive. Children's behaviour is observed and interpreted by the adults caring for them. In the empathy research (Hodgkins, 2023), Aadiya said of a child she works with,

> Behaviours are a window of what's going on inside. She is expressing that something is not right, but is unable to articulate what it is at the moment.
>
> (Aadiya)

Aadiya understands that the child's behaviour is an outward sign of their inner emotion, which the child is not yet capable of relaying verbally. She knows the child sufficiently to be able to interpret her behaviour. Egan's (2013) description of advanced empathy, which involves picking up and acting on emotion recognised from non-verbal clues, may explain what Aadiya is doing when she says of the child,

> something is not right.
>
> (Aadiya)

The idea of 'sensing what is being felt but not said or consciously realised by the other person' is labelled advanced empathy by Egan (2013, p. 48). However, Claxton (2003) terms it intuition, which he explains is when people use implicit learning as unconscious 'ways of knowing' (p. 33). Aadiya may be unconsciously noticing tiny physical clues and using her experience with the child to pre-empt what may happen next.

Factors influencing behaviour

A child's emotions and behaviour are influenced by a multitude of circumstances. If we return to the previously mentioned scenario of the child lying down, kicking and screaming in the supermarket, we can try to surmise what has led to the emotional outburst. It may be that the child is overtired, bored, or struggling with being told that he cannot have something that he wants. But it may also be the case that the child has a learning difficulty, which makes understanding the situation difficult, or a neurodiversity which causes the child to feel overwhelmed by the sights and sounds around him. A recent event may have caused the child to feel unsettled, or the child's parent/carer may have responded to him insensitively.

One of the most well-known models to describe the factors affecting a child's life is the bio-ecological framework (Bronfenbrenner, 1979). The theory views child development as a complex system of relationships. It describes how a child's life and development is affected by multiple levels of the surrounding environment, from immediate family and childcare settings to broader cultural values, laws, and customs. These levels are called the microsystem, mesosystem, exosystem, macrosystem, and chronosystem (see Figure 6.1). Factors at each of these levels/layers can affect a child's emotions and behaviours.

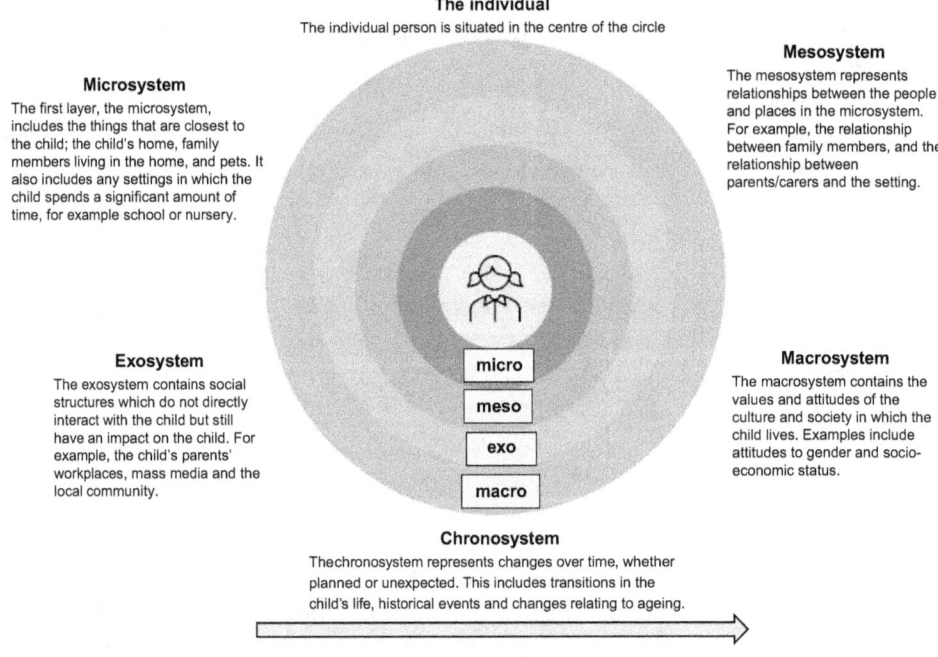

Figure 6.1 Bronfenbrenner's bio-ecological systems theory

> **Individual activity**
>
> Think of a child you know well and try to identify factors affecting the child at all levels. Reflect on the usefulness of the exercise; does it make you consider the child more holistically?

Table 6.1 Bio-ecological systems activity

Microsystem
Mesosystem
Exosystem
Macrosystem
Chronosystem

A focus on the mesosystem

The mesosystem is particularly important to the early years profession, as it concerns relationships between the people and places in the child's microsystem. The relationship between home and the setting and the relationships between the family and setting staff are key. Empathic and compassionate relationships within the setting have a positive impact on the child, but any problems within those relationships may have a detrimental effect.

As children's social and emotional skills develop, they learn the social rules of their microsystem. They learn what is acceptable and what isn't and about the relationship between their behaviour and its consequences. This is the essence of Social Learning Theory (Bandura, 1971), but there can be challenges when there is more than one setting involved.

> ***Reflective prompt*** - What are the consequences of children attending more than one setting? Imagine a child who attends nursery three days a week and who goes to a childminder one day a week. What are the potential challenges for the child? For the nursery staff? For the child's family? How can these challenges be managed?

Children who attend more than one setting can experience difficulty in adjusting to the different routines and expectations of each setting. However, some children may adapt very well with no problems, particularly if the expectations of the settings are similar. Having an awareness of the potential difficulty and observing the child for signs of struggle is important. The same concern applies to a child whose parents are not living together and who spends time in two different homes. This can be very challenging unless care is taken to discuss and agree on boundaries and routines for the child. McDowall-Clark (2016) explains that young children today often have more than one microsystem, meaning that they have more than one mesosystem. The interactions and communication between these various microsystems impact the child.

> **Individual activity**
>
> How might you manage the following situations?

Table 6.2 Different rules in different settings

A child refuses to wash his hands after using the toilet at nursery because no one at his house does that.
A child uses swear words regularly because his family uses them in everyday conversation. The child does not seem to realise that some words should not be used.
There has been a minor incident between two children. It has been handled positively, but you overhear a parent say to her son, 'If it happens again, you hit him back'.
A child at nursery is sometimes collected by his parent and sometimes by his childminder. Messages sent home to the parent are often not passed on to the childminder.

The solution to all of the examples in Table 6.2 is partnership and collaboration between all people and places within the child's microsystem(s). Sometimes, children have to learn that there are some rules that relate to one particular place only, but this takes time for them to comprehend. When individuals all work together for the benefit of the child, this can be very powerful. A study by Childs and Scanlon (2022), which aimed to find a solution to school absenteeism, drew upon the bio-ecological systems theory. The researchers investigated ways of building positive relationships between those in the children's mesosystem (families and school staff) and liaising with community resources in the local exosystem. By coordinating support from families and cooperation from community partners (e.g. shop staff and public transport services), they were able to make a difference in school attendance. The example was in a school and with older children, but community involvement can be a great way of forging links with your own exosystem.

Case study – community links

A large nursery is in an area of deprivation; the majority of the children attending are in receipt of pupil premium funding, and a large percentage of the children are known to social services; many are on child protection plans. The area that the nursery is situated in is a multi-cultural one, with families from a variety of races, ethnicities, and religions. There has been some racial tension in the area.

The nursery manager has worked hard to make links within the local community. The children are regularly taken for walks around the local area and have been involved in litter picking and planting wildflowers. The nursery has taken over a small plot on the local allotment where they grow food and exchange some of the things they have grown with other allotment holders. On a visit to the local greengrocer, the children were given different fruits to try. The greengrocer now sells small bags of fruit for 10p for children to buy. When out shopping, some of the children now ask their parents if they can buy a bag of grapes instead of sweets.

One of the first things the new manager did when she first arrived was to arrange a meeting with the Imam of the local mosque. The children have since visited the mosque to learn all about what happens there, as well as the local church. The Imam is a regular visitor to the nursery and even dressed as Santa at their Christmas party!

 Group activity

Reflect on the case study and then think about your local area. Are there links that you could make which would benefit both children and their community?

Locus of control

The term 'locus of control' refers to how much control a person feels they have in their own behaviour (Rotter, 1966). Children's value judgements come from either their internal or external locus. Evidence suggests that a high locus of control can result in higher academic achievement and better psychological adjustment for children (Nowicki et al., 2018). Boddey (2020) explains,

> If a child or person is operating from an internal locus of evaluation, then they trust their own instincts and the evaluation of their actions comes from within. However, many people, and especially children, operate from an external locus of evaluation – this means they use the values of others as a guide to evaluating their actions and ideas.

Internal locus of control

I make things happen
I can decide my future
If I work hard, I can do it
I am in control
I can make my life better

External locus of control

Things happen to me
It's too hard, I can't do it
I have terrible luck
It's not my fault
My teacher doesn't like me, so I'll probably fail

Figure 6.2 Locus of control

Figure 6.2 illustrates the difference between having an internal or external locus of control.

Young children starting to attend an early years setting are unlikely to have a high level of self-confidence. A child of preschool age will naturally want approval from the adults around them; they rely on adults to nurture them, celebrate their successes, and support them through challenges. Young children gain self-worth through the reactions of others, but as they grow and develop, they begin to develop a sense of themselves as capable people. As early years practitioners, we can help to foster children's belief in themselves and their capabilities.

Research by Nowicki et al. (2018) identified some factors that impact children's locus of control. They found that a nurturing home life that includes cuddling and being read stories improved a child's internal locus of control. Conversely, situations where the child's caregivers are less focussed on the child, for example, having the TV on all day, were associated with an external focus. Boddey (2020) suggests that the practice in the early years focuses on evaluating children's development and achievements against universal norms and judgements (external locus) and does not help young children believe in themselves as individuals (internal locus). Behaviour management techniques can also be damaging to children's self-esteem.

Critiquing 'behaviour management' approaches

In other parts of the world, children are not expected to obey adult-sanctioned rules. In an aboriginal tribe, there is a saying, 'The Anbarra child hears of no rules and receives no punishment' (Ruggeri, 2022). In this and similar Aboriginal tribes, children have a choice whether or not to obey an adult's command, and there is no consequence if the child chooses not to. There are no rewards or punishments, and children learn ways of behaving through trial and error. Conversely, there are cultures where physical discipline and/or psychological aggression

Supporting and promoting positive behaviour

are used to control children's behaviour (UNICEF, 2024). In Western society, behaviour management has traditionally been based on the long-established operant conditioning theory (Skinner, 1963), where positive behaviour is rewarded, and negative behaviour is given consequences. Rewards given for following the behaviour rules, particularly in schools, include stickers, star charts, house points, and verbal praise. Sanctions can include warnings, isolation, and detention. As recently as 2014, the DfE emphasised the need for discipline, threats, and punishment for managing behaviour. However, research by Rose (2023) suggests that,

> Current behavioural policies and practices which utilise the systems of sanction and reward do not necessarily address the complexities of social and emotional needs of pupils, particularly those who are vulnerable, in need and/or high-risk of under achievement.

A report by the Children and Young People's Mental Health Foundation showed that 60% of children experienced a form of punishment during their school days (Rainer et al., 2023). In the early years, punishment is used much less often, but there are still practices which do not demonstrate compassion or empathy for the child. A strategy that has recently been criticised is reward charts.

Reward charts

In the early years, stars, stickers, and behaviour charts are often used to 'manage' children's behaviour. The intention of these charts is to encourage children to behave in particular ways in order to be rewarded. Children then copy others, hoping to be rewarded similarly. Davis (2022) points out the problem with this strategy, as such charts are a visual representation of children's rewards and punishments for all to see. Apart from the obvious potential damage to children's self-esteem, Davis (2022) points out that 'we are making the assumption that all children in the setting have control over their behaviour'. This, of course, is not the case for very young children. Between the ages of two to three, children are learning to develop self-control, but this requires warm interactions with attachment figures and a secure base, which not all children have.

 Individual activity

Table 6.3 shows two examples of potentially damaging 'behaviour management' that the author has observed in early years settings within the past 20 years. Read each one and write down your thoughts about the effects on the child.

The examples in Table 6.3 are very poor examples of how to treat young children. The second one, in particular, is extremely damaging to a child's sense of self. I am pleased to say

Table 6.3 Reward and punishment examples

1. The teacher of a preschool class within a primary school has developed a reward system for the children.

   Each child has a sticker chart kept in their drawer in the classroom. Whenever they do something that the teacher thinks deserves praise, they are given a sticker to put on their sticker chart.

   When the child gets to five stickers, a large sticker is placed by the child's name on another chart on the wall of the classroom. Some children never manage to get five small stickers; others get up to 20 small stickers over a week.

   Every Friday afternoon, just before the children go home, the teacher counts the large stickers on the wall chart and gives the child with the most stickers a lollipop.

2. On their first day, when children start at this school nursery, they are all given a wide variety of arts and crafts resources to use to decorate their name cards (previously prepared by the teacher).

   The children enjoy decorating their names with colours, sequins, and glitter, and these are then displayed on the wall of the classroom.

   Throughout the year, every time a child 'misbehaves', their name card is taken off the wall, and the child is given scissors and asked to cut a piece off their card, which is then replaced on the wall.

that this strategy was challenged and did not continue. Often, reward systems are too complicated for a child to understand, as in Example 1. In that example, a child who struggles socially but has a good day and gets four stickers for doing four positive things will never be rewarded with a lollipop. These strategies do not consider the emotions of the child; they do not demonstrate empathy or compassion.

'Time out' or 'time in'

The concept of 'time out' first appeared in the 1960s (Staats et al., 1962) but grew in popularity in the UK and USA with the introduction of TV programmes like Supernanny. The idea

Table 6.4 Time out or time in?

Time out	Time in
The child may not understand why they have been separated from the person who loves them	The child still has their trusted adult with them, so they feel safe
Strong feelings are magnified when alone	With nurturing support, strong feelings are calmed
The child is not learning how to manage the emotion	The child is helped to identify and accept the emotion
The child will not know how to react if the situation happens again	With support, the child learns to manage their own emotions

of giving children 'time out' was to withdraw attention from the child and isolate them for a short period of time. In the UK, this has included placing children on 'the naughty step' or 'the naughty chair', and it has been a feature of the management of behaviour in early years settings. The word 'naughty' is frowned upon in the early years profession these days due to our understanding of the dangers of labelling children with negative words, but the 'time out' strategy can still be seen in some settings. Older children at school are often sent to work in another classroom or even put into isolation as a punishment. New thinking leads us to see the practice as damaging to children, particularly very young children. What children need, within a nurturing and compassionate relationship, is help from adults to manage their own emotions and behaviour. 'Time in' helps children to understand; in this scenario, the child can be moved away from the situation, causing the emotional outburst, but is not separated from the adult. The adult is there to help the child to cope, learn, and move on.

Using a 'time in' approach, the adult role is to calm the situation and support the child. Techniques such as distraction are also a much more positive way of managing the situation.

Emotion coaching

Emotion coaching is gaining popularity in the UK (Rose and Gilbert, 2018). At its core, it requires early childhood practitioners to demonstrate empathy to help young children understand and regulate their emotions. Early childhood is a time when children are learning to control their overwhelming emotions and to behave in socially acceptable ways. There are three stages of emotional development in early childhood: stage one (age birth to one) is noticing emotions, stage two (age two to three) is expressing emotions, and stage three (age three to five) is managing emotions (Meinke, 2019). Throughout this age phase, there is rapid socio-emotional development, and there is evidence that high-quality interactions with adults increase children's development in this area exponentially (Malik and Marwaha, 2022). Goleman (2020) agrees that the interactions between young children and adults that influence their future emotional intelligence. Goleman (2020, p. 13) says that a child's earliest years are 'a critical opportunity for setting down the essential emotional habits that will govern our lives'. In this approach, adults working with the child are encouraged to provide scaffolding and support to help the child recognise and label the emotion they are feeling (Krawczyk, 2017). It is important to validate the child's emotion (Gus et al., 2015), so the child feels listened to and understands that their emotions are accepted. In order to do this, empathy must be a requirement. In the empathy study (Hodgkins, 2023), there were examples of practitioners using the approach very effectively. The first example is from Harriet,

> I used empathy by using emotion coaching, 'I think you are feeling sad, shall we try . . .'
>
> (Harriet)

The quote by Harriet echoes Gottman et al.'s (1996) view that emotion coaching involves the two elements of empathy and guidance to help children recognise their emotions. In the example, Harriet has used empathy 'I think you're feeling . . .' to ascertain the child's emotional state (sadness) and has then tried to guide the child ('Shall we try . . .') to consider ways of coping with the emotion. Another example from Cheryl's diary demonstrates the way she helps a child to understand his own emotions,

> I explained to him that our tummy can sometimes hurt if we feel nervous, and it is okay to feel that way, but we can tell a grown-up or adult if we feel that way.
>
> (Cheryl)

Here again, empathy is illustrated ('I explained . . .') and guiding/assurance enacted ('It is okay. . .'). In the next excerpt from the research, Cheryl explains how she uses a resource, 'feelings cards', to help the child to recognise his emotions,

> I sat next to him and showed him my feelings cards . . . happy, sad, angry, worried. He pointed to sad, and said his tummy hurts. I asked if he knew why his tummy hurts. He replied, 'No'. I explained to him that our tummy can sometimes hurt if we feel nervous, and it is okay to feel that way, but we can tell a grown-up or adult if we feel that way.
>
> (Cheryl)

Cheryl is giving the child an explanation of why he feels the way he does and what this feels like in his body; she is also reiterating that feelings like this are normal and that he can ask for help. Some participants had used emotion coaching to manage children's unwanted behaviour. An example of this is seen in Debbie's diary, where she is speaking to a child who has angrily hit out at another child. Debbie says to the child,

> I can imagine it made you feel a little bit angry; I think I might have felt a little bit angry, too. How do you think we could show we are angry instead of using unkind hands?
>
> (Debbie)

In the example, Debbie encourages the child to think about choices in how he responds, supporting him to talk about his emotions using empathy and guidance (Krawczyk, 2017).

Children's conflicts

Sometimes, in an early years setting, there are conflicts and arguments between children; this is human nature. The compassionate way to handle such conflicts is by coaching children in ways to manage conflict themselves, rather than an adult punishing them. It is important to listen to all sides of the conflict whilst remaining calm and getting down to the children's level. The early childhood consultation partnership (ECCP, 2024) suggests that 'rather than solving the problem for children, help generate ideas of how they might solve the problem'. Practitioners see examples of anger and frustration regularly as young children learn to build relationships and manage their emotions. One of the key purposes of emotion coaching by practitioners in a setting is to promote behavioural self-regulation by the children. Rose et al. (2015), academics from the USA who piloted the first emotion coaching study in UK schools and early childhood settings, propose that adults can support and empower children to 'build a repertoire of internal and external socio-emotional regulatory skills that promote prosocial behavior' (p. 1766). Practitioners in the empathy study gave examples of this. Mel described talking to two children who had been arguing angrily. She says,

> I spoke to each child, validating their feelings and explaining how the other is feeling.
>
> (Mel)

This is a clear example of using emotion coaching to manage children's behaviour by trying to get them to imagine how another child is feeling, thus promoting empathy to children as a social skill (Gottman et al., 1996). Watzlawick et al.'s (1967) assertion that 'all behaviour is communication' (p. 31) means that the adult's role is to ascertain what the child is communicating and to respond accordingly. In another example, Jake explains the way he assesses a situation in order to identify ways of supporting the child to manage it without stepping in to sort out the problem himself,

> I was quick to spot the potential conflict and move over to carefully observe the situation. With conflict and things, we try not to rush in and take over the situation because they're all learning experiences, and if you don't experience conflict, then you're never going to learn how to deal with conflict.
>
> (Jake)

Social pedagogy

Social pedagogy offers a holistic way of working with children, young people, and families in ways that support their well-being, learning, and growth (Thempra, 2024). In an early years context, the ethos of social pedagogy seeks to ensure that every child is treated with dignity. There are many aspects of social pedagogy, all of which are relevant to working with

98 Nurturing Compassionate Connections

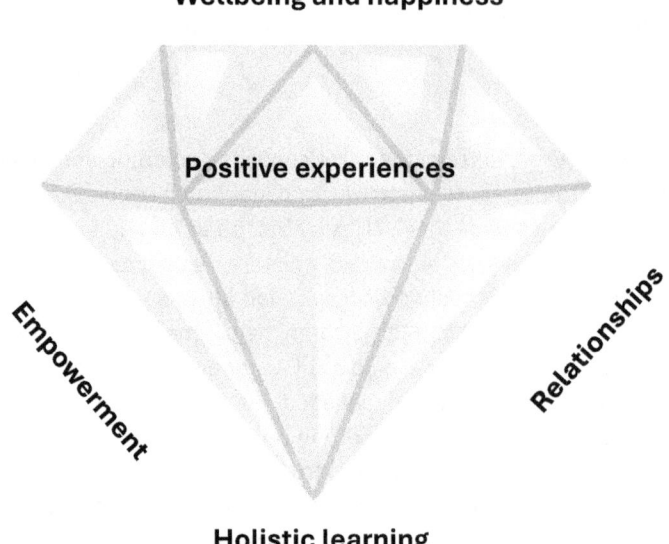

Figure 6.3 The diamond model

children and families, but one of the linked concepts, the diamond model, is particularly applicable here. Figure 6.3 is a representation of the diamond model. The model describes an approach to working with children that is based on positive experiences, empowerment, relationships, well-being, and happiness. When all of these things are in place, then holistic learning can happen. Social pedagogic practice is very specific and responsive to the individual rather than a 'one-size-fits-all approach'. The following activity should help you to apply the diamond model to a child you know.

 Individual activity

Think of a child in your care, then answer the prompts in Table 6.5. Then, reflect and identify any areas of improvement in the care of children in your setting.

Table 6.5 Applying the diamond model

Well-being and happiness	What makes the child feel happy? What does the child need in order to feel a lasting sense of physical, mental, emotional, and social well-being?
Relationship	Does the child have a supportive personal relationship with a member of staff who cares for them and who they can trust?

(Continued)

Table 6.5 (Continued)

Empowerment	Is the child able to take responsibility for their own experiences and learning? How often are they encouraged to be independent?
Positive experiences	Does the child regularly experience something positive (a new skill, caring support, friendship, making someone happy)?
Holistic learning	The approach sees everything in the child's life as an opportunity for learning and growth. Is the child supported to learn in all situations? Is the child aware of what they have learned?

 Group activity

Examine any policies or documents that mention 'behaviour management' and describe rewards and punishment. How can you adapt your policies to make a move from 'managing' children's behaviour to supporting children's social and emotional development? If your setting already has a positive behaviour policy, can you take anything from 'emotion coaching', 'locus of control' or 'the diamond model' to enhance it? How can you share messages about your approach to children's behaviour with all staff and with parents?

Chapter summary

In this chapter, we have examined the role of empathy in understanding and interpreting behaviour, with examples from empathy research to illustrate practitioners' skills in this area of practice. The chapter has taken a positive, non-judgemental approach to children's behaviour, appreciating the factors affecting children and how these may affect behaviour. Traditional 'reward and punishment' methods of managing behaviour have been critiqued, and alternative strategies suggested. Strategies such as emotion coaching help children to understand their own emotions and learn to find ways of coping with them. Alongside emotion coaching, awareness of children's locus of control, and understanding of social pedagogy's relationship-based pedagogy, a compassionate view of children's behaviour has been examined.

Key messages

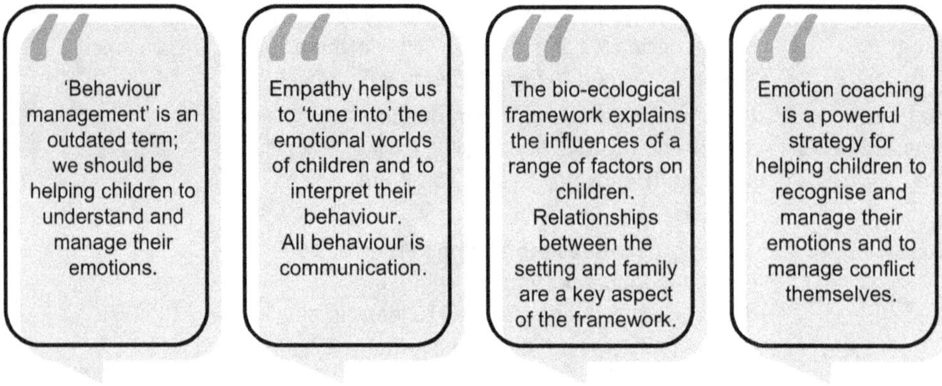

- 'Behaviour management' is an outdated term; we should be helping children to understand and manage their emotions.

- Empathy helps us to 'tune into' the emotional worlds of children and to interpret their behaviour. All behaviour is communication.

- The bio-ecological framework explains the influences of a range of factors on children. Relationships between the setting and family are a key aspect of the framework.

- Emotion coaching is a powerful strategy for helping children to recognise and manage their emotions and to manage conflict themselves.

Figure 6.4 Key messages from Chapter 6

Note

1 The term 'tantrum' is used here to illustrate a popular view, but it has negative connotations, signifying 'bad' behaviour that needs to be controlled. Children exhibiting this behaviour are sometimes viewed as trying to manipulate their parents, whereas it is a natural way to release accumulated stress, feelings, and trauma through the body. The view in this book is that the word *tantrum* should be renamed, maybe as 'struggles', 'emotional overload', 'release of feelings', or even 'storms of feeling' (Sunderland, 2006). Even worse is the label 'terrible twos'; children aged two are certainly not 'terrible'. Between the ages of one and two, there is tremendous brain development; children experience strong and powerful emotions and are not yet able to manage these. Children at this stage need to learn that such emotion can be tolerated and resolved.

References

Bandura, A. (1971) *Social learning theory*, New York: General Learning Press.
Boddey, J. (2020) 'Why we need to nurture early learners' self-belief', *Teach Early Years*, available at: www.teachearlyyears.com/a-unique-child/view/why-we-need-to-nurture-early-learners-self-belief
Bronfenbrenner, U. (1979) *The ecology of human development: Experiments by nature and design*, Cambridge, MA: Harvard University Press.
Childs, J. and Scanlon, L. (2022) 'Coordinating the mesosystem: An ecological approach to addressing chronic absenteeism', *Peabody Journal of Education*, 97(1), pp. 74–86.
Claxton, G. (2003) 'Chapter 2: The anatomy of intuition', in Atkinson, T. and Claxton, G. (eds) *The intuitive practitioner: On the value of not always knowing what one is doing*, Maidenhead: Open University Press, pp. 32–52.
Davis, E. (2022, March 1) 'Behaviour charts: Good or bad?', *Nursery World*.
DfE. (2014) *Behaviour and discipline in schools: Advice for headteachers and school staff*, available at: https://assets.publishing.service.gov.uk/government/uploads/system/uploads/attachment_data/file/353921/Behaviour_and_Discipline_in_Schools_-_A_guide_for_headteachers_and_school_staff.pdf
Early Childhood Consultation Partnership (ECCP). (2024) *Supporting young children: Help young children with conflict resolution*, available at: www.eccpct.com/Resources/Child/Tips-for-Tots/Help-Young-Children-with-Conflict-Resolution

Egan, G. (2013) *The skilled helper: A problem-management and opportunity-development approach to helping*, 10th edn, CA: Brooks/Cole, Cengage Learning.

Goleman, D. (2020) *Emotional intelligence: Why it can matter more than IQ*, 25th anniversary edn, London: Bloomsbury.

Gottman, J. M., Katz, L. F. and Hooven, C. (1996) 'Parental meta-emotion philosophy and the emotional life of families: Theoretical models and preliminary data', *Journal of Family Psychology*, 10(3), pp. 243-268.

Gus, L., Rose, J. and Gilbert, L. (2015) 'Emotion coaching: A universal strategy for supporting and promoting sustainable emotional and behavioural well-being', *Educational and Child Psychology*, 32(1), pp. 31-41.

Hodgkins, A. (2023) *Exploring early childhood practitioners' perceptions of empathic interactions with children and families*. PhD thesis, University of Worcester, available at: https://eprints.worc.ac.uk/13525/

Krawczyk, K. M. (2017) *A whole school single case study of Emotion Coaching (EC) training and the impact on school staff*. Unpublished PhD thesis, University of Birmingham.

Malik, F. and Marwaha, R. (2022) 'Developmental stages of social emotional development in children', *National Library of Medicine*, available at: www.ncbi.nlm.nih.gov/books/NBK534819/

McDowall-Clark, R. (2016) *Childhood in society for the early years*, 3rd edn, London: Sage.

Meinke, H. (2019) 'Understanding the stages of emotional development in children', *Rasmussen University Early Childhood Education Blog*, available at: www.rasmussen.edu/degrees/education/blog/stages-of-emotional-development/ (accessed 4th June 2023).

Nowicki, S., et al. (2018) 'Early home-life antecedents of children's locus of control', *Frontiers in Psychology*, 9, pp. 1-12.

Rainer, C., Le, H. and Abdinasir, K. (2023) *Behaviour and mental health in schools, children and young people's mental health coalition*, available at: https://cypmhc.org.uk/wp-content/uploads/2023/06/Behaviour-and-Mental-Health-in-Schools-Full-Report.pdf

Robinson, M. (2010) *Understanding behaviour and development in early childhood: A guide to theory and practice*, Taylor & Francis Group.

Rogers, C. (1980) *A way of being*, Boston: Houghton Mifflin.

Rose, J. (2023) 'Improving behaviour – why rewards and sanctions are just not enough', *Teaching Times*, available at: www.teachingtimes.com/improving-behaviour-why-rewards-and-sanctions-are-not-enough/

Rose, J. and Gilbert, L. (2018) 'Developing resilience with emotion coaching', *Early Childhood Journal*, 7(1), pp. 35-44.

Rose, J., McGuire-Snieckus, R. and Gilbert, L. (2015) 'Emotion coaching – a strategy for promoting behavioural self-regulation in children/young people in schools: A pilot study', *The European Journal of Social & Behavioural Sciences*, 13(2), pp. 1766-1790.

Rotter, J. B. (1966) 'Generalized expectancies for internal versus external control of reinforcement', *Psychological Monographs*, 80 (Whole No. 609). [online], available at: https://www.neshaminy.org/site/handlers/filedownload.ashx?moduleinstanceid=34376&dataid=51132&FileName=Article%207-Are%20You%20the%20Master%20of%20Your%20Fate.pdf (accessed 4th September 2024).

Ruggeri, A. (2022) 'The truth about "time out"', *BBC Family Tree*, available at: www.bbc.com/future/article/20220607-what-should-you-do-when-a-child-misbehaves

Skinner, B. F. (1963) 'Operant behaviour', *American Psychologist*, 18(8), pp. 503-515.

Staats, A., Staats, C., Schutz, R. and Wolf, M. (1962) 'The conditioning of textual responses using "extrinsic" reinforcers', *Journal of the Experimental Analysis of Behavior*, 5(1), pp. 33-40.

Sunderland, M. (2006) *The science of parenting*, London: Dorling Kindersley.

Thempra. (2024) *An introduction to social pedagogy*, available at: https://thempra.org.uk/downloads/Social%20Pedagogy%20-%20Comprehensive%20Handout.pdf

UNICEF (2024) 'Hidden in plain sight: A statistical analysis of violence against children', *UNICEF*, available at: www.unicef.org/media/66916/file/Hidden-in-plain-sight.pdf

Watzlawick, P., Beavin-Bavelas, J., Jackson, D. and O'Hanlon, B. (1967) *Pragmatics of human communication – A study of interactional patterns*, Pathologies and Paradoxes, New York: W. W. Norton.

7
Embracing empathy and compassion in challenging situations

Chapter outcomes

- To analyse obstacles to empathy and compassion
- To explore empathy across diversity and address personal biases
- To explore empathy in a range of challenging situations:
  - Conflict and aggression
  - Safeguarding concerns
  - Inspection and judgement
  - Language barriers
  - Trauma and adversity

Empathy and compassion undoubtedly foster a nurturing atmosphere of care for others, yet there are instances when focusing on the positives and embracing diverse perspectives can pose a challenge. Within this chapter, we explore various demanding scenarios, analysing strategies for their empathetic and compassionate management. Empathy, the ability to understand and share the feelings of others, is a crucial component of human connection and effective communication. However, various obstacles can impede our capacity to empathise with others. These barriers are detailed in Figure 7.1. Understanding these challenges is essential for fostering more empathetic interactions and building stronger, more compassionate relationships.

Embracing empathy and compassion in challenging situations 103

Obstacles to empathy

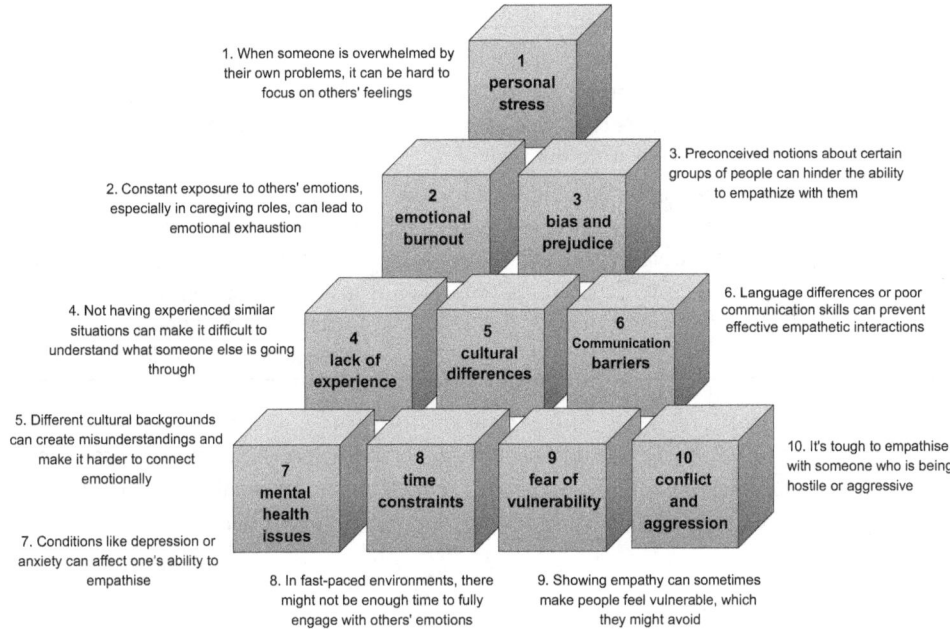

Figure 7.1 Obstacles to empathy

The 'empathy gap'

The empathy gap refers to the difficulty people have in understanding or feeling what others are experiencing, especially when they are in a different emotional state. For example, when someone is calm, they might find it hard to understand how someone else feels when they are angry or stressed. We can easily underestimate the influence of mental states on our own behaviour, and we can make decisions based only on our current emotions. This gap can make it challenging to connect with others and respond empathetically. There are different types of 'empathy gap':

Table 7.1 Empathy gaps

Empathy gap	Description	Example
Intrapersonal prospective empathy gap	The inability to effectively predict our own future behaviour when we are in a different state.	Deciding to give up alcohol and going to a party, failing to predict how your social anxiety will make not having a drink difficult.
Intrapersonal retrospective empathy gap	Struggling to recall or understand our own behaviour that happened in a different state.	Not being able to understand why you did so badly at an interview that you were well prepared for.

(Continued)

Table 7.1 (Continued)

Empathy gap	Description	Example
Interpersonal empathy gap	The difficulty in evaluating and understanding the behaviour of another person who is in a state different from our own.	Not being able to understand someone becoming aggressive in a heated argument.
Parochial empathy gap	Bias leading to higher empathy for people perceived as similar to yourself and a 'gap' in empathy towards 'outsiders'.	The public outcry in the UK over the disappearance of Madeline McCann versus the lack of action following an earthquake causing devastation to hundreds of people living on the other side of the world.

Behler and Berry (2022, p. 1) explain that parochial empathy presents itself as preferential higher empathy for people similar to us, and it can be 'a promoter of intergroup conflict and antipathy'. This can cause problems in interpersonal relationships with others in a diverse community.

Diversity and bias

Bias, prejudice, and stereotypes can hinder the ability to empathise with people from different backgrounds. Sadly, we live in a world where prejudice and discrimination are still rife. 'With depressing regularity, individuals respond toward others in racist, sexist, homophobic, or otherwise disagreeable stereotype-related ways' (Falbén et al., 2019, p. 1228). Although we may not like to admit it, everyone has prejudice; we may not be overtly racist or sexist, but we all make assumptions based on a single interaction. Do you maybe assume that all librarians are introverts, that salespeople are untrustworthy, or that born-again Christians will try to convert you?

> **Reflective prompt** - Imagine that you are in the school playground in the morning, and you see a parent wearing pyjamas, a dressing gown, and slippers to bring their child to school. What would your initial view of the parent be? Why is it important to be aware of your own prejudice?

Being aware of our own prejudices is essential, particularly when working with children and families who have different needs, strengths, and abilities and who must all be appropriately included, valued, and supported (Prowle and Hodgkins, 2020). Taking the time to get to know people and find out about their lives is crucial in order to identify both needs and strengths.

> **Individual activity**
>
> Look at the stereotypes in Table 7.2; consider where these stereotypes come from and then identify ways of negating these stereotypes with examples. Add other stereotypes that you are aware of.

Table 7.2 Stereotyping exercise

Stereotype	Flawed reasoning	Counter-arguments
Women are incapable of understanding 'the offside rule'	Gender stereotype – male assumption that football is a man's game.	Alex Scott MBE is a BBC football commentator. She has vast experience as a professional footballer as a player for Arsenal and for the England team.
		Understanding the 'offside rule' is about training and experience, not gender.
Teenagers are rebels		
Immigrants come to the UK to exploit the public finances		
Homeless people have made bad decisions		
Asian girls are docile and want to please others		
Older people are 'set in their ways' and don't like change		
Millionaires have no morals		

Different cultural norms and values can make it challenging to fully understand and empathise with someone's perspective.

➡ An important point: While it is crucial to empathise with others' points of view, especially in a diverse society that values acceptance and equality, it is equally vital to challenge prejudice and discrimination, particularly in professional settings. Understanding someone else's perspective does not mean tolerating racism, sexism, homophobia, or any form of discrimination. These issues must always be addressed and confronted.

106 *Nurturing Compassionate Connections*

'Problem families'

Have you ever heard a family referred to as a 'problem family'? Or had a child start in your class or group and heard negative comments about having 'another child from *that* family' who is likely to cause you trouble? Sadly, this sort of labelling still happens in schools and early years settings, and it means that children and families are disadvantaged even before they enter the building. Labelling children or families 'undermines their uniqueness and instead pigeon-holes children by a particular characteristic' (Davis, 2024), for example, 'disadvantaged', 'troublemaker' or 'the one to watch'. In a research project examining the views of teachers, Hannon and O'Donnell (2021) found that there is a tendency for teachers to see parents as different from them due to class differences in many cases. This leads to stereotyping children and families who they believe do not value education and who need to change. This can unfortunately become a self-fulfilling prophecy when one person's or one group's expectations for the behaviour of a person can help to bring about the behaviour expected (Rosenthal, 2012). Figure 7.2 gives an example of how a self-fulfilling prophecy can impact a child. However, by recognising that assumptions are being made, we can ensure that this does not affect a child's potential success and happiness. Empathy is important in this situation; by empathising with the child, we can identify his feelings and needs, and also his strengths.

> **Individual activity**
>
> Look at the stages in Figure 7.2. At each stage, identify what could/should change to ensure that this child can reach his full potential. Then ask yourself, do you appreciate how situations like this can happen? What would you do if you were aware of this happening in your workplace?

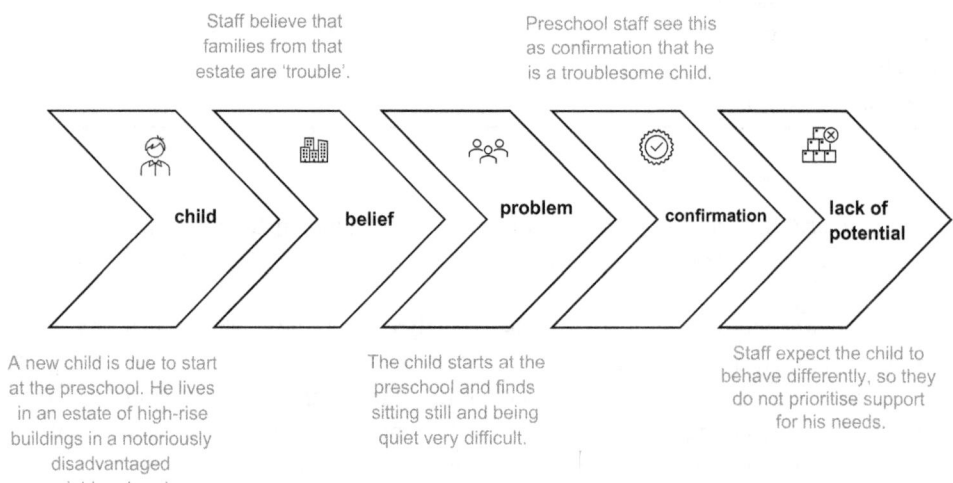

Figure 7.2 Self-fulfilling prophecy

Challenging situations

In this next part of the chapter, specific situations which may make empathy more difficult are examined.

Conflict and aggression

Positive communication is a cornerstone of working with others as a professional. In early years work, practitioners generally understand the need for active listening, and they communicate positively with young children, families, staff members, and other professionals. Using the core conditions of empathy, congruence, and unconditional positive regard (see Chapter 1) allows people to feel heard and respected. However, there will inevitably be times when people are upset or angry and, at these times, additional skills are needed to handle situations. Managing conflict with others requires a profound understanding of each person's viewpoint. Diplomacy emerges as a crucial tool when addressing situations, such as differences of opinion on matters encompassing care, behaviour, and Special Educational Needs, Disabilities, and Inclusion (SENDI). There are also times when things happen that make practitioners feel angry or upset too, so it is important to remain professional and to endeavour to empathise with the other person. Here are some examples from participants in the empathy research (Hodgkins, 2023). In the first excerpt, George (deputy manager of a private day nursery) talks about the family of a new two-year-old child who has started at the nursery. The child has been crying and upset when left in the morning.

> The mother is always blaming me and saying, 'She must be scared of the man'. I've been taking a really delicate and positive approach to building a relationship with the family. I understand that the family is looking for reasons why their child won't settle, so when they are around, I am very gentle and try to develop a relationship with them. However, when they aren't around, my emotions differ, and I feel sad and angry and wonder why they have blamed me right from day one.
> (George)

In George's example, the parents clearly have a view on George's gender, suggesting that a man is scary for the child. George is understandably upset about this, and he tries hard to be extra gentle when dealing with the family. He does empathise with the parents, though, and he understands that they are worried and are looking for an excuse for their child's upset. In the next example, Joel (manager of a private day nursery) talks about his feelings when he has to tell a parent that they cannot stay at the setting with their child.

> I had to inform them that they couldn't stay with their child for a stay and play session due to Covid restrictions. I knew they would be unhappy and possibly aggressive, so I felt a combination of nervous about telling them but also sad for them.
> (Joel)

In Joel's example, he feels nervous as he is expecting the parent to become aggressive, presumably because he knows the parent and is able to predict how they will react. However, he also feels sad for them, showing that he empathises with their wish to accompany their child. These examples demonstrate the importance of empathy in conflict situations. Research evidence suggests that empathy and compassion reduce aggression, create 'more favourable intergroup attitudes during conflicts', and establish more willingness for reconciliation following conflict situations (Klimecki, 2019, p. 322).

> **Reflective prompt** – Reflect on a difficult conversation you have had with another adult at work; this could be another member of staff or a parent/carer. Use the following question prompts to look at the situation from all points of view.

- What was the situation/context?
- How were you feeling at the time?
- How do you think the other person was feeling?
- How did you handle the situation?
- How do you think your reaction affected the other person?
- To what extent did you show empathy, congruence, and unconditional positive regard?
- What did you learn?
- Would you do anything differently next time?

Courageous conversations

A courageous conversation is 'a planned discussion about an uncomfortable topic or a negative experience where the goal is to share different perspectives, build mutual understanding, and develop respect, not to persuade or *win*' (Jackson et al., 2023, p. 80). In the early years profession, there are many times when we have to be very courageous in order to have important conversations with parents/carers about their children. They can be difficult but are necessary and cannot be avoided. Cliffe (2022, in Solvason and Cliffe, 2022, p. 87) reflects on her experiences with this:

> There will still be times when you will see a parent coming, and your stomach will flip because you know just how awful the conversation is likely to be... you can spend hours overthinking them, running through scenarios that might occur and what you might say.

Cliffe's feelings about these conversations are familiar to anyone working with children, but if we start with the core conditions, then we will handle these conversations with empathy, positive regard, and congruence. This is another example of the importance of developing good working relationships with parents/carers. If a relationship built on trust has already been established, then these conversations are easier to tackle. Cliffe (2022) points out that these conversations can even improve trust and respect in the parent/carer: practitioner relationships, as they show 'a willingness to deal with the hard stuff' (p. 90).

Having the foundation of a positive, trusting, and empathic relationship with parents/carers will help when conversations about difficult situations are necessary. When we talk to parents/carers about sensitive subjects such as special needs or safeguarding concerns, it is important to be aware that the words we choose are likely to stay with them and will never be forgotten, so the choice of words is crucial. Here are some golden rules for having courageous conversations (Figure 7.3).

Sometimes, if you are really worried about an upcoming difficult conversation, it can be a good idea to rehearse your words with a colleague. Reflection is also important; a debriefing session with a colleague, which includes reflection on the experience, will ensure that learning from experiences will feed into future practice.

Safeguarding concerns

Child protection interactions can understandably be stressful and worrying for practitioners. There is evidence in the research pointing to the burden and concerns that safeguarding imparts upon practitioners, as these excerpts from Debbie, deputy manager of a nursery, attest:

> Dealing with a complaint, having to tell a parent that we've noticed some additional needs, or talking to them about safeguarding concerns . . . I do enjoy working with parents, and I use my own experiences because my son is diagnosed with ADHD . . . I always say to parents, 'Look, I do totally know where you're coming from; I've been in your shoes'.
>
> (Debbie)

Golden rules for courageous conversations
• Be honest
• Remember that parents are the experts in their own children
• Make sure the environment is private, warm, and unthreatening
• Prepare for the conversation
• Don't put off the conversation
• Focus on the facts
• Listen
• Empathise
• Don't make assumptions
• Be open to changing your mind
• Collaborate and ask for their opinions and ideas
• Clarify the outcomes(s)

Figure 7.3 Golden rules for courageous conversations

> All the time I'm constantly thinking about it, especially safeguarding children ... it's quite difficult to switch off ... hopefully, we're just doing what we have to do, and hopefully, people understand that, but I don't know how I switch off.
>
> (Debbie)

What Debbie describes as her difficulty 'switching off' is echoed in the next example. For a manager, the weight of ultimate responsibility often extends into their home life as well. This sentiment is echoed in the words of Jake, a kindergarten manager:

> I'll take it home and start worrying about it ... I feel a sense of responsibility, and that's the thing that causes me to, like, overthink it, be anxious, and sometimes not be able to sleep. Am I doing enough for these children? If not, why not? And I know it's everyone's responsibility shared, but ultimately, as the manager of that setting, it is my responsibility, and I need to have the answers if there is a safeguarding risk, so that's the bit that gets me.
>
> (Jake)

What Debbie and Jake describe could be 'empathic distress', where the burden of responsibility can result in tiredness and/or emotional upset, which prevails outside work. This is further discussed in Chapter 9.

Balancing empathy with the need to protect vulnerable individuals can be complex. Safeguarding stands as the paramount responsibility for Early Years practitioners. This is underscored by The Children Act (1989), which firmly declares that 'the welfare of the child is paramount', thus making children's safety the foremost concern. Even so, it remains essential to exhibit empathy towards all parties, skilfully balancing safeguarding, risk assessment, and family relationships with the child's best interests. The practices of 'professional curiosity' and 'respectful uncertainty' (BHSCP, 2017) are examined through a lens of empathy and compassion.

Engaging in respectful dialogues with parents remains essential, though a delicate balance is maintained by adhering firmly to policies and procedures. Research with child protection social workers by Forrester et al. (2008) suggests that 'empathic social workers produced less resistance and achieved more disclosure of information from clients. Furthermore, they did so while managing to raise concerns and be clear about their role' (p. 48). A strength-based approach is important, even in safeguarding situations. Although talking to parents/carers about safeguarding concerns will be worrying, it is still possible to discuss strengths, skills, and resources to effect positive change, using approaches like 'Solution-focussed practice' and 'Signs of safety' (Hodgkins and Prowle, 2023, p. 139). Being a designated safeguarding lead (DSL), although a critically important role, can be a rewarding one, with an opportunity to educate others and to make a real difference.

Embracing empathy and compassion in challenging situations 111

Individual activity

Read the case study below about an upcoming conversation with a parent about a safeguarding concern. How would you manage your conversation with the parent? Consider the following:

- Where would you talk to Daniel's Mum?
- How would you start the conversation?
- How can you show empathy and compassion?
- How can you demonstrate 'respectful uncertainty'?
- How can you ensure that things change for Daniel's sake?
- How would you end the conversation?

Case study - Daniel

You work with a family who have five children all attending the same primary school. The youngest child, Daniel, is in your preschool class. Over the three months that Daniel has been with you, you have noticed that he never looks very clean. The staff team has been discussing whether this constitutes neglect. Now that the weather is turning cold, he comes in wearing thin clothes and doesn't have a warm winter coat or gloves. Earlier this week, Daniel had a fall in the playground and grazed his knees. Although they were cleaned up at the time by staff, you notice today that his knees are very dirty, and there is still dried blood on his legs. Clearly, no one at home has bathed him since. As Daniel's key worker, you think the time has come to talk to Daniel's mother when she comes to collect him.

Inspection and judgement

Situations where one is being judged or inspected can create defensive barriers to empathy. During Ofsted inspections, the perspective shifts to a critical appraisal of the setting, which is understandably a stressful time for practitioners. Osgood's (2010) viewpoint underscores the challenge of being evaluated against external criteria, a stance that potentially clashes with the ethos of individualised care. The approach advocated in this book accentuates highlighting the positives while maintaining an honest assessment without explicitly pinpointing the negatives.

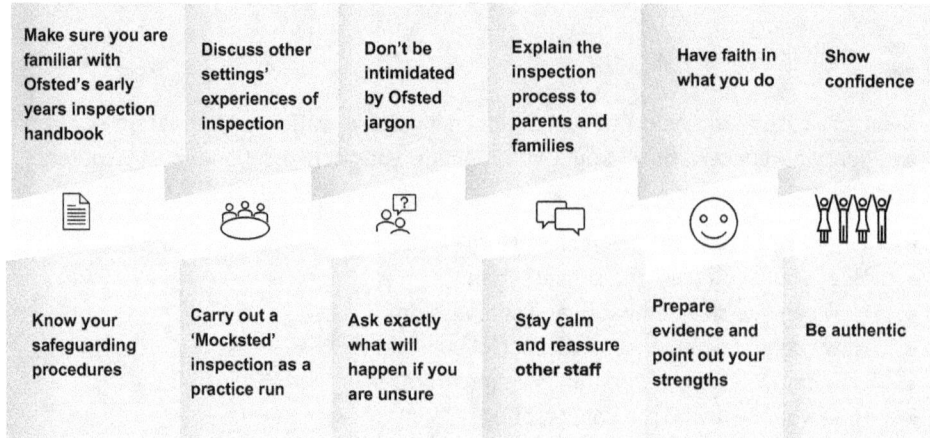

Figure 7.4 Preparing for inspection

During an Ofsted inspection, it is important to be assertive. If you disagree with an inspector's decision or feel they haven't understood your approach to an area of practice, it is reasonable to question them. Assertiveness does not require aggression; you can be firm while showing respect, empathy, and compassion. By putting ourselves in the inspector's shoes and recognising their role, we can discuss matters calmly and persuasively. For example, if an inspector says that they have not seen something they expected to see, it is perfectly reasonable to show them exactly where they might see it. Inspectors are with you for a short time, and they will understand that there are things happening which they did not see on their visit. Botten (2024) has this advice, written for schools but relevant to all settings:

> There's no point being delusional – if your data clearly says one thing, it's hard to argue the opposite. However, don't give up on a point too easily. Don't be rude or aggressive, but ask the inspector, 'What evidence would you like me to show you to convince you that I'm right?' Ofsted isn't some all seeing eye. The inspector will be constantly shifting their opinion as the Ofsted inspection proceeds, so keep providing evidence if you think they've got the wrong end of the stick.

Remember that the principal aim of inspection is to raise standards and to provide guidance on how to improve services for the benefit of children and families.

Language and communication barriers

Communication difficulties can hinder our ability to understand and empathise with others' feelings. These challenges can stem from various sources, such as language barriers, disabilities, and sensory impairments (e.g. deafness), emotional difficulties (e.g. severe anxiety), and learning difficulties, including illiteracy. I recall an experience as a young teaching assistant when I asked a child's father to read and sign a disclaimer slip at Sports Day. I was puzzled by his anger and abrupt departure. It hadn't occurred to me that he might not be able to read the form, and his embarrassed response was to react with anger instead of explaining the issue. According to the National Literacy Trust (n.d.), 16% of adults in England (5.2 million people) are functionally illiterate. 'This means that they can understand short, straightforward texts on familiar topics, but may have difficulty reading unfamiliar topics or information from unfamiliar sources'. This means that it is important to provide important information in a range of formats, for example, explaining verbally anything of importance in a newsletter, and writing down verbal feedback so it can be read by a relative or friend later.

English as an additional language

Statistics in the UK show that 9% of people speak English as a second or additional language. A further 7% are proficient in spoken English, although this is not their main language. The most common languages, other than English in England and Welsh in Wales, are Polish (1.1%), Romanian (0.8%), Punjabi (0.5%0 and Urdu (0.5%) (ONS, 2022). This implies that many families may find communication in English challenging. Additionally, for families arriving in the UK from other countries, differences in culture and customs can further complicate communication. This is where empathy is particularly important. Taking the time to get to know people and finding out about their background and their views and needs will help you to 'tune into' the people you are working with. Communicating with people who speak a different language and/or who are from a different culture is becoming more commonplace as we welcome refugees and immigrants into the country. According to the United Nations Refugee Agency (Refugee Action, 2022), at the end of 2020, there were 132,349 refugees, 77,245 pending asylum cases, and 4,662 stateless persons in the UK. Despite what we may believe by reading some newspapers, this still only constitutes 0.5% of the population of the UK.

Figure 7.5 gives advice on communicating empathically with people who do not speak English as a first language.

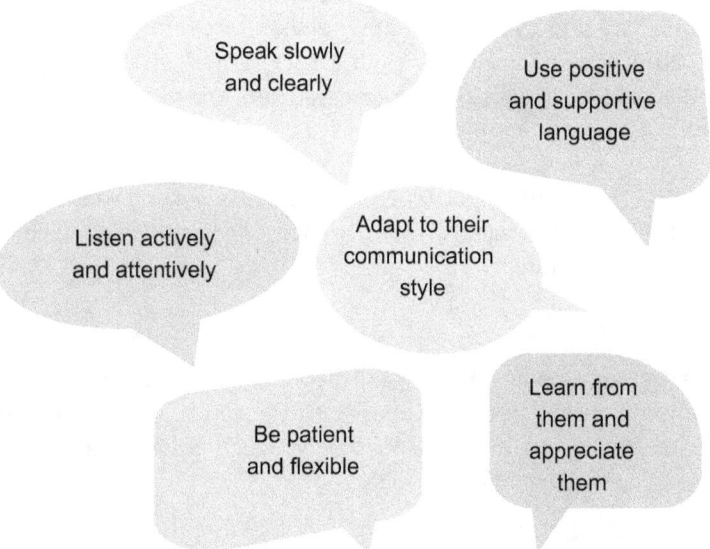

Figure 7.5 Empathic communication

Patience and respect are the key to building relationships with others who do not speak English as a first language. Empathising with those who are trying to communicate and finding ways of building trust and compassion will improve relationships. As practitioners, we can learn so much from getting to know people from different backgrounds with different experiences, and our practice will be expanded and enhanced.

Trauma and adversity

Trauma and adverse life experiences can significantly hinder effective communication. Everyone goes through adversity in their lives, but for some people, multiple difficulties can be overwhelming, and this can make all areas of life difficult. Multiple adversity is complex and often spans health and social issues, including mental health problems, substance misuse, disabilities, and social exclusion (Rankin and Regan, 2004). Poverty can be a compounding factor within this adversity, with lack of resources making everything else more difficult to address' (Prowle and Stobbs, 2025).

Empathising with individuals who have experienced significant trauma can be challenging and emotionally taxing. Working with trauma-affected children can be very difficult, as this description by Prowle and Stobbs (2025, p. 52) attests:

> [Children] may replicate a familiar emotional environment. Accustomed to chaos and disappointment, when rewarded with kindness by a new caregiver the child may unwittingly self-sabotage the attachment by becoming violent, destroying objects and being verbally abusive (ibid). From the child's perspective, the loving response is unexpected and goes against their internal working model as being unworthy of love. To protect themselves from rejection insecure attached children will sometimes reject the caregiver before they are rejected. This relationship sabotaging cycle frequently persists throughout the child's whole life (Slade, 2019). Thankfully however, the cycle is reversible (Bergin and Bergin, 2009; Black, 2019) and well-informed caregivers and professionals can be hugely influential in addressing this.

In this excerpt by Prowle and Stobbs (2025), they discuss working with children who have attachment difficulties as a result of an abusive and/or neglectful upbringing. Working with such children can be very tough.

 Reflective prompt – Have you experienced working with a child who has suffered serious trauma or abuse? If not, can you imagine what this might be like? What are the challenges for you as a practitioner? What are your personal underpinning guidelines?

This demanding work can result in 'vicarious trauma' (or 'secondary trauma'), which occurs when we soak up a child's trauma and experience it ourselves. This is a form of affective empathy, and it can be overwhelming. It is important to remember that although caring for children and families is often a core part of our identity and includes sacrificing our own needs for theirs, this is not sustainable. We must set professional boundaries to protect ourselves and ensure that we can carry on working and making a difference. This involves being self-aware and able to recognise times when you are feeling overwhelmed. A caring, empathic person does not have to be everything to everyone. See Chapter 9 for more about this.

Covid-19

In 2019, the Covid-19 pandemic introduced unique stressors that complicated the early years profession. This event of worldwide magnitude had profound and often traumatic repercussions. Very young children, at a crucial stage of their development, were denied access to outdoor play areas and opportunities for socialising. Families were unable to access professional services and unable to turn to family for help, thanks to social distancing rules. The consequences of the pandemic and subsequent lockdowns on both children and staff manifested in mental health concerns. Nelinger et al. (2021, p. 3) reported that 69% of early years practitioners were now working with children affected by trauma or abuse. Practitioners reported feeling upset and struggling to manage the adversity faced by the families they worked with. However, armed with understanding, empathy, and compassion, a pathway toward recovery is possible. The National Children's Bureau (NCB), in partnership with a range of other charitable organisations, produced a plan for Early Years recovery following the pandemic, detailing their recommendations to prevent 'a long-term impact that could last well into childhood and beyond' (NCB, n.d.). Their recommendations for the long term included making the early years a government priority with improved financial investment, funding for parenting and community support, and a primary focus on physical safety and personal, social, and emotional development for young children, above all else. Policy change takes time, but empathy and compassion are things we can all do to help mitigate the damage and optimise recovery.

It is scientifically proven that empathy helps with this process. Sunderland (2019), a child psychology expert, describes empathy as having a healing impact on the brain and mind. It calms the heart rate and supports emotional regulation.

> When a child is emotionally regulated, the medulla in the brain is calmed and a trauma response is lessened. Vagal tone is about an internal process in the body involving the vagus nerve which originates from the medulla part of the brain that is a key component of the nervous system operating our heart, lungs and digestion. An increase in vagal tone slows the heart down. So, this means that empathy from

an adult to a child creates good vagal tone and thus helps the child to calm down and emotionally regulate.

(Sunderland, in Gunning, 2019)

> **Group activity**
>
> As a team, work through the situations in Table 7.3 and discuss how you would manage each one with empathy and compassion.

Table 7.3 Communication with parents/carers

The situation	What is your priority?	What are the potential difficulties with this conversation?	How can you show empathy and compassion?
You need to inform a parent that you think their child may have a learning difficulty.			
You need to phone a parent to let them know that their child has had an accident and that you have called for an ambulance.			
You need to talk to a child's parents about the bruises that you have noticed and which you are concerned might be non-accidental.			
A child has been hurting other children. There have been a couple of complaints from parents whose children have gone home with bite marks on them, so you need to speak to the child's parent.			
When giving verbal feedback at the end of an inspection, an Ofsted inspector has made a comment which you feel is unfairly negative.			
A parent has been making sexual advances towards a young member of staff in the nursery, which is making her feel very uncomfortable. You need to address this with the parent.			

(Continued)

Table 7.3 (Continued)

The situation	What is your priority?	What are the potential difficulties with this conversation?	How can you show empathy and compassion?
A parent has come to collect their child from your preschool to drive them home. However, you believe that the parent is drunk.			
A new member of staff has started at your nursery. You are aware that some of the other staff are not treating him well, and you think it amounts to bullying. You want to talk to the staff members before going to the manager.			

The decline of empathy?

Rhetoric has arisen recently which suggests that empathy is in decline. Rubin (2023), writing in the Washington Post, suggests that empathy is in decline because 'too many people live alone, cut off from others . . . people's capacity for empathy decreases as their stress intensifies . . . the deluge of negative news can make us less empathetic'. Narcissistic personality disorder is a formally diagnosed condition, but narcissistic tendencies appear as a continuum and can be mild or situational (Lebow, 2022). Ukwu (2024) describes the difference between empathy and narcissism,

> While empathy acts as a bridge, facilitating understanding and connection, narcissism often erects barriers, isolating individuals and corroding the foundations of trust and mutual respect necessary for healthy relationships.

The decline in empathy is often attributed to social media, which objectifies people and promotes narcissism (Rubin, 2023). This rise in narcissism, particularly among young people, is linked to their use of social media (Jenkins, 2019). However, Martingano (2024) points out that criticising the younger generation is not a new phenomenon, as this quote from nearly 1,000 years ago illustrates, 'The world is passing through troublous times. The young people of today think of nothing but themselves' – Peter the Hermit (1050-1115 AD, in Martingano, 2024).

Contrary to this view, my own observations and research reveal a different picture. I see caring, nurturing individuals working tirelessly with young children, demonstrating deep empathy and compassion. Interestingly, Martingano (2024) identified a rise in empathic concern over the last 15 years, stating,

> Young people are not uniformly less empathetic than their forebears; instead, the empathy of youth today ebbs and flows, much like the societal currents they are part of.

This perspective offers a more hopeful outlook.

Chapter summary

This chapter acknowledges the challenges of empathy, exploring obstacles such as stereotyping, prejudice, and discrimination. It emphasises the importance of recognising and questioning our assumptions to enhance empathy in our interactions, particularly with parents, families, and children. The chapter highlights the dangers of labelling children and the impact of self-fulfilling prophecies.

Various situations where empathy is challenging are examined, including conflicts with parents or colleagues, where diplomacy and active listening are crucial. The value of empathy in courageous conversations, especially regarding sensitive topics like safeguarding, is discussed. Respectful dialogue and empathy are essential in these complex practices to foster cooperation.

The chapter also addresses the stress of inspections, suggesting that empathy can help us understand the purpose behind them and reduce pressure. It explores communication difficulties, working with individuals who have experienced trauma, and the unique challenges posed by the pandemic, emphasising the role of empathy and compassion.

Finally, the chapter counters the narrative of a decline in empathy, encouraging us to observe the empathy, compassion, and care within our profession, reaffirming that these qualities remain both fundamental and widespread.

Key messages

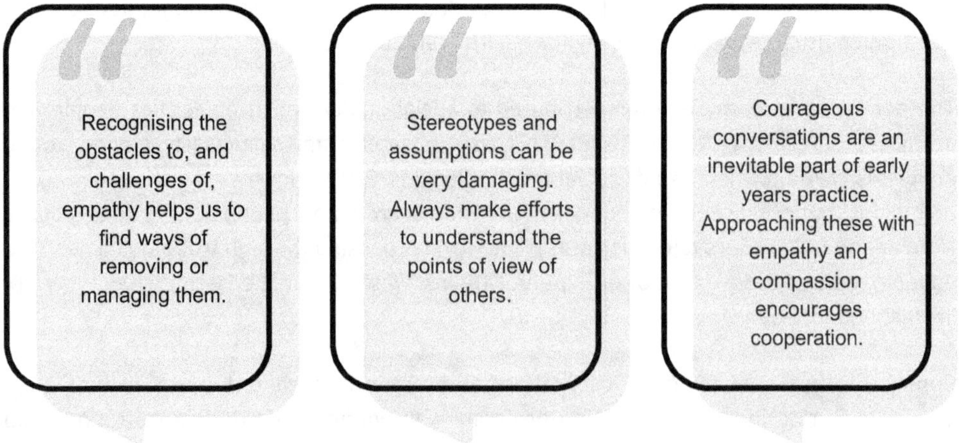

> Recognising the obstacles to, and challenges of, empathy helps us to find ways of removing or managing them.

> Stereotypes and assumptions can be very damaging. Always make efforts to understand the points of view of others.

> Courageous conversations are an inevitable part of early years practice. Approaching these with empathy and compassion encourages cooperation.

Figure 7.6 Key messages from Chapter 7

References

Behler, A. M. C. and Berry, D. R. (2022) 'Closing the empathy gap: A narrative review of the measurement and reduction of parochial empathy', *Social and Personality Psychology Compass*, 16(9), pp. 1-14.

Bergin, C. and Bergin, D. (2009) 'Attachment in the classroom', *Educational Psychology Review*, 21, pp. 141-170.

Brighton and Hove Safeguarding Children Partnership (BHSCP). (2017) *Working together to improve professional curiosity*, available at: https://www.bhscp.org.uk/wp-content/uploads/sites/3/2019/11/Professional-Curiosity-Bulletin.pdf (accessed 14th March 2025).

Botten, O. (2024) 'Ofsted inspections – How to prepare for one like a pro', *The Headteacher*, available at: www.theheadteacher.com/attainment-and-assessment/ofsted/how-to-plan-and-prepare-for-an-ofsted-inspection (accessed 8th December 2024).

The Children Act (1989) available at: www.legislation.gov.uk/ukpga/1989/41/contents (accessed 18th December 2024).

Cliffe, J. (2022) 'Chapter 5: Tackling difficult conversations', in Solvason, C. and Cliffe, J. (eds) *Creating authentic relationships with parents of young children*, London: Speechmark, Routledge, pp. 87-104.

Davis, E. (2024, February 27) 'How to avoid labelling children', *Nursery World*, available at: www.nurseryworld.co.uk/content/features/how-to-avoid-labelling-children/ (accessed 4th December 2024).

Falbén, J. K., et al. (2019) 'Stop stereotyping', *Attention, Perception & Psychophysics*, 81(5), pp. 1228-1235.

Forrester, D., Kershaw, S., Moss, H. and Hughes, L. (2008) 'Communication skills in child protection: How do social workers talk to parents?', *Child and Family Social Work*, 13, pp. 31-51.

Gunning, C. (2019) 'Showing empathy creates calm', *Early Education*, available at: https://early-education.org.uk/attachment-and-trauma-awareness/ (accessed 15th December 2024).

Hannon, L. and O'Donnell, G. (2021) 'Teachers, parents, and family- school partnerships: Emotions, experiences, and advocacy', *Journal of Education for Teaching*, 48(2), pp. 241-255.

Hodgkins, A. (2023) *Exploring early childhood practitioners' perceptions of empathic interactions with children and families*. PhD thesis, University of Worcester, available at: https://eprints.worc.ac.uk/13525/

Hodgkins, A. and Prowle, A. (2023) *Strength-based approaches with children and families*, St Albans: Critical Publishing.

Jackson, H., et al. (2023) 'Coaching in difficult conversations', *YC Young Children*, 78(3), pp. 80-87.

Jenkins, J. (2019) 'I feel for you: Narcs and narcissists', *BBC Radio Four – Seriously . . .*, available at: www.bbc.co.uk/programmes/p06y2j6v (accessed 16th December 2024).

Klimecki, O. (2019) 'The role of empathy and compassion in conflict resolution', *Emotion Review*, 11(4), pp. 310-325.

Lebow, H. (2022) 'Narcissism vs. Narcissistic personality disorder: Telling them apart', *Psych Central*, available at: https://psychcentral.com/disorders/narcissistic-personality-disorder/the-difference-between-narcissism-narcissistic-personality-disorder (accessed 16th December 2024).

Martingano, A. (2024) 'The surprising surge of compassion in modern youth', *Psychology Today*, University of Wisconsin, available at: https://news.uwgb.edu/phlash/mediacoverage/03/19/the-surprising-surge-of-compassion-in-modern-youth-psychology-today/#:~:text=Empathyincreased when socializing decreased, on social interactions and worldviews (accessed 16th December 2024).

National Children's Bureau (n.d.) 'Early years recovery briefing', *NCB*, available at: www.ncb.org.uk/sites/default/files/uploads/attachments/early-years-recovery-briefing.pdf (accessed 15th December 2024).

National Literacy Trust (n.d.) 'Adult literacy', *Literacy Trust*, available at: https://literacytrust.org.uk/parents-and-families/adult-literacy/ (accessed 13th December 2024).

Nelinger, A., Album, J., Haynes, A. and Rosan, C. (2021) 'Their challenges are our challenges – a summary report of the experiences facing nursery workers in the U.K. in 2020', *The Anna Freud Centre*, available at: www.annafreud.org/media/13013/their-challenges-are-our-challenges-survey-report.pdf

Office for National Statistics (ONS). (2022) *Language, England and Wales: Census 2021*, available at: www.ons.gov.uk/peoplepopulationandcommunity/culturalidentity/language/bulletins/languageenglandandwales/census2021 (accessed 13th December 2024).

Osgood, J. (2010) 'Reconstructing professionalism in ECEC: The case for the "critically reflective emotional professional"', *Early Years*, 30(2), pp. 119-133.

Prowle, A. and Hodgkins, A. (2020) *Making a difference with children and families: Reimagining the role of the practitioner*, London: Red Globe books, Bloomsbury.

Prowle, A. and Stobbs, N. (2025) *Supporting children's mental health and wellbeing-therapeutic approaches for working with children and families*, London: Routledge (in production).

Rankin, J. and Regan, S. (2004) 'Meeting complex needs in social care', *Housing, Care and Support*, 7(3), pp. 4–8.

Refugee Action. (2022) 'Facts about refugees', *Refugee Action*, available at: www.refugee-action.org.uk/about/facts-about-refugees/#:~:text=According%20to%20UNHCR%20statistics%2C%20as,UK%20including%20recent%20Ukrainians%20refugees (accessed 13th December 2024).

Rosenthal, R. (2012) 'Self-fulfilling prophecy', in *Encyclopaedia of human behavior*, 2nd edn, CA: Academic Press.

Rubin, J. (2023, February 15) 'We are suffering from an empathy gap, but we can fix it', *The Washington Post*, available at: www.washingtonpost.com/opinions/2023/02/15/empathy-gap-fix/ (accessed 16th December 2024).

Sunderland, M. (2019) 'Creating mentally healthy schools', *Conference & Common Room*, Spring, pp. 12–14.

Ukwu, P. (2024) *Empathy vs. Narcissism: Unpacking the influence on emotional intelligence and social connections*, conference paper, available at: www.researchgate.net/publication/379333693_Empathy_vs_Narcissism_Unpacking_the_Influence_on_Emotional_Intelligence_and_Social_Connections#fullTextFileContent (accessed 16th December 2024).

8

Developing and enhancing empathy skills

Chapter objectives

- To examine the development of empathy throughout childhood
- To examine empathy as an innate quality or a skill to be learned
- To examine trauma and empathy
- To explore emotional labour in early years practice
- To explore the relationship between empathy and reflective practice

This chapter describes theories about the development of empathy in children, starting with the seminal work of Piaget and Vygotsky and examining contemporary research, such as Gopnik's findings that babies as young as one year old demonstrate empathy. It discusses two views on developing empathy: as an innate ability and as a skill to be learned. The chapter also presents ideas about empathy developed from childhood trauma and the concept of the wounded healer (Jung).

Concepts of intuition versus advanced empathy are explored, and a new theory of intuitive empathy is proposed as an accurate depiction of what occurs in early years settings. Intuition and empathy are closely related to reflective practice, which is also examined as a crucial aspect of early years professionalism. A key component of reflective practice is the development of self-awareness. The chapter investigates emotional labour within the early years practitioner role and suggests reflective practice and reflective supervision as effective methods for enhancing self-awareness skills.

Development of empathy throughout childhood

Some of the earliest child development theorists published their views on the age at which young children first develop empathy. Piaget (1957) and Vygotsky (1978) both proposed that children's social and emotional development develops through stages, but they differed in their views. Piaget believed that children develop through experience as 'little scientists'. He believed that empathy developed in what he called the 'concrete operational stage' (age 7-11), when a child develops the capability to think about how other people think

122 Nurturing Compassionate Connections

and feel. Vygotsky, on the other hand, saw children as 'little apprentices', being guided in their development of social skills through interaction with more knowledgeable others.

Later, theories developed which suggested that empathy is present at a much earlier age. Decety (2010) believes that children's ability to empathise develops as they grow, with the urge to comfort others appearing around 12 months old. In Gopnik's (2010) experiment with 1-year-olds, the children watched a researcher's reaction to eating different foods, and they chose to give her the foods that made her look happy, demonstrating their appreciation for the view of another person. To empathise with others, children must have developed a theory of mind, 'the ability to attribute mental states to oneself, and to others, and to understand that others have beliefs, desires, intentions, and perspectives that are different from one's own' (Premack and Woodruff, 1978, p. 155). As they develop a 'theory of mind' and interact with others in their first three years, they rapidly gain an understanding of emotions (Hoffman, 2000). This continues to develop through adolescence with the improvement of emotional regulation, which facilitates a more nuanced understanding of helping others (Decety, 2010; Hoffman, 2000).

Stages of empathy development

Belzung (2014) describes emotional contagion as the most basic form of empathy, where reactions like yawning when others yawn occur unconsciously and instinctively. This can be seen in very young babies, which explains why, when one baby in a nursery is upset and crying, the others often join in! The second level of empathy involves recognition of others' distress and the beginnings of a desire to help. This requires understanding others' feelings, facilitated by the theory of mind, which is the ability to attribute mental states to oneself and others (Premack and Woodruff, 1978). Empathy involves feeling with someone while maintaining a clear distinction between oneself and the other person. Without this distinction, it is merely emotional contagion (Singer and Klimecki, 2014). Throughout childhood, there is a growing understanding of the feelings of others; children learn about others through social interactions, education, and role models. This develops, in middle childhood,

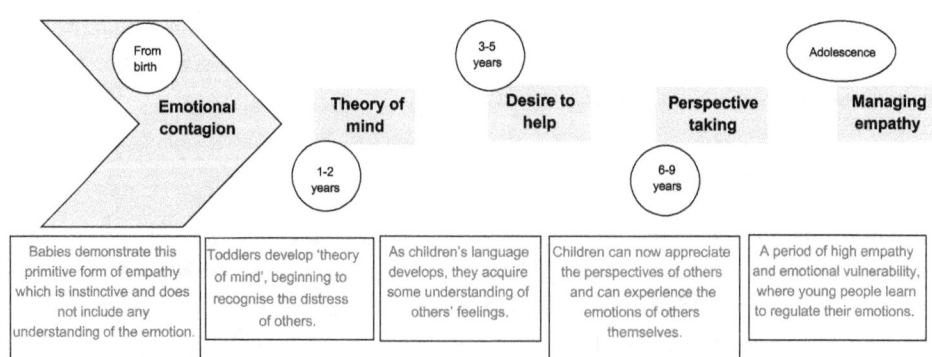

Figure 8.1 Empathy development

into both cognitive and affective empathy. At this stage, children can imagine what it would be like to be the other person (cognitive empathy) and they sometimes experience the feelings themselves (affective empathy).

There are conflicting ideas about whether empathy is innate (we all have the potential for empathy) or whether it is a skill which can be learned and developed.

Empathy as an innate quality

Genetic behaviour studies (for example, Knafo and Uzefovsky, 2013) have shown that there are both hereditary and environmental influences on the development of empathy. This genetic link suggests that empathy is, to some extent, a natural quality. Reiss (2017) points out that in the earliest tribal communities, the ability to observe and share others' pain motivates us to respond; therefore, the survival of our species depends on mutual aid, and providing it reduces our own distress. As long as people have the prerequisites for empathy, then empathy is a natural response. Rogers (1951) consistently maintained that, although empathy is a natural human trait, we still need to develop an appropriate mindset. According to McNaughton (2016), the pre-requisites for empathy are,

For the majority of people, the three prerequisites are present in adulthood, although there are conditions and circumstances which may preclude them. For example, a mental illness which prevents a person from being aware of their own emotional state will make empathy difficult. Psychopathy often results in a lack of empathy. In the past, a popular opinion evolved that Autistic people are unable to show empathy. However, contemporary research has revealed a huge diversity of empathic experiences ranging from low empathy to strong 'hyper-empathic' responses within this group (Verrier et al., 2024). It is important to challenge the assumption/stereotype that Autistic people cannot empathise.

Empathy is experienced in different ways by different people, and it appears that some people are more naturally empathic than others. Baron-Cohen (2003) contends that there

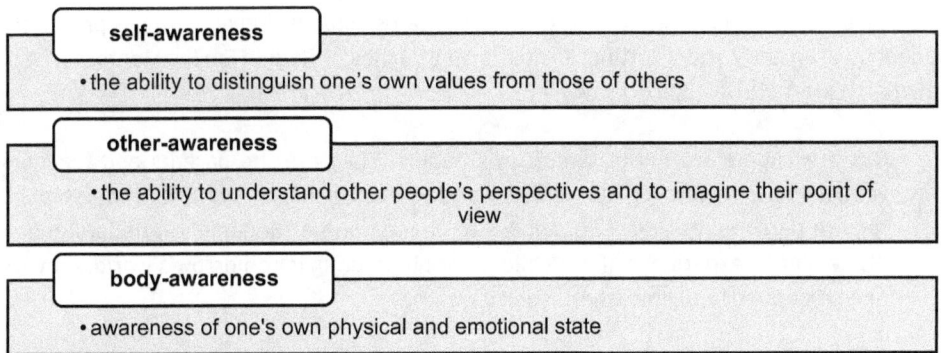

Figure 8.2 Prerequisites for empathy

are people who continually think about the feelings and thoughts of others. He describes these as natural-born empathisers. Baron-Cohen says of these individuals, 'you are not empathizing in order to appear appropriate, or as an intellectual exercise. You are doing it because you can't help doing it' (2003, p. 24). In recent years, the term 'empath' has been used to describe a person with extreme empathic awareness and emotional connection. Jeong and Lee (2015) claim that these people have an increased number of mirror neurons in their brains, resulting in increased sensitivity to the feelings of others. The challenges of being an empath are further discussed in Chapter 9.

Mirror neurons

Over the past decade, studies (for example, Manassis, 2017) have explored the idea of a genetic predisposition for empathy, with a particular emphasis on mirror neurons. Mirror neurons are brain cells which activate when we take action or when we see someone else taking action. Research into mirror neurons began with animal experiments in the 1990s when Rizzolatti (cited in Decety and Jackson, 2004) discovered that the activation of neurons in primates' brains during their own actions coincided with the activation observed when they were merely observing another individual performing the same action. Iacoboni (2009) suggests, therefore, that mirror neurons are the basis of the capacity for empathy. However, a critique of the theory suggests that because much of the research in this area was carried out on primates rather than humans, this casts doubt about whether mirror neurons exist or whether the mirroring that is seen is an occasional phenomenon (Dinstein et al., 2008; Lingnau et al., 2009; Hickok, 2009).

Empathy as a skill to be developed

Although the capacity to empathise is innate, the environment also has an influence. Research by Liu et al. (2022) showed that when mothers demonstrated higher levels of empathy, this increased the empathy of their young children. A nurturing environment with empathic role models fosters the development of empathy skills throughout childhood. The early years are a critical period, with 90% of a child's brain developing between birth and age 5 (NHS, 2024); the quality of care and experiences during this significant phase helps to shape brain development. Garnett (2018) advocates establishing empathy as part of the pedagogy in an early years setting, as do the approaches of Reggio Emilia, Montessori, and Te Whariki. Garnett (2018, p. 9) says,

> Our preschools are full of tomorrow's people. They are the parents and teachers, workers and leaders of our future world. Effective parenting and leadership will require personal resilience, openness to change and a fundamental understanding of the human experience. If our children are to flourish in tomorrow's world, they will need emotional and empathetic toolkits.

Everyone can take some responsibility to help children develop emotional intelligence and empathy; parents, families, teachers, practitioners, the media, etc. Empathy is closely connected to emotional intelligence, a broad concept that encompasses the capacity to recognise, understand, and manage our own emotions, as well as the ability to recognise, influence, and navigate the emotions of others. It involves self-awareness, self-regulation, motivation, social awareness, and interpersonal skills.

 Individual activity

Identify as many ways as possible of encouraging empathy in young children. Table 8.1 contains some prompts as a starting point.

Table 8.1 Encouraging empathy in young children

Empathy skill	Ideas
Describing and labelling emotions	Model talking about what makes you feel sad, angry, etc.
	'Feelings' faces
	Talking about the feelings of story characters
	Reflect back children's emotions ('I can see you are feeling angry because the teddy was taken away from you')
	Songs, rhymes, and stories about emotions
Helping children recognise feelings within their body	
Teaching children about different emotions	
Embracing and celebrating diversity	
Books and stories	
Resolving conflict	
Role play	

Social Pedagogy is discussed throughout this book, as it has empathy at the heart of its ethos. A social pedagogical concept which recognises the importance of empathy is 'head, heart, hands' (Thempra, 2024). The concept combines cognitive knowledge (head), emotional and spiritual learning (heart), and practical and physical skills (hands). The 'heart' component is concerned with following our intuition and feelings and considering relationships in every aspect of our work with children. Dachyshyn's (2015) definition of heartful practice is 'responding from the heart, from a place of deep compassion and empathy' (p. 37). In working with children and young people, the heartful practice advocates *being with* them rather than *doing to* them, so listening to the child's voice and following the interests of the child are imperative.

Teaching empathy

If empathy skills can be developed, then, presumably, they can also be taught. There are examples of empathy training in nurse education (see, for example, Galetz, 2019). These studies describe simulation-based learning and communication training, focussing on empathy. Galetz' study found that it was not possible to create empathy in the students – the training did raise their awareness of the importance of showing empathy. In the education field, Roberts et al.'s (2019) research with preschool teachers suggested that training should include the management of their emotions to decrease the likelihood of stress and burnout. Although there is little training available specifically focussed on empathy, a proven method of developing professional skills is learning from others. All of us can be a role model for others; anyone can facilitate change in the workplace. Leading and influencing others is not just for managers; any member of the team can be an 'agent of change', whether they are a manager, room leader, or a student on placement. Change can happen quietly and can be initiated by the most introverted people. Susan Cain's work on the 'power of introverts' (2013) describes how we can all lead change through role modelling.

Enhancing and developing skills can be achieved through mentoring and coaching, each offering unique avenues for growth. Mentoring, involving an experienced professional supporting the skill development of someone less experienced, proves particularly valuable for honing specific skills. For instance, it aids in effectively conducting empathic conversations with parents and carers. Conversely, coaching is a more comprehensive approach dedicated to aiding individuals in reaching their full potential. When coupled with the practice of being a role model, coaching becomes a potent method for nurturing a caring and empathetic practitioner persona.

Developing your own empathy skills

Some people believe that the development of empathy needs to be driven by the individual (e.g. Su, 2014). There are ways of increasing one's own empathic understanding; some of these are detailed in Figure 8.3. Watching a TV documentary about ADHD will help you understand the emotions of people with ADHD and their families and so will help you to empathise with them in the future. Taking to a homeless person instead of walking by will help you to understand and empathise with homeless people in the future. The more we learn about people, the higher our capacity for empathy.

Developing empathy through experience

Just as we develop empathy through learning about others, our empathic understanding increases as we have our own experiences. For example, if we experience the death of a parent, we may be more able to feel empathy for another person who is similarly bereaved. Some people believe that to empathise with someone; we need to have been through something similar ourselves. If we are faced with someone who has been in prison, and we have

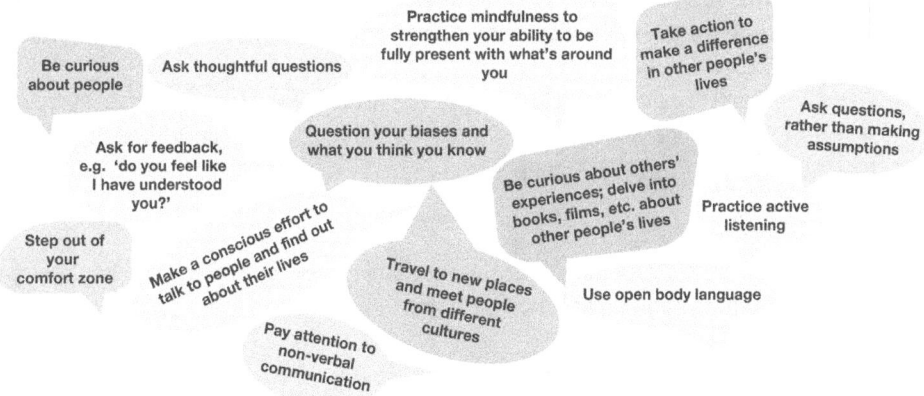

Figure 8.3 Ways of increasing your empathic understanding

not experienced that ourselves, can we really empathise with the person as much as someone who has experienced that themselves?

> **Reflective prompt** - Reflect on something you have experienced in your past; will this help you to empathise with others? What do you need to consider when using your own experiences in discussion?

The important thing to remember here is that we are all individuals; no two people will react in the same way or feel the same way as another person. So, if someone says, 'That happened to me; I know exactly how you feel', this is unlikely to be true; we cannot know exactly what it is like to be the other person. All we can do is try to put ourselves in their position and imagine how it might feel. In the empathy research, there were several examples of practitioners drawing on past experiences to help them empathise. In the first example, George is empathising with a child who is struggling with being away from a parent,

> One child had to say goodbye to their parent as they went away for a few days with work, and this made them very upset. I myself was a military child, which meant at a young age, my dad used to go to sea for long periods. So, I spoke to the child about this happening to me when I was their age, and this put the child at ease a little more and helped them settle.
>
> (George)

In another example, George talks to a young child whose pet had recently died. George talked about his own experience of losing a dog as a child and said that, although those memories were painful to bring to mind, he felt that it would really help the child. There were examples of using past experiences to empathise with parents too. Jake described talking to a parent who had recently had a miscarriage. As Jake and his wife had been through that, too, he used his experience in order to empathise,

> There's some things you experience, you live through them, and it helps you understand it . . . because of what we'd been through, I could really understand, and I could help them as best I could.
>
> (Jake)

Jake also reflected on his experience as a parent and wondered whether he could empathise as effectively if he hadn't had his own children,

> I do think it helps. I know it shouldn't, but I'm also starting to think that it helps to do the job that we do if you've had children yourself.
>
> (Jake)

It is certainly the case that many people who do not have their own children exhibit excellent empathy skills, so past experience is just one influencing factor. Yarrow's (2015) research with childcare practitioners in Australia describes how the experiences practitioners go through shape their attitudes to the children they work with. This use of personal experience to understand the child's reality is one expounded by Neukrug et al. (2013), who claim that one can experience empathy by applying one's own personal experience to understand another person; however, Neukrug et al. also state that intuition and imagination are used alongside this personal experience. In contrast, Nussbaum's (2001, p. 302) definition of empathy as the 'imaginative reconstruction of another person's experience' seems to suggest that one does not need to have had the experience oneself that it is possible to imagine how another person feels even if you have not been through a similar experience yourself.

Trauma and empathy

The earlier examples from George and Jake suggest that experiencing a traumatic event may increase empathy. Another participant from the empathy research, Debbie, talked about practitioners developing empathy through the experiences of the Covid-19 pandemic; she says,

> This last year has been like a roller coaster for everyone, and hopefully, everybody's learned a bit of empathy from going through it.
>
> (Debbie)

Eadie et al.'s (2021) discussion on the effects of the Covid-19 pandemic on early childhood practitioners highlights a negative impact on their own health but an enduring positive relationship with the children they cared for, suggesting that empathic relationships had improved, but at the detriment of the practitioners' own emotional/mental health. This could be due to empathic distress, the feelings of others triggering distress in the empathiser (Hoffman, 2000). The report by Nelinger et al. (2021) on the emotional impact of early childhood work during the Covid-19 pandemic echoes Debbie's response about its influence on the profession.

There are conflicting views on whether childhood trauma has an impact on empathy in later life. Greenberg et al. (2018) found that people who had experienced significant trauma in their early years tended to have higher levels of empathy than those who had not, particularly affective empathy. However, research by Cerqueira and Almeida (2023) found that childhood adversity was associated with lower empathy, as well as more difficulty recognising and describing their own emotions. What is certain is that childhood trauma can have long-term effects on a person's life.

The wounded healer

The concept of the wounded healer is that people who have successfully dealt with a specific challenge may have a unique capacity to help people dealing with a similar problem and that this may benefit both parties (Kali and Malka, 2023). The term was first used by Jung (Dunne, 2015), and it describes people who use their own painful experiences to help others. There are lots of examples of people going through a difficulty and then wanting to help others with the same difficulty. For example, a high percentage of counsellors and therapists have a history of mental ill health; many women working in women's refuges have a history of domestic abuse. A study by Victor et al. (2022) found that 82% of psychology students in the United States and Canada had experienced mental health conditions at some point in their lives.

 Reflective prompt - Reflect on your own childhood. Can you identify any experiences that influenced your desire to work with young children? Do you have any strong views which originate from your own past experiences?

Intuitive empathy

The empathy research (Hodgkins, 2023) identified many examples of empathy which could be described as either 'advanced empathy' or 'intuition'. I suggest that there are elements of both concepts at play and that 'intuitive empathy' is an appropriate way of describing the phenomenon (see Figure 8.4).

Egan (2013), a counselling theorist and writer, describes advanced empathy as a type of empathy involving perceiving another person's feelings when the person themselves may not be consciously aware of them. Egan (2013) describes the interpretation of nonverbal clues such as body language and voice tone and explains that skilled therapists can use this to determine how someone is feeling. There were examples of practitioners interpreting children's nonverbal behaviour in the findings of this research (see Chapter 2). The following example by Mel illustrates this skill,

130 *Nurturing Compassionate Connections*

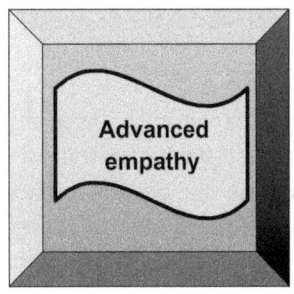
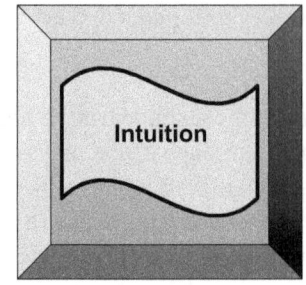
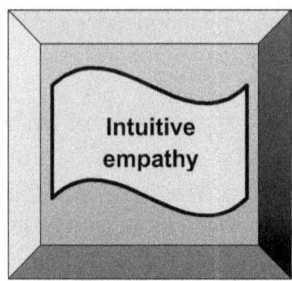

Picking up feelings recognised from body language and voice tone, sensing what is felt

(Egan, 2013)

Using knowledge and experience to unconsciously identify changes in behaviour

(Claxton, 2003; Brown, 2012)

Unconsciously using knowledge, experience and empathy to sense what is being felt, often without the other person's awareness

(Hodgkins, 2023)

Figure 8.4 Advanced empathy, intuition, or intuitive empathy?

> I think I am a very empathetic person. I pick up on people's emotions a lot of the time … I quite often know how other people are feeling, or if somebody's quieter than usual, I pick up on that really quickly. I'm always talking to people and saying, 'Are you ok? You seem a bit quiet', or 'Is there something wrong?'
>
> (Mel)

Mel considers this to be a form of empathy. However, what Egan (2013, p. 48) terms 'advanced empathy', Claxton (2003) and Brown (2012) might call 'intuition', which is developed through experience, the idea that it is possible to 'just know … without reasoning' (Brown, 2012, p. 65) what people are thinking and feeling. It is suggested, therefore, that advanced empathy and intuition may be elements of the same phenomenon. Figure 8.4 compares the terms and suggests 'intuitive empathy' as a suitable term for the synthesis of the two terms into one overarching phrase.

Participants in the empathy research identified times when they were able to identify signs of children's emotional states, particularly when a child is too young to be able to articulate such emotion verbally. Practitioners demonstrated a keen ability to decode non-verbal clues, such as body language and facial expressions, to interpret how children are feeling. This interpretative process often occurs unconsciously, with practitioners drawing on their perceptive knowledge of the child and their professional experience to tune into the child. The term 'intuitive empathy' encapsulates the practitioner's capacity to grasp a child's emotions through non-verbal signals, informed by their accumulated knowledge and experience, further enhanced by what is colloquially described as a 'gut feeling' (Sipman et al., 2021). This amalgamation of skills demonstrates a high level of intuitive empathy and emphasises practitioners' advanced understanding of a child's emotional state.

> **Individual activity**
>
> Look at the descriptions and previous examples. Can you identify times when you have used intuition, advanced empathy, or intuitive empathy? Which term makes the most sense to you? Why?

Emotional labour

Emotions, then, are integral to the profession, and workers are expected to display the emotion appropriate to the rules and expectations of employers (Barry et al., 2019). This includes empathy (Findlay et al., 2009; Henshall et al., 2018). The 'commercialisation of feelings' is examined by Hochschild (2013), who terms this *emotional labour*. Hochschild asserts that the management or suppression of emotions that are seen as inappropriate and the introduction of positive emotion cues, or 'feeling rules' (p. 50), are expected to be consistent with the image required for the job. She describes two types of emotional work: surface acting and deep acting.

Surface acting involves showing outward signs of a particular emotion; for example, smiling when smiling is socially appropriate. Ellis and Tucker (2015, p. 138) use the example of attending the funeral of someone you were not close to, following hearing the good news that you will inherit lots of money from the person. Surface acting would involve looking sad at the funeral, which is the socially acceptable emotion for the occasion.

Deep acting, in comparison, is concerned with not only deceiving others that you are feeling a certain way but also deceiving oneself, so you are genuinely feeling the emotion (Hochschild, 1983). This could entail, for example, listening to a co-worker whose husband has left her by thinking back to when that happened to you and feeling the emotion you felt at the time. This deep acting has a close affinity with empathy. Jonggab (2018) explains that in deep acting, we identify with another person and feel as if we are the other person; we share in the emotion, which is synonymous with affective empathy. Jonggab's research with nurses indicates that when a nurse smiles at a patient and does so only to satisfy the emotional needs of a patient, this is emotional labour. However, if the emotion of the patient is shared with the nurse and the smile becomes a real smile for the nurse, then this is empathy. Jonggab (2018) agrees with Hochschild (2013) in the belief that surface acting is more likely to result in stress, depression, and burnout than deep acting. Although deep acting involves more depth of feeling, the emotion is genuine. Surface acting, on the other hand, produces conflict between one's outward expression and one's internal feelings, which in turn produces conflict between mind and body (Hülsheger and Schewe, 2011), leading to stress. The effects of surface and deep acting are depicted in Figure 8.5.

132 *Nurturing Compassionate Connections*

Surface acting

Showing outward signs of a socially appropriate emotion

"Everything is great!"

Conflict between outward expression and inner feelings causes stress

Deep acting

Genuinely making an effort to feel the emotion of others

"You must feel devastated"

Deep but honest feeling, closely related to affective empathy

Figure 8.5 Emotional labour: surface acting vs. deep acting. Image from FreePik.

Page and Elfer (2013) assert that prioritising the emotions of the child over their own is not merely a skill but rather an instinct rooted in practitioners' deep understanding of the child and their strong bond with them. This aspect of ethical practice is crucial for practitioners in their interactions with children. Taggart (2019, in Langford, 2019), also sees care and compassion as a feature of ethical practice,

> The implication is that, if we can reconceptualise the capacity for love, caring and intimacy as ethical dispositions, the way is then open towards cultivating such dispositions in professional programmes.
>
> (p. 99)

The list of attributes required in someone who works with young children includes caring (Noddings, 2013), loving (Cousins, 2017), and demonstrating emotional warmth (Cameron and Maginn, 2008). A caring, warm, loving person appears to be the right sort of person for this profession. Colley (2006, p. 14) explores this in her case study research with childcare students in a Further Education college. Colley found that childcare trainees were expected to adopt specific ways of behaving with gentleness and sensitivity. Colley's research, which was with a solely female sample, also revealed a belief among these childcare students that, as they were caring for other people's children, it was important that they were seen as 'nice girls' (p. 24), resulting in Colley's concern that the role produces 'docile' and 'uncomplaining caregiving' (p. 27). Colley suggests that it is the lack of power and the exploitation of the early childhood worker's emotional labour, rather than the demands of the children, which are emotionally draining. This passivity and lack of control is a threat to practitioners' wellbeing (Tebben et al., 2021). Basford's (2019) research further unveils an emotional burden experienced by practitioners, resulting in feelings of incompetence and a perceived lack of trust in their professional competence.

Case study – interviewing Harriet

As part of the empathy research, I carried out an interview with Harriet, an early years educator working in the baby room of a private day nursery. It was a virtual interview using MS Teams, as we were still experiencing the Covid-19 pandemic. As usual in these sessions, I started by thanking her for completing her reflective diary and for taking the time out of her busy day to talk to me. I asked her how her day had been, as she'd just got back from work. She had caught a bus home from work, and the interview with me started 20 minutes after she arrived home.

Harriet talked about struggling at work. She told me that the nursery is short-staffed and that she had to look after the babies on her own for part of the day. She began to get tearful as she started describing how one of the babies had cried nearly all day. Harriet said she was so tired and stressed, and she didn't know how she would cope with another day the same tomorrow. At this point, Harriet's emotional state was my priority, not my research, so my focus was on how to manage the situation and make sure she felt listened to. I used some of the techniques from my counselling experience, like active listening and paraphrasing, so Harriet knew my attention was on her. Harriet talked for around 5–10 minutes, and she stopped crying. I felt that it would not be appropriate to return to a conversation about the research, so I decided to just use the input I already had from Harriet. At the end of the conversation, I asked what she was going to do now, and I asked if she had anyone at home that she could talk to about things like this. I asked if there was anyone else at home with her, and she said that her mother was downstairs and she would go and talk to her after our meeting. I finished the meeting by giving her some positive messages and thanking her for her input. I also emailed her the following day to check that she was ok, and she responded letting me know she was fine.

 Individual activity

Read the case study 'interviewing Harriet' and reflect on the following questions:

- Why do you think Harriet was upset?
- What sort of empathy is Harriet displaying?
- How does the relationship with the child impact Harriet's emotions?
- Which skills did the researcher use in the conversation with Harriet?
- If you were Harriet's colleague or manager, what could you do to help her?

Empathy and reflective practice

There is a close link between reflective practice and empathy development; McNaughton's (2016) research with nursing students showed that reflective practice increased their understanding of others' perspectives. Grant's (2014) research with social work students had similar findings and an indication that reflection both increases empathy and protects emotional wellbeing. Reflective conversations within early childhood settings, therefore, have merit in developing empathy and in the management of the impact of empathic interactions. Elfer (2012) identified supportive relationships among staff in early years settings as crucial to wellbeing. Elfer recommends 'work discussion groups', where practitioners discuss a particular issue relating to their role. The research concluded that there was a strong need for practitioners to talk about their work, particularly about relationships with others at work. Elfer (2012) and Basford (2019) recommend professional reflection to help contain the stress and anxiety arising from close emotional work with children.

Work discussion groups

Elfer (2024) describes a work discussion group as 'a safe space to talk, think about, and strengthen professional relationships at work' (p. xi) and what it is not:

> it is not therapy! It is not a space to off-load personal worries, and it is not a space to have a competition with others in the group about who copes best with the work.
>
> (Elfer, 2024, p. xi)

Wilson (p. 10 in Elfer, 2024) describes a work discussion group as,

> A forum for nursery practitioners to think with colleagues about the children and families they work with in which particular attention is given to both the positive and negative feelings that may be stirred up through their work.

A work discussion group should meet regularly and there should be a theme for discussion at each meeting. These are identified by members of the group and could be areas of practice that a practitioner has found challenging emotionally (Chapter 9 gives some examples of these areas of practice). Elfer (2024) suggests that the practitioner brings an observation with them to the meeting for discussion. Often, it is a good idea to begin the meeting with a general chat about the working week to encourage conversation and to make people feel comfortable. A facilitator is needed to manage the meeting; this must be done compassionately and with empathy for group members. Everyone in the group should feel heard and valued.

 **Group activity**

Revisit the reflective practice activity from Chapter 1. Can you add any more to your notes on reflective practice? How well would 'work discussion groups' work for your organisation?

Chapter summary

In this chapter, we have explored ways that empathy is attained or developed. Stages of empathy development have been identified and discussed, starting before birth and continuing to develop into the adolescent years. However, diverse ideas exist about whether empathy is innate or whether it is a skill which can be further developed in adulthood.

In support of empathy as an innate human quality, we examined mirror neurons and genetic behaviour studies, which identified some prerequisites required before empathy can be experienced. The chapter also acknowledged the idea that some people are more pre-disposed to empathy, 'natural born empathisers' (Baron-Cohen, 2003).

There is, however, much research suggesting that empathy is both a teachable skill and one that is impacted by life experiences. Environmental factors were explored, including a nurturing environment and quality of care as children's brains develop. Ways of developing our own empathic understanding further as adults were identified and links between life experiences and our ability to empathise with others. Trauma can affect the way we feel empathy, and this was explored briefly; this is revisited in Chapter 9.

Empathy is closely related to intuition and reflection; the terms can be amalgamated into 'intuitive empathy'. Therefore, reflective practice is an important aspect of the development of empathy. Group reflection within the early years, in the form of work discussion groups, was discussed and suggested as a useful vehicle for professional reflection and development.

Key messages

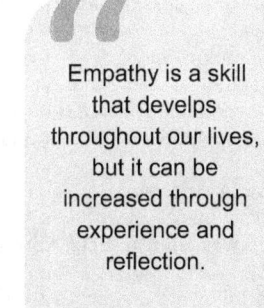 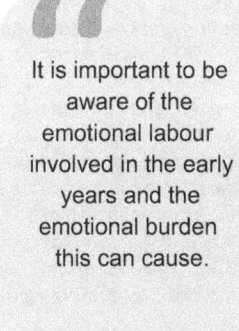

Figure 8.6 Key messages from Chapter 8

References

Baron-Cohen, S. (2003) *The essential difference: Males, females, and the truth about autism*, New York: Basic Books.
Barry, B., Olekalns, M. and Rees, L. (2019) 'An ethical analysis of emotional labour', *Journal of Business Ethics*, 160, pp. 17-34.
Basford, J. (2019) 'Being a graduate professional in the field of early childhood education and care: Silence, submission and subversion', *Education*, 47(7), pp. 862-875.
Belzung, C. (2014) 'Empathy', *Journal for Perspectives of Economic, Political, and Social Integration*, 19(1-2), pp. 177-191.
Brown, A. (2012) 'Assessment strategies for teaching empathy, intuition and sensitivity on the labour ward', *Evidence Based Midwifery*, 10(2), pp. 64-70.
Cain, S. (2013) *Quiet: The power of introverts in a world that can't stop talking*, London: Penguin.
Cameron, R. and Maginn, C. (2008) 'The authentic warmth dimension of professional childcare', *British Journal of Social Work*, 38, pp. 1151-1172.
Cerqueira, A. and Almeida, T. (2023) 'Adverse childhood experiences: Relationship with empathy and alexithymia', *Journal of Child and Adolescent Trauma*, 16, pp. 559-568.
Claxton, G. (2003) 'Chapter 2: The anatomy of intuition', in Atkinson, T. and Claxton, G. (eds) *The intuitive practitioner: On the value of not always knowing what one is doing*, Maidenhead: Open University Press, pp. 32-52.
Colley, H. (2006) 'Learning to labour with feeling: Class, gender and emotion in childcare education and training', *Contemporary Issues in Early Childhood*, 7(1), pp. 15-29.
Cousins, S. (2017) '"Practitioners" constructions of love in early childhood education and care', *International Journal or Early Childhood Education*, 25(1), pp. 16-29.
Dachyshyn, D. M. (2015) 'Being mindful, heartful, and ecological in early years care and education', *Contemporary Issues in Early Childhood*, 16(1), pp. 32-41.
Decety, J. (2010) 'The neurodevelopment of empathy in humans', *Developmental Neuroscience*, 32(4), pp. 257-267.
Dinstein, I., Thomas, C., Behrmann, M. and Heeger, D. (2008) 'A mirror up to nature', *Current Biology*, 18(1), pp. 13-18.
Dunne, C. (2015) *Jung: Wounded healer of the soul*, London: Watkins.
Eadie, P., Levickis, P., Murray, L., Page, J., Elek, C. and Church, A. (2021) 'Early childhood educators wellbeing during the COVID-19 pandemic', *Early Childhood Education Journal*, 49(5), pp. 903-913.
Egan, G. (2013) *The skilled helper, a problem-management and opportunity-development approach to helping*, 10th edn, CA: Brooks/Cole, Cengage Learning.
Elfer, P. (2012) 'Emotion in nursery work: Work discussion as a model of critical professional reflection', *Early Years*, 32(2), pp. 129-141.
Elfer, P. (2024) *Talking with feeling in the early years: 'Work discussion' as a model of supporting professional reflection and wellbeing*, London: Routledge.
Ellis, D. and Tucker, I. (2015) *Social psychology of emotion*, London: Sage.
Findlay, P., Findlay, J. and Stewart, R. (2009) 'The consequences of caring: Skills, regulation and reward among early childhood Workers', *Work, Employment and Society*, 23(3), pp. 422-441.
Galetz, E. (2019) 'The empathy-compassion matrix: Using a comparison concept analysis to identify care components', *Nursing Forum*, 54(3), pp. 448-454.
Garnett, H. (2018) *Empathy in the early Years*, London: Jessica Kingsley.
Gopnik, A. (2010, July) 'How babies think', *Scientific American*, pp. 76-81.
Grant, L. (2014) 'Hearts and minds: Aspects of empathy and wellbeing in social work students', *Social Work Education*, 33(3), pp. 338-352.
Greenberg, D., et al. (2018) 'Elevated empathy in adults following childhood trauma', *PLoS ONE*, 13(10).
Henshall, A., Atkins, L., Bolan, R., Harrison, J. and Munn, H. (2018) '"Certified to make a difference": The motivation and perceptions of newly qualified early years teachers in England', *Journal of Vocational Education and Training*, 70(3), pp. 417-434.
Hickok, G. (2009) 'Eight problems for the mirror neuron theory of action understanding in monkeys and humans', *Journal of Cognitive Neuroscience*, 21(7), pp. 1229-1243.
Hochschild, A. (1983) *The managed heart: Commercialization of human feeling*. Berkeley, CA: University of California Press.

Hochschild, A. (2013) *The managed heart – commercialization of human feeling*, 3rd edn, Berkeley, CA: University of California Press.

Hodgkins, A. (2023) *Exploring early childhood practitioners' perceptions of empathic interactions with children and families*. PhD thesis, University of Worcester, available at: https://eprints.worc.ac.uk/13525/

Hoffman, M. (2000) *Empathy and moral development*, New York: Cambridge University Press.

Hülsheger, U. R. and Schewe, A. F. (2011) 'On the costs and benefits of emotional labor: A meta-analysis of three decades of research', *Journal of Occupational Health Psychology*, 16(3), pp. 361-389.

Iacoboni, M. (2009) 'Imitation, empathy and mirror neurons', *Annual Review of Psychology*, 60, pp. 653-670.

Jeong, H. and Lee, Y. (2015) 'Smartphone addiction and empathy among nursing students', *Advanced Science & Technology Letters*, 88, pp. 224-228.

Jonggab, K. (2018) 'Emotional labor in the care field and empathy-enhancing education by reading literature: A brief review', *Iranian Journal of Public Health*, 47(8), pp. 1084-1089.

Kali, D. and Malka, M. (2023) 'It's not just me, it's us, together: The embodied of the wounded healer in the role of sex trade survival mentors-a critical mentoring perspective', *International Journal of Environmental Research and Public Health*, 20(5), p. 4089.

Knafo, A. and Uzefovsky, F. (2013) 'Chapter 5 – variation in empathy: The interplay of genetic and environmental factors', in Legerstee, M., Haley, D. and Bornstein, M. (eds) *The infant mind: Origins of the social brain*, New York: The Guildford Press, pp. 97-122.

Lingnau, A., Gesierich, B. and Caramazza, A. (2009) 'Assymetric fMRI adaptation reveals no evidence for mirror nuerons in humans', *Proceedings of the National Academy of Sciences*, 106(24), pp. 9925-9930.

Liu, H., et al. (2022) 'The relationship between maternal and infant empathy: The mediating role of responsive parenting', *Frontiers in Psychology*, 13, pp. 1-11.

Manassis, K. (2017) *Developing empathy: A biopsychosocial approach to understanding compassion for therapists and parents*, London: Routledge.

McNaughton, S. (2016) 'Developing pre-requisites for empathy: Increasing awareness of self, the body and the perspectives of others', *Teaching in Higher Education*, 21(5), pp. 501-515.

Nelinger, A., Album, J., Haynes, A. and Rosan, C. (2021) *Their challenges are our challenges – a summary report of the experiences facing nursery workers in the U.K. in 2020*, available at: https://www.annafreud.org/media/13013/their-challenges-are-our-challenges-survey-report.pdf (accessed 14th March 2025).

Neukrug, E., Bayne, H., Dean-Nganga, L. and Pusateri, C. (2013) 'Creative and novel approaches to empathy: A neo-rogerian perspective', *Journal of Mental Health Counseling*, 35(1), pp. 29-42.

NHS. (2024) *Early learning and development*, available at: www.nhs.uk/start-for-life/early-learning-development/ (accessed 27th June 2024).

Noddings, N. (2013) *Caring: A relational approach to ethics and moral education*, 2nd edn, Berkeley, CA: University of California Press.

Nussbaum, M. C. (2001) *The upheavals of thought: The intelligence of emotions*, New York: Cambridge University Press.

Page, J. and Elfer, P. (2013) 'The emotional complexity of attachment interactions in nursery', *European Early Childhood Education Research Journal*, 21(4), pp. 553-567.

Piaget, J. (1957) *Construction of reality in the child*, London: Routledge & Kegan Paul.

Premack, D. and Woodruff, G. (1978) Does the chimpanzee have a theory of mind? *Behavioural and Brain Sciences*, 1(4), pp.515-526.

Reiss, H. (2017) 'The science of empathy', *Journal of Patient Experience*, 4(2), pp. 74-77.

Roberts, A., LoCasale-Crouch, J., Hamre, B. and Jamil, F. (2019) 'Preschool teachers' self-efficacy, burnout, and stress in online professional development: A mixed methods approach to understand change', *Journal of Early Childhood Teacher Education*, 41(3), pp. 262-283.

Rogers, C. (1951) *Client-centered therapy: Its current practice, implications and theory*, London: Constable.

Singer, T. and Klimecki, O. (2014) 'Empathy and compassion', *Current Biology*, 24(18), pp. 875-878.

Sipman, G., Martens, R., Tholke, J. and McKenny, S. (2021) 'Professional development focused on intuition can enhance teacher pedagogical tact', *Teaching and Teacher Education*, 106, pp. 1-17.

Su, Y. (2014) 'Self-directed, genuine graduate attributes: The person based approach', *Higher Education Research and Development*, 33(6), pp. 1208-1220.

Taggart, G. (2019) 'Chapter 5: Cultivating ethical dispositions in early childhood practice for an ethic of care: A contemplative approach', in Langford, R. *Theorizing feminist ethics of care in early childhood practice: Possibilities and dangers*, London: Bloomsbury Academic.

Tebben, E., Lang, S., Sproat, E., Tyre-Owens, J. and Helms, S. (2021) 'Identifying primary and secondary stressors, buffers, and supports that impact ECE teacher wellbeing: Implications for teacher education', *Journal of Early Childhood Teacher Education*, 42(2), pp. 143-161.

Thempra. (2024) *An introduction to social pedagogy*, available at: https://thempra.org.uk/

Verrier, D., Connolly, S. and Kimber, L. (2024) 'Autism and empathy, news', *National Autistic Society*, available at: www.autism.org.uk/advice-and-guidance/professional-practice/autism-and-empathy (accessed 27th June 2024).

Victor, S., Devendorf, A., Lewis, S., Rottenberg, J., Muehlenkamp, J., Stage, D. and Miller, R. (2022) 'Only human: Mental-health difficulties among clinical, counseling, and school psychology faculty and trainees', *Perspectives on Psychological Science*, 17(6), pp. 1576-1590.

Vygotsky, L. S. (1978) *Mind in society: The development of higher psychological processes*, Cambridge, MA: Harvard University Press.

Yarrow, A. (2015) 'What we feel and what we do: Emotional capital in early childhood work', *Early Years*, 35(4), pp. 351-365.

9

Understanding and managing empathic distress

Chapter objectives

- To evaluate the outcomes of empathy and emotional labour
- To examine stress, burnout, and empathic distress
- To analyse the emotional impact of early years work on practitioners' lives
- To explore self-awareness and self-care
- To evaluate support and supervision in early years settings

The impact of empathy on the self has been briefly discussed in Chapter 1, which explored two different outcomes of (particularly affective) empathy. A positive outcome is compassion; we feel empathy for someone, and this leads to us taking compassionate action. Another reaction to empathy, one that occurs if no action can be taken or if a person is overwhelmed with emotion, is empathic distress. However, the outcomes of empathy differ depending on the type of empathy displayed. Cognitive empathy, as discussed in Chapter 2, is concerned with thinking through how another person may be feeling. When people use cognitive empathy, they make an effort to imagine themselves in the person's position, using reason to interpret how they might be feeling. Cognitive empathy can result in compassionate action, or it can result in fatigue, as the effort required can be tiring. With affective empathy, however, there is no effort required, as we share the feelings of the other person and feel the emotion ourselves. Again, this can lead to compassionate action, or it can result in personal, empathic distress for the empathiser. Figure 9.1 shows the potential consequences of both types of empathy: cognitive and affective.

Stress and burnout

Although the term empathic distress is not widely known, the terms stress and burnout are, and they are synonymous with the caring professions.

140 *Nurturing Compassionate Connections*

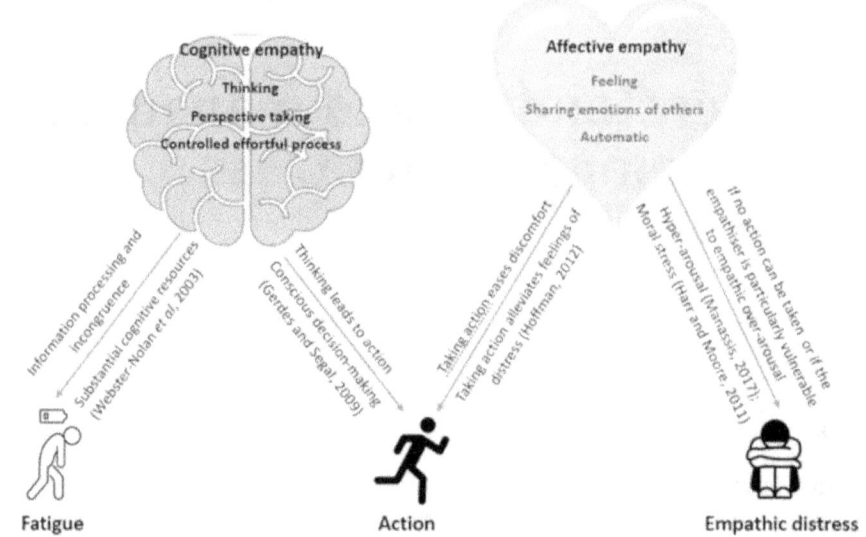

Figure 9.1 Consequences of empathy

Stress

The World Health Organisation defines stress as 'a state of worry or mental tension caused by a difficult situation' (WHO, 2023). Stress is the body's natural reaction to feeling threatened or under pressure and is universal, but the way individuals respond to stress affects their wellbeing. Feeling under pressure can be positive in some situations, for example, in competitive sport, but too much pressure at work can become negative and can cause the body to go into a state of *fight, flight,* or *freeze*. In an acute stress situation, the sympathetic nervous system is activated; 'hormones such as adrenaline and cortisol are released in order to prepare the body for action. Impairment of the prefrontal cortex causes difficulty in thinking logically, which can affect our work as well as our home lives' (Prowle and Hodgkins, 2020, p. 154). If negative stress is not controlled, it can cause both mental and physical ill health. Chronic stress can adversely affect the cardiovascular, neural, immune, and metabolic systems (McEwen, 2017). Prolonged stress can affect people's resilience and can lead to the more serious condition of burnout.

Burnout

Burnout, *a state of physical, mental, and emotional exhaustion,* occurs as a consequence of long-term stress. The signs of burnout are quite different from the signs of stress.

> Where stress causes emotional overreactions, burnout causes a lack of emotion; where stress causes urgency and hyperactivity, burnout makes us feel helpless and hopeless.
> (Prowle and Hodgkins, 2020, p. 154)

Mental Health UK conducted The Burnout Report in 2024 and found that 24% of adults living in the UK feel unable to manage the stress and pressures in their lives. The report

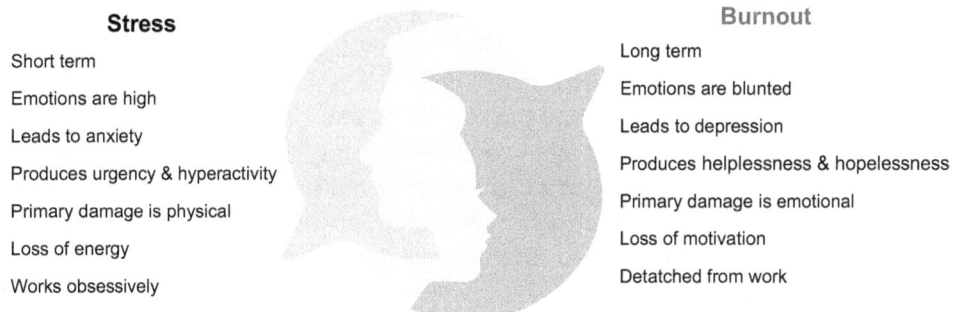

Stress	Burnout
Short term	Long term
Emotions are high	Emotions are blunted
Leads to anxiety	Leads to depression
Produces urgency & hyperactivity	Produces helplessness & hopelessness
Primary damage is physical	Primary damage is emotional
Loss of energy	Loss of motivation
Works obsessively	Detatched from work

Figure 9.2 Stress vs. burnout

suggests that the changes in society caused by the Covid-19 pandemic have had a negative effect on our mental health as a nation and, consequently, the UK is becoming 'a burnt out nation' (Mental Health UK, 2024, p. 12). Burnout is a much more serious condition than stress, so it is important to be able to identify the signs. Smith and Reid (2024) suggest that you may be at risk of burnout if:

- 'Every day is a bad day.
- Caring about your work or home life seems like a total waste of energy.
- You're exhausted all the time.
- The majority of your day is spent on tasks you find either mind-numbingly dull or overwhelming.
- You feel like nothing you do makes a difference or is appreciated'.

If you ever feel that you are experiencing burnout, then please seek support. It is important to be able to recognise the signs and to take action to reverse the effects.

 **Group activity**

How can you, as a staff team, recognise the signs of staff struggling with stress? How can you identify burnout? Develop an action plan for supporting staff mental health and wellbeing.

Empathic distress

Empathic distress is a particular stress which results from the very close empathic relationships that practitioners have with the children in their care. Whilst empathy is essential, at times, we can feel overloaded with emotion, which can result in our own distress. It is important to note that empathy can also result in empathic satisfaction (discussed further in Chapter 10). Empathic distress is not something that happens to everyone but, again, it is useful to know the signs.

The empathy research (Hodgkins, 2023) identified a range of effects of empathy on practitioners, including tiredness, feeling the burden of responsibility, and emotional upset, which was identified as empathic distress. Findings from the research substantiate the views of many, including Datler et al. (2010), Taggart (2016), and Elfer et al. (2018), that being around young children with 'catastrophic emotions' (Datler et al., 2010) and developing close empathic relationships with them can cause emotional distress. Transitions, in particular, were a time of intense emotion for many of the participants, who described feeling the emotional pain of young children. This example from Mel illustrates the emotion she feels and picks up from the child,

> If there's a child who's really struggling with separation from their parents and they're really upset, it used to get to me a lot, and I'd get really upset about it.
>
> (Mel)

In this example, Mel feels upset about the separation. She senses the emotion of the child and appears to literally feel the child's pain (Neukrug et al., 2013), a clear example of affective empathy.

Hoffman's (2000) description of the personal distress of empathy being too painful to bear is evident in participants' reports of their own crying. These participants appear to be literally feeling the emotional pain of the child themselves. This intense emotional reaction is labelled by various writers as 'emotional overexcitability' (Smith, 2016), 'hypersensitivity' (Pietchowiski, 2009), 'empathic distress' (Hoffman, 2000), 'empathic over-arousal' (Eisenberg, 2005), and 'hyper-arousal' (Manassis, 2017). One of the research participants, Harriet, had been working in the baby room of a nursery, which was understaffed, and she was overwhelmed with the amount of responsibility she had. In the following examples, Harriet's distress is evident,

> I'm always upset. I come home and cry.
>
> I do really struggle at work a lot of the time . . . especially if you can't help them, even with emotion coaching and all these different strategies. If they're still really unsettled, it is hard.
>
> You take it home, and then you can't stop thinking about it.
>
> (Harriet)

Harriet's reaction supports Datler et al.'s (2010) view that being around young children with 'catastrophic emotions' and developing close empathic relationships with them can cause emotional distress. Debbie, a deputy manager, also talked about emotional upset, saying,

> *we cry daily to each other over something.*
>
> (Debbie)

Understanding and managing empathic distress 143

However, for Debbie, the reasons for her distress were different. Debbie's nursery was in financial difficulty and in danger of closing, which caused stress for the staff and the families using the nursery. Peer support within the setting was clearly important in offering support for each other during the working day. Both Harriet's and Debbie's comments indicate empathy overload.

An ethical dilemma?

In the next research excerpt, there are conflicting emotions, empathy, guilt, and uncertainty. This example of practice is discussed as a case study in Chapter 4, where we examined it from the perspective of relationships with parents. Here, we examine the effect on Mel herself, the tension between Mel's own emotions, her empathy for the parent, and the conflict between her own values and what is expected of her in her role. The example describes Mel's feelings after telling a parent that her child had been settled when, in fact, he had been distressed. Mel said,

> At first, I was feeling good at not adding to the guilt, seeing Mom's relief at not being told her son had struggled again... I chose to tell Mom about the positives to spare her feelings. I had mixed emotions; I was feeling glad at sparing Mom's feelings, feeling guilty about omitting the truth, and worried because I wasn't sure whether it was the right thing to do!
>
> (Mel)

In the example, Mel is clearly feeling conflicted. There is a tension and uncertainty between the rules of her role and her own ethical beliefs. Barry et al. (2019) ethical analysis of emotional labour suggests that this is what causes burnout, emotional exhaustion, and a perceived lack of personal accomplishment (p. 20), which is clear in Mel's uncertainty. Colley's (2006) view that it is the lack of power and the exploitation of the early childhood worker's emotional labour that is emotionally draining, rather than the demands of children, seems relevant here. If Mel had the power to handle the situation the way she felt was best, she would not have felt so conflicted.

Reflective prompt - Consider the options if you were to find yourself in Mel's position. What is most important to you personally? What is your opinion of the nursery's 'rule' of not passing on details of a child's distress?

Empathic distress, stress, and burnout do not just affect practitioners at work; they often affect people's home lives, too. Figure 9.3 gives examples from all nine of the empathy research participants, illustrating the effects on people outside the working day.

144 *Nurturing Compassionate Connections*

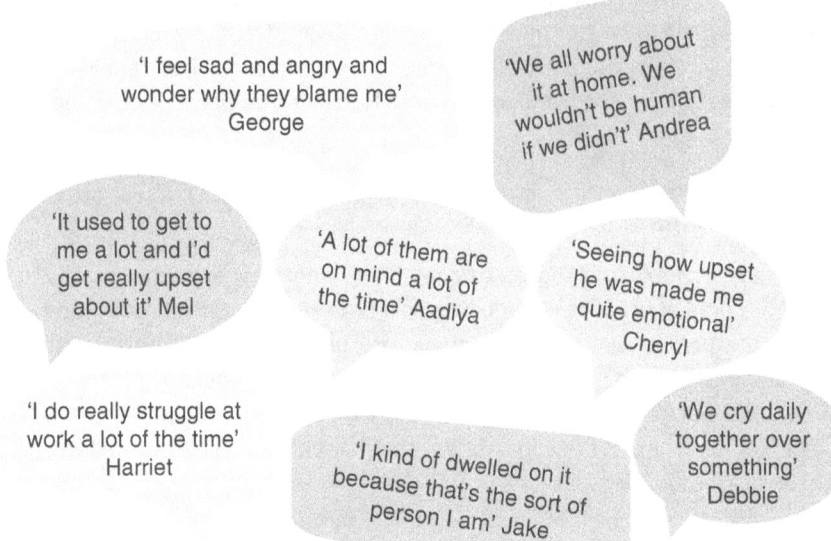

Figure 9.3 Examples of emotional impact on participants' home lives

 Individual activity

Keep a diary of emotion over a week and identify the impact of emotional labour on your life. Assess whether this is manageable or whether you need support. Where do you go/what do you do for support?

Avoiding empathy

Empathic distress, if extreme and long-lasting, can lead to a protective withdrawal from the situation. Cameron et al. (2016) suggest that people may avoid empathy to protect themselves against being exhausted and overwhelmed. Another study by Cameron et al. (2019) suggests that people choose whether to empathise by weighing up the rewards and costs to themselves. Rewards are in the form of satisfaction and pride in helping, but the costs can be distress and exhaustion. Cameron et al. (2019) concluded that empathy is emotionally costly.

In the empathy research (Hodgkins, 2023), one participant described concern over her conceived decreasing empathy. Mel made three comments about this. The first comment,

> thinking a lot about if it's a good or bad thing that I am getting less emotionally attached.
>
> (Mel)

This seemed important, so it was followed up in Mel's interview when she was asked about the comment. Mel reflected on this and replied, with her second comment,

> When I first started in baby room, I would use empathy a lot, and quite often, it would make me quite emotional, and I'd think about it a lot afterwards, but then having to think of those things everyday, it kind of impacts on you less, I think, so that you become less stressed.
>
> (Mel)

Here, Mel appears to be reflecting upon the way that her emotional state has changed over time in her job role. In the interview, Mel continued to talk about her interactions with the babies in her third comment and her frustration over the rules of the nursery, which meant that she could not give the babies the attention she thought they wanted,

> I felt really sympathetic, but then I found I was just getting really frustrated because, personally, there was nothing I could do, and I wonder if that's me becoming less empathetic or maybe putting up a barrier to not get as stressed out.
>
> (Mel)

Mel's conflicting emotions are evident. Csaszar et al. (2018) suggest that people whose empathy causes them stress may show decreasing empathy for others as a protection against exhaustion and burnout. It may be, therefore, that in Mel's example, she became aware of becoming stressed and in danger of burnout and was therefore protecting herself, as she seems to have realised in her reflection.

Emotional labour

In Chapter 8, the subject of emotional labour was examined. Emotional labour concerns a requirement to display the emotion appropriate to the rules and expectations of employers. In early years practice, this usually means being very positive and patient at all times. Although there may be variations in expectations, there has long been an expectation of the qualities that early years practitioners should display. An early book by Tietze et al. (1996, p. 452) stated that the ideal early childhood worker should display 'sensitivity, gentleness, enthusiasm, effort, and enjoyment of contact with children'. Elfer et al. (2018) suggest that early years practitioners are expected to show a love of children and endless patience.

When managed well, emotional labour can have positive outcomes for fostering and nurturing meaningful relationships; however, as Hochschild (1983) says, the outcomes for practitioners are often guilt and stress, as the expectations can be unsustainable. Research by Faulkner et al. (2016) with early childhood practitioners highlighted high levels of depression in the profession and its effects on wellbeing, such as 'exhaustion, sleep disturbances and physical health problems' (p. 280).

146 *Nurturing Compassionate Connections*

It is worth noting that in early years settings in England, there is a focus in recent years on children being encouraged to express their true emotions. In comparison, the literature on emotional labour suggests that practitioners are not encouraged to do the same. Practitioners are expected to display a specific persona at work, regardless of their frustrations and negative emotions. I recently heard a practitioner refer to this as her 'children's TV presenter persona'.

> **Individual activity**
>
> Do you feel that you display a specific persona at work? What are the unwritten rules for the expression of feelings at work? (Mark these on Figure 9.4). For example, are you expected to have 'endless patience' as Elfer et al. (2018) suggest? Do you often find yourself concealing your true emotions when working with children? Reflect on the advantages and disadvantages of emotional labour within your role. Do you believe that hiding true feelings leads to increased stress?

Managing stress and empathy overload

In recent years, there has been growing research interest in the emotional demands of early childhood work. Findlay et al. (2009), Taggart (2016), Elfer et al. (2018), and Page (2018) have all conducted investigations into this area and, in some cases, into compassion fatigue within the sector (Taggart, 2016; Elfer et al., 2018). A study by Nelinger et al. (2021) investigated the emotional impact of the work during the Covid-19 pandemic, which has understandably affected the whole profession. The report showed that over 70% of early years practitioners felt stressed or upset by challenging situations at work. Although the pandemic is now behind us, the effects remain and are likely to continue to impact on people's physical health, mental health, and social wellbeing for a decade (BMA, 2024).

Figure 9.4 Identifying unwritten 'feelings rules'. Image from FreePik.

Self-awareness

Being self-aware means knowing yourself and understanding your own views, feelings, strengths, and weaknesses. According to Vanourek (2023), *'self-awareness is critical in our life, work, and relationships'*. Self-awareness helps us communicate who we are and be authentic. It also helps us to understand what we want and identify ways of succeeding. Self-awareness can be perceived in two ways: intrapersonally (understanding yourself) and interpersonally (understanding how others see you); see Figure 9.5 (Carden et al., 2022, p. 170).

Self-awareness is a necessary step in developing self-acceptance and self-compassion.

 Reflection point - Reflect on yourself and on how others see you. Use the exercise in Chapter 1, where you considered your values and beliefs. Read further about the Johari window model and consider ways of decreasing your blind and hidden areas.

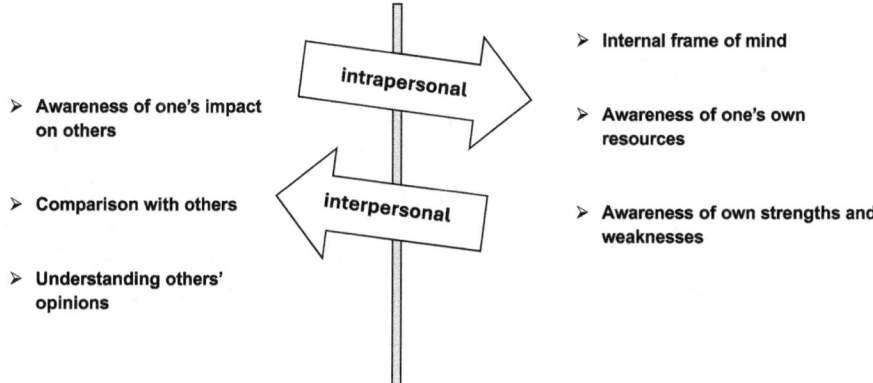

Figure 9.5 Intrapersonal and interpersonal self-awareness

Figure 9.6 Self-awareness activity. Image from FreePik.

148 *Nurturing Compassionate Connections*

A popular strategy for finding out how you perceive yourself and how others perceive you is to consider the Johari window model (Luft and Ingram, 1955). The Johari window model is comprised of four quadrants:

- The Open Area (things you and others know about yourself)
- The Blind Area (things that others know about you but you are unaware of)
- The Hidden Area (things you know about yourself, but others don't)
- The Unknown Area (things that are unknown to you and to others)

The idea behind the model is that the more we expand the blind and hidden areas, the larger the open area becomes. When we are open to feedback from others, we learn more about ourselves, and the blind area decreases. When we openly give information about ourselves to others, the hidden area decreases. As these two areas decrease, the open area expands. The unknown area also begins to expand and reveals things previously unknown, such as our future potential. The Johari window model is one method of uncovering both intrapersonal and interpersonal self-awareness.

Personalised self-care

Practitioners experience and manage stress within the profession in different ways. Research by Tebben et al. (2021), based on a case study with early childhood teachers in Ohio, USA, identified similar stressors as in England, with staffing crises, the emotions of young children struggling with attachment, and staff feeling undervalued as professionals (p. 153). In Tebben et al.'s research, staff described the coping strategies they had developed. Strategies included creating routines and structure, deep breathing and mindfulness, positive self-talk, and supportive relationships with colleagues.

Different strategies work for different people, so it is advisable to reflect on what would work for you individually. Whilst one person may go for a run to de-stress, another might prefer a long hot bath, while for another, cleaning the house might be their preferred way to relieve stress.

 Individual activity

Consider possible self-care strategies (see Figure 9.7 for some ideas), then write yourself a self-care prescription.

Understanding and managing empathic distress   149

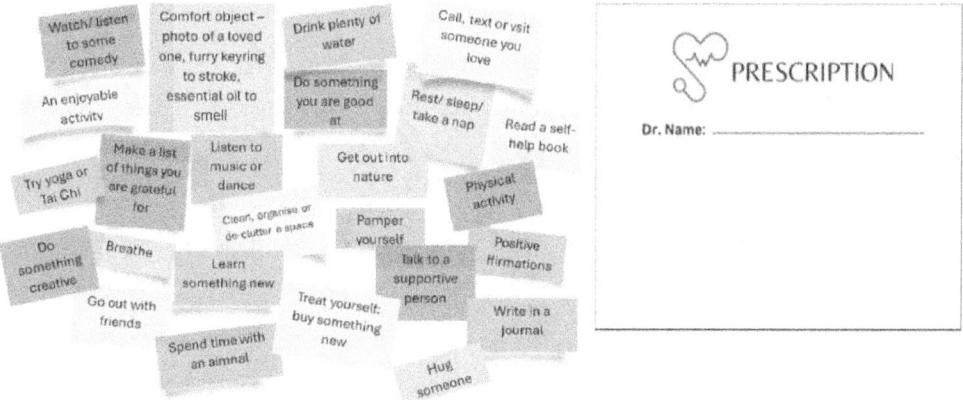

Figure 9.7 Self-care strategies and self-care prescription

 Case study – Ashanti

Ashanti has been working in the early years for ten years and has been at her current setting, a school nursery, for four years. She has two children, aged 7 and 5, who both attend the primary school that her nursery is attached to. Ashanti enjoys her job very much, but lately, she has been feeling very stressed.

Ashanti's 5-year-old daughter has recently been experiencing tummy aches and vomiting. Ashanti has taken her to the doctor, who cannot find anything worrying wrong with the child, telling Ashanti that it is probably a simple stomach bug. Ashanti accepts this until her daughter starts to have the same symptoms every couple of weeks. The GP cannot find anything wrong and suggests that the child's tummy aches could be due to anxiety.

Ashanti struggles to find anyone to care for the children when they are sick. She is a single parent with no extended family living nearby. She has taken a couple of days off to look after her daughter but worries about how the nursery is managing without her, as they are already short-staffed. The other day, she took a day off to look after her daughter, who seemed fine for most of the day, so Ashanti felt really guilty about being at home. On another occasion, she sent her daughter to school, and she was sent home after vomiting in assembly. Ashanti feels that whatever she does, she feels guilty.

> **Individual activity**
>
> Answer the following questions about the case study of Ashanti:
>
> - To what extent do you appreciate how Ashanti feels?
> - If you were a friend or colleague of Ashanti's, what would you say to her?
> - What can Ashanti do to help her feel more in control over the situation?
> - What could Ashanti's manager do to help?

Absenteeism and presenteeism in the early years

The sickness absence rate in the UK is currently at the highest level since 2010 (Kinman and Clements, 2023). Stanton (2024) identifies three types of absenteeism that managers have to deal with:

- Occasional short-term – these are unlikely to cause a problem
- Long-term – these can be difficult to deal with, so they require specialist advice and support
- Frequent short-term – these can cause difficulties for a business

There are many reasons for frequent absence; according to research by Culture Shift (2023), 61% of participants took time off due to workplace bullying or harassment, and 71% admitted to calling in sick due to not wanting to see a particular person they didn't get on with at work. Many people said they did not tell their manager the real reason for the absences, so they were unaware of the problems within the workplace.

However, presenteeism (working while sick) is also at a high level, particularly in the early years profession. There are many reasons for this, including worry about losing pay and possibly losing employment. Workload pressures, including staff shortages, make people feel that they need to go to work before they are fully recovered from sickness; however, 'a strong sense of duty and responsibility for the welfare of others' is also a key factor.

There is some evidence that returning to work before a person is fully recovered from illness can be therapeutic (Karanika-Murray and Biron, 2020), but there is also a possibility that presenteeism may delay recovery, increase future sickness absence, and increase the risk of mistakes and illness to the employee, colleagues, children and families (Kinman and Grant, 2021).

> **Group activity**
>
> Discuss the issues of absenteeism and presenteeism as a staff team. Consider:
>
> - The difficulties with absenteeism in the workplace and the challenges for managers of balancing staff support with running a sustainable, high-quality service
> - The potential impact of absenteeism on the staff team and children
> - The potential impact of presenteeism on the staff team and children
> - The emotional impact of guilt when taking time off from work
> - What might make someone call in sick when they are not sick?
> - What could be done about this?
> - How can the work culture be improved so that people are happy and committed?
> - Does your setting have an absence policy? Is it fit for practice?

Communication between the staff team is important; the more people know each other, the more they understand what people are experiencing and the support they need. Regular supervision is a good place to discuss issues of absenteeism and presenteeism.

Supervision

Since the Tickell review of the early years (DfE, 2012), it has been a requirement of early childhood settings in England to provide supervision for staff. The requirements state that supervision should include discussion of children's development and well-being, solutions to issues with children, and coaching to improve personal effectiveness (DfE, 2021). Although recent studies recommend incorporating emotional support for practitioners, the current approach seems to lack such provisions. Nagasawa and Tarrant (2020) stress the importance of emotional support following the recent trauma of the Covid-19 pandemic. Hunter (2023) also urges the sector to keep the emotional wellbeing of all staff as a priority, recommending supervision based on respect and honest communication. Reflective supervision is a very effective method of supporting each other within an early years setting. Supervision and work-discussion groups are discussed further in Chapter 8.

Helping others to help yourself

Hoffman (2000) claimed that there is an optimal state of empathy. He described an experiment where observers were shown vignettes of distressing situations. As the subjects' distress increased, the observer's distress also increased. A problem occurs when the observer's distress is greater than that of the person being observed. At this point, the observer can no longer help the other person, as they are suffering from empathic over-arousal.

Figley (1995), a colleague of Hoffman's, examined his previous career as a reporter; he had interviewed Vietnam veterans about their war experiences. He remembered the interviews making him feel angry and frustrated, leaving him feeling traumatised himself. In Figley's example, he coped with this by doing something to help the situation, such as establishing a charity to help veterans. There is evidence to suggest that doing something to help others can help us to feel better when we are suffering with empathic distress. For example, watching people living in a war zone or a natural disaster area can make us feel upset, but if we donate money or volunteer to help, our personal distress lessens.

The case for rational compassion

The term 'rational compassion' was coined by Bloom (2016) in his book 'Against empathy'. The book title is misleading; Bloom does not disagree with concern and care for others or trying to understand how people are feeling. Bloom (2016) advocates consideration of moral principles, considering the costs and benefits of actions, and attempting to make people's lives better without putting oneself in the other person's position. This notion of 'rational compassion' could be understood as a form of cognitive empathy (see Chapter 2), which results in compassion for others. The premise of Bloom's argument is that the attempt to feel the emotions of others is flawed. He suggests that empathy is biased; that we are more likely to feel empathy, for example, for someone who is like us (racially, socially, etc.) or who is more attractive. Bloom (2016) uses the example of people feeling more empathy for a news story of a little girl stuck in a well than the multitude of people affected by climate change, which seems illogical.

Conversely, Morgan (2017, p. 1), writing about compassion in healthcare, considers rational compassion to be lacking in 'richness and clarity' and believes that empathy, which has an emotional component, is far superior in understanding the multiple responses to others' distress.

Reflective prompt - Consider the view of Bloom (2016) described previously. Do you agree that empathy can be biased and that we tend to feel more empathy for people who are like us? Do you think that we should use logic and moral thinking to decide who, how, or when to help? Or do you think that affective (emotional) empathy is a more advantageous way to understand others?

Support for early years practitioners

A document by the Department for Education which focuses on early years practitioners' mental health and wellbeing states,

> The early years workforce makes a huge contribution to young children's lives, and a role in early years can be enjoyable and rewarding. However, it can also be a

challenging and demanding career. As in any workplace, this can take a toll on an individual's mental health and wellbeing. It is therefore essential that early years practitioners are properly supported within their setting to feel happy and fulfilled both inside and outside of work.

(DfE, 2023)

The document was published as a response to the recruitment and retention crisis in the UK; it lists a range of resources and guides to support early years practitioners and managers. An NCFE report (2023) highlighted an increasing skills gap within the sector and rising demand for staff. Among its recommendations, the NCFE calls for a change in the narrative, with more recognition of 'the value and incredible impact the early years and childcare sector has on society' (NCFE, 2023, p. 18). The report identifies sources of outside support for practitioners as well as wellbeing toolkits and resources for managers. One of these is an excellent resource for early years managers and teams from the Anna Freud Centre (Douglas-Osborne et al., 2021). The resource is based on the findings of research which highlighted four areas of support for practitioner wellbeing:

- *Supporting each other:* Being open, trusting each other, knowing each other, and making time for each other
- *Supportive management:* Making staff wellbeing a priority; being available and approachable; recognising and appreciating contribution; wellbeing support for managers
- *The physical environment:* Access to safe spaces; access to wellbeing information; small touches and creature comforts; regular wellbeing activities
- *Outside support:* Staff training; signposting; access to external support; self-care

Support for managers

The empathy research highlighted the unique stress on early years managers, who show empathy with children, families, and staff. The role of an early years manager is often associated with a sense of 'overwhelming responsibility, being described as a professional who is many things; to many people' (Preston, 2013). The responsibility of a manager frequently requires them to juggle several roles and skills at the same time to be successful with their vast workload. Debbie, deputy manager of a large inner-city nursery, explains,

> I've got a lot of roles at work, so I'm the deputy manager, I'm the deputy safeguarding lead, and I'm the setting SENCO, and I see parents on all different levels. So, one day, I'm dealing with a complaint; next, I'm having to tell a parent that we've noticed some additional needs in a child, and then I have safeguarding concerns to manage too.
>
> (Debbie)

One of these responsibilities would be challenging, but Debbie is juggling many very significant concerns on a daily basis. Empathy was evident in the interactions they portrayed;

managers were clearly attempting to see things from their colleagues' points of view. Joel describes this well in one of his interviews,

> I spend the large part of each day thinking about how the team members feel – what motivates and demotivates, their strengths and interests – how they might act in different scenarios.
>
> (Joel)

Joel's words are an example of the effective interpersonal skills proposed by Swindells (2023), the way that managers tune into the needs and anxieties of their staff. Research participants who are managers gave many examples of being attuned to their staff, demonstrating what Goleman (2020, p. 176) refers to as 'managing with heart'. In his diary reflections, Jake recognised this,

> Staff members discuss their concerns . . . feedback is always good, and morale is high. One-to-one talks are very important in building and maintaining relationships.
>
> (Jake)

> As the manager, I support them if they need support for the personal stuff, but then the day-to-day stuff, we know when someone is a bit down because we work so closely together.
>
> (Jake)

This second quote by Jake points to the team culture of the setting and the relationships between staff, which help promote understanding and empathy. Joel, too, recognises the importance of close contact with staff,

> I think it's that open culture of being with the staff, of working alongside them or just checking on their well-being.
>
> (Joel)

This added responsibility for staff wellbeing, on top of having overall responsibility for the children and obligations towards their families, amounts to 'overwhelming responsibility' (Preston, 2013).

 Group activity

Read through the early years staff wellbeing resource (Douglas-Osborn et al., 2021) together as a team. In each section, make notes of things that your setting does well and any ideas that you think could be adopted. Include support for managers. Use the activities at the back of the resource to identify good practice.

Chapter summary

In this chapter, the effects of empathy on practitioners have been examined, highlighting how different types of empathy impact individuals in various ways. Empathy generally has a positive influence, often leading to compassionate action. However, the information processing involved in cognitive empathy can sometimes result in fatigue, while the deep emotional involvement in affective empathy may lead to empathic distress. Managing high levels of emotion and stress can be challenging, and this may cause individuals to avoid empathy to protect themselves from distress. The chapter discusses empathic distress, stress, and burnout, using examples from empathy research to illustrate their effects on practitioners.

The emotional labour required in early years practice can lead to incongruence and subsequent depression, making it crucial to recognise these issues and identify a range of personal self-care strategies. Recognising warning signs is essential, and self-awareness is a key component of effective practice. Furthermore, practitioners must be well supported by managers and colleagues. The chapter explores the importance of supervision and support for all team members, drawing on strategies and insights from empathy research.

Key messages

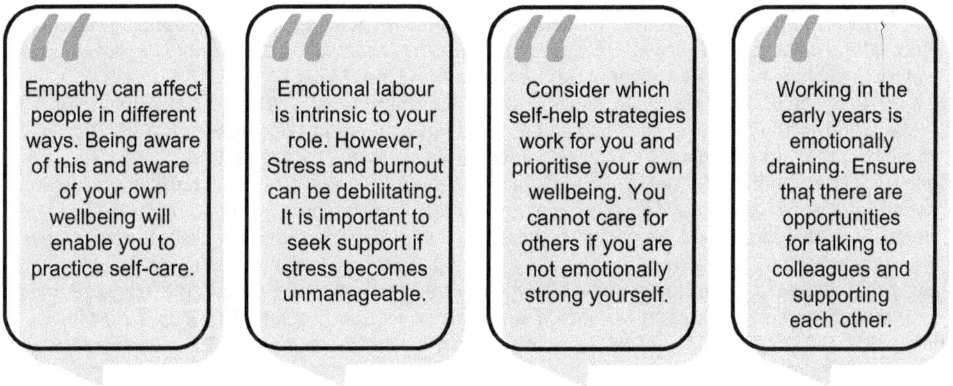

> Empathy can affect people in different ways. Being aware of this and aware of your own wellbeing will enable you to practice self-care.

> Emotional labour is intrinsic to your role. However, Stress and burnout can be debilitating. It is important to seek support if stress becomes unmanageable.

> Consider which self-help strategies work for you and prioritise your own wellbeing. You cannot care for others if you are not emotionally strong yourself.

> Working in the early years is emotionally draining. Ensure that there are opportunities for talking to colleagues and supporting each other.

Figure 9.8 Key messages from Chapter 9

References

Barry, B., Olekalns, M. and Rees, L. (2019) 'An ethical analysis of emotional labour', *Journal of Business Ethics*, 160, pp. 17–34.

Bloom, P. (2016) *Against empathy: The case for rational compassion*, London: Penguin.

British Medical Association (BMA). (2024) *The impact of the pandemic on population health and health inequalities*, available at: www.bma.org.uk/advice-and-support/covid-19/what-the-bma-is-doing/the-impact-of-the-pandemic-on-population-health-and-health-inequalities

Cameron, D., Harris, L. and Payne, K. (2016) 'The emotional cost of humanity: Anticipated exhaustion motivates dehumanization of stigmatized targets', *Social Psychological and Personality Science*, 7(2), pp. 105–112.

Cameron, D., Hutcherson, C., Ferguson, A., Scheffer, J., Hadjiandreou, E. and Inzlicht, M., (2019) 'Empathy is hard work: People choose to avoid empathy because of its cognitive costs', *Journal of Experimental Psychology: General*, 148(6), pp. 962–976.

Carden, J., Jones, R. J. and Passmore, J. (2022) 'Defining self-awareness in the context of adult development: A systematic literature review', *Journal of Management Education*, 46(1), pp. 140–177.

Colley, H. (2006) 'Learning to labour with feeling: Class, gender and emotion in childcare education and training', *Contemporary Issues in Early Childhood*, 7(1), pp. 15–29.

Csaszar, I. E., Curry, J. R. and Lastrapes, R. E. (2018) 'Effects of loving kindness meditation on student teachers' reported levels of stress and empathy', *Teacher Education Quarterly*, 45(4), pp. 93–116.

Culture Shift. (2023) *The impact of workplace absenteeism and presenteeism*, available at: https://culture-shift.co.uk/workplace-issues/workplace-absenteeism

Datler, W., Datler, M. and Funder, A. (2010) 'Struggling against a feeling of becoming lost: A young boy's painful transition to day care', *Infant Observation*, 13(1), pp. 65–87.

Department for Education. (2012) *Foundations for quality: The independent review of early education and childcare qualifications*, available at: https://assets.publishing.service.gov.uk/government/uploads/system/uploads/attachment_data/file/175463/

Department for Education. (2021) *Statutory framework for the early years foundation stage*, available at: www.gov.uk/government/publications/early-years-foundation-stage-framework-2 (accessed 30th May 2023).

Department for Education. (2023) *Early years practitioner wellbeing support*, available at: https://help-for-early-years-providers.education.gov.uk/get-help-to-improve-your-practice/early-years-practitioner-wellbeing-support (accessed 23rd August 2024).

Douglas-Osborne, E., Lyons, R., Nelinger, A. and Linehan, T. (2021) *Early years staff wellbeing: A resource for managers and teams*, available at: www.annafreud.org/resources/under-fives-wellbeing/early-years-staff-wellbeing-a-resource-for-managers-and-teams (accessed 23rd August 2024).

Eadie, P., Levickis, P., Murray, L., Page, J., Elek, C. and Church, A. (2021) 'Early childhood educators wellbeing during the COVID-19 pandemic', *Early Childhood Education Journal*, 49(5), pp. 903–913.

Eisenberg, N. (2005) 'The development of empathy-related responding', in Carlo, G. and Edwards, C. P. (eds) *Moral development through the lifespan: Theory, research, and application: The 51st Nebraska on motivation*, Lincoln, NE: University of Nebraska Press, pp. 73–117.

Elfer, P., Greenfield, S., Robson, S., Wilson, D. and Zachariou, A. (2018) 'Love, satisfaction and exhaustion in the nursery: Methodological issues in evaluating the impact of Work Discussion groups in the nursery', *Early Child Development and Care*, 188(7), pp. 892–904.

Faulkner, M., Gerstenblatt, P., Lee, Ahyoung, Vallejo, V. and Travis, D. (2016) 'Childcare providers: Work stress and personal well-being', *Journal of Early Childhood Research*, 14(3), pp. 280–293.

Figley, C. R. (1995) *Coping with secondary traumatic stress disorder in those who treat the traumatized*, New York: Brunner/Mazel.

Findlay, P., Findlay, J. and Stewart, R. (2009) 'The consequences of caring: Skills, regulation and reward among early childhood workers', *Work, Employment and Society*, 23(3), pp. 422–441.

Goleman, D. (2020) *Emotional intelligence: Why it can matter more than IQ*, 25th anniversary edn, London: Bloomsbury.

Hodgkins, A. (2023) *Exploring early childhood practitioners' perceptions of empathic interactions with children and families*. PhD thesis, University of Worcester, available at: https://eprints.worc.ac.uk/13525/

Hoffman, M. (2000) *Empathy and moral development*, New York: Cambridge University Press.

Hochschild, A. (1983) *The managed heart: Commercialization of human feeling*. Berkeley, CA: University of California Press.

Hunter, C. (2023) 'Team morale in early years – How to create an emotionally positive environment for everyone', *Teach Early Years*, available at: www.teachearlyyears.com/positive-relationships/view/staff-morale (accessed 23rd August 2024).

Karanika-Murray, M. and Biron, C. (2020) 'The health-performance framework of presenteeism: Towards understanding an adaptive behaviour', *Human Relations*, 73, pp. 242–261.

Kinman, G. and Clements, A. J. (2023) 'Presenteeism – the case for action', *Occupational Medicine (Oxford)*, 73(4), pp. 181–182.

Kinman, G. and Grant, C. (2021) 'Presenteeism during the COVID-19 pandemic: Risk factors and solutions for employers 2021', *Society of Occupational Medicine*, available at: www.som.org.uk/Presenteeism_during_the_ COVID-19_pandemic_May_2021.pdf

Luft, J. and Ingram, H. (1955) 'The Johari window, a graphic model of interpersonal awareness', in *Proceedings of the Western Training Laboratory in Group Development*, Los Angeles: University of California.

Manassis, K. (2017) *Developing empathy: A biopsychosocial approach to understanding compassion for therapists and parents*, London: Routledge.

McEwen, B. (2017) 'Neurobiological and systemic effects of chronic stress', *Chronic Stress*, 1(24).

Mental Health UK. (2024) *Burnout report: One in five needed to take time off work due to stress in the past year*, available at: https://mentalhealth-uk.org/blog/burnout-report-one-in-five-needed-to-take-time-off-work-due-to-stress-in-the-past-year/ (accessed 23rd August 2024).

Morgan, A. (2017) 'Against compassion: In defence of a "hybrid" concept of empathy', *Nursing Philosophy*, 18(3), pp. 1–6.

Nagasawa, M. and Tarrant, K. (2020) 'Who will care for the early care and education workforce? COVID-19 and the need to support early childhood educators' emotional well-being', *Educate*. New York Early Childhood Professional Development Institute, available at: https://educate.bankstreet.edu/sc/1 (accessed 29th May 2023).

NCFE. (2023) *Sector spotlight: Early years and childcare*, available at: www.ncfe.org.uk/media/q5ofx4pz/175-sector-spotlight-reports-early-years.pdf

Nelinger, A., Album, J., Haynes, A. and Rosan, C. (2021) *Their challenges are our challenges – a summary report of the experiences facing nursery workers in the U.K. in 2020*, available at: www.annafreud.org/media/13013/their-challenges-are-our-challenges-survey-report.pdf (accessed 2nd June 2023).

Neukrug, E., Bayne, H., Dean-Nganga, L. and Pusateri, C. (2013) 'Creative and novel approaches to empathy: A neo-rogerian perspective', *Journal of Mental Health Counseling*, 35(1), pp. 29–42.

Page, J. (2018) 'Characterising the principles of Professional Love in early childhood care and education', *International Journal of Early Years Education*, 26:2, pp. 125–141.

Pietchowiski, M. (2009) 'The inner world of the young and bright', in Cross, T. and Ambrose, D. (eds) *Morality, ethics, and gifted minds*, Dordrecht, Netherlands: Springer.

Preston, D. (2013) 'Being a manager in an English nursery', *European Early Childhood Education Research Journal*, 21(3), pp. 326–338.

Prowle, A. and Hodgkins, A. (2020) *Making a difference with children, young people and families: Re-imagining the role of the practitioner*, London: Red Globe Books, Bloomsbury.

Smith, F. (2016) 'Walking in another's shoes and getting blisters: A personal account of the blessing and curse of intense empathy', *Advanced Development Journal*, 15, pp. 96–107.

Smith, M. and Reid, S. (2024) *What is burnout?* available at: www.helpguide.org/mental-health/stress/burnout-prevention-and-recovery

Stanton, V. (2024) 'Tips on addressing staff absence for nursery managers', *Teach Early Years*, available at: www.teachearlyyears.com/nursery-management/view/addressing-absence

Swindells, R. (2023) 'Nursery management: What can we learn from the managers of successful, private, voluntary and independent day nurseries in England?', *Early Years Educator*, 24(6) [online]. (Accessed: 18 February 2024).

Taggart, G. (2016) 'Compassionate pedagogy: The ethics of care in early childhood professionalism', *European Early Childhood Education Research Journal*, 24(2), pp. 173–185.

Tebben, E., Lang, S., Sproat, E., Tyre-Owens, J. and Helms, S. (2021) 'Identifying primary and secondary stressors, buffers, and supports that impact ECE teacher wellbeing: Implications for teacher education', *Journal of Early Childhood Teacher Education*, 42(2), pp. 143–161.

Tietze, W., Cryer, D., Bairrao, J., Palacios, J. and Wetzel, G. (1996) 'Comparisons of observed process quality in early child care and education programmes in five countries', *Early Childhood Research Quarterly*, 4, pp. 447–475.

Vanourek, G. (2023) *Why self-awareness is so important – and how to develop it*, available at: https://greggvanourek.com/why-self-awareness/

World Health Organisation. (2023) *What is stress?* available at: www.who.int/news-room/questions-and-answers/item/stress

10
Experiencing satisfaction through positive empathy and compassion

Chapter objectives

- To identify empathy satisfaction in working with children and families
- To explore positive and joyful empathic experiences
- To explore the rewards of relationship-based practice
- To examine practitioners' empowerment and resilience
- To explore ways of attaining self-actualisation at work

Empathy is not only about recognising and sharing the negative feelings of others; it also involves sharing their positive emotions. Experiencing empathy for those who are joyful can create an atmosphere of positivity and happiness. This chapter focuses on these positive effects, featuring examples from research participants who describe the joy and fulfilment that come with being an early years practitioner.

Building close relationships with children and families can be highly rewarding, and the chapter explores these intrinsic rewards. The experience of early years practice is diverse and dynamic; no two days are ever the same. Practitioners who thrive in this environment often feel empowered and have developed resilience in their roles. The chapter examines strategies for building resilience to support a long and rewarding career.

Empathy satisfaction

It is widely accepted that there is a strong relationship between emotion and job satisfaction. Williams et al. (2023) identified pride, joy, happiness, contentment, hope, and optimism as the emotions that impact high job satisfaction. Of these six emotions, they assert, pride is the only one that is concerned with the person themselves whereas the other five emotions are dependent on circumstances within the workplace. Pride, say Williams et al. (2023) is associated with an individual's confidence and self-esteem and their motivation to maintain good achievement within the workplace. The researchers suggest that managers should prioritise the emotional experiences of their staff to promote job satisfaction. They suggest regular 'emotional check-ins' to identify the emotional state of their employees. This supports the suggestion by Elfer et al. (2018) for emotional supervision in early years settings.

Chapter 9 discusses the benefit of emotional supervision for practitioners to prevent compassion fatigue and empathic distress in early years practice. However, we also encounter much compassion satisfaction (Figley, 2013) and empathic satisfaction (Galetz, 2019) within the profession. The study by Galetz (2019) suggests that these are different things: compassion results in satisfaction with the action (helping another person), whereas empathy results in satisfaction with self, increasing understanding and awareness of one's own feelings.

Most people have had the experience of having to go out to an event and not wanting to go, but then picking up on the atmosphere of others while you're out and ending up really enjoying yourself. Just as we can be affected by negative emotions, we can be personally affected by positive emotions too. This is especially true for people who identify as empaths (see more about this in Chapter 8).

 Reflective prompt - Reflect on how you felt when you were last around someone who was happy or excited.

When asked about the influence of positive emotions and job satisfaction in the context of the empathy research, five overarching themes emerged as contributors to practitioners' well-being. In the following sections, each of these themes will be explored, accompanied by a practitioner's example for clarity.

1. Enjoyment, fun and laughter
2. Observing children's progress

Figure 10.1 Compassion satisfaction vs. empathy satisfaction. Images from FreePik.

3. Pride in making a difference
4. Pleasure in relationships
5. Receiving positive feedback and praise

1. Enjoyment, fun and laughter

In the empathy research (Hodgkins, 2023), Jake reflects on an example of the fun and enjoyment of working with young children,

> Today, we sat down. Nine children and me just eating our snack of cheese and crackers, and we were talking about apples. We cut them in half, and I was pretending to karate chop them, and we were all laughing together so much, and it was just lovely. It was one of those moments where you go, 'Crikey, this is the best job in the world', you know?
>
> (Jake)

There is real joy in Jake's response, which may go some way in mitigating the negative emotional effects of the work. Andreychik (2019) writes 'feeling your joy helps me to bear your pain' (p. 147), to describe this phenomenon. Andreychik (2019) asserts that increasing professionals' 'positive empathy' through fulfilling relationships, and sharing triumphs and successes, results in reduced stress and an improved quality of professional life, as 'empathising with the positive emotions of others is a personally pleasant experience' (Andreychik, 2019, p. 149).

Working relationships between practitioners can also be enjoyable and can include fun and laughter. Again, Jake, who is the owner-manager of a preschool, says,

> We just all get on really well, and we tease each other a little bit in a nice, friendly way, and it just helps to set the right mood really.
>
> (Jake)

Workplace friendships can be instrumental in supportive working environments and can develop a sense of belonging, trust, and support (Hamilton et al., 2022). Research suggests that workplaces with a positive, friendly atmosphere also have high creativity and innovation (Cao and Zhang, 2020). This appears to be the case for Jake and his team.

2. Observing children's progress

The empathy research highlighted many examples of fulfilment and pride arising from sharing in children's achievements. Here are just a few examples,

> Just to see the little changes that have happened over the last six months, the breakthroughs, that makes it all worth it.
>
> (Cheryl)

> To watch their progression, how they come in being unconfident, and then seeing them go out with tons of confidence.
>
> (Cheryl)

> When they have left nursery and I see them out in the street later, or when parents contact me to babysit for them, they show off their early reading and their writing, and it's so nice to see the impact that the early teaching at nursery has given them, the first stride in their educational life.
>
> (George)

In early years practice, one of the most significant roles of practitioners is to document and celebrate children's accomplishments. This practice not only helps boost children's self-esteem but also brings a sense of satisfaction and pride to the practitioners themselves. According to Elfer and Page (2015), working with babies can be particularly rewarding, as their milestones evoke powerful feelings of pride in us.

Andreychik (2019) describes positive empathy as a motivation for us to help others increase their positive emotions and pursue growth and development. Early childhood practice is fundamentally about supporting children to grow, develop, and achieve their full potential, ensuring their happiness. In turn, this nurturing role brings joy and fulfilment to the practitioners who care for them.

3. Pride in making a difference

De Castella (2020) writes that the majority of people who work with children have an intrinsic desire to 'change the course of a person's entire life'. More recently, there is much evidence that practitioners can and do make a real difference to the children and families that they work with (Prowle and Hodgkins, 2020, p. xviii). These are some of the examples of making a difference from the empathy research,

> The difference you make in children's lives is just unbelievable . . . the difference we're making to the children and their families, the community and everything, I wouldn't change it for the world.
>
> (Jake)

> I felt pride in myself for encouraging the boys to make good choices . . . . I find it rewarding, seeing the impact my practice has on the children and other staff.
>
> (Mel)

> It's all about having an impact, seeing a difference . . . whether it's in staff practice or in a child's development. I like to feel that I'm making a difference, not necessarily by working with the children but through the staff team and making sure we are providing high-quality practice.
>
> (Joel)

> It's lovely the difference I make to some of the children. Sometimes, if I'm out on the high street and they see me from over the road, and they scream my name and wave at me. Obviously, I've made some sort of positive impact on them.
>
> (George)

Jake and Joel are managers of their settings, but it is important to note that everyone is capable of making a difference. In the past, managers held ultimate power over their employees and rewarded them for doing a good job. Contemporary thinkers today, however, believe that true motivation is internally motivated. Pink (2011), for example, believes that people are motivated when they can see a higher purpose and perceive their own contributions as meaningful. Pink (2011) believes that 'the true secret to high performance and satisfaction in today's world is the deeply human need to direct our own lives, to learn and create new things, and to do better by ourselves and the world'.

4. Pleasure in relationships

Relationships are at the heart of early years practice, and relationship-based practice is advocated in the 'social pedagogy' approach. Practitioners are an important part of the child's 'relationship universe', a feature of Social Pedagogy (see Chapter 3 for more on this), and, as such, connections grounded in care and support are reciprocal (Eichstellar, 2023). The mutual benefit of such a relationship is clear in practitioners' comments,

> The relationship, the bonds you make with the children and the families are really rewarding.
>
> (Cheryl)

> We have a staff display by the door . . . a child's mom was looking at it and said to her child, 'Jake' is the owner, he's the boss', and the child said, 'Jake isn't the boss, Jake is just our best friend'.
>
> (Jake)

The second example, by Jake, demonstrates this reciprocity well; in the children's eyes, the staff are their friends. These reciprocal relationships make working with children enjoyable, and the work is very varied; as McIntyre (2020) says, when working with children, 'no two days are the same'. All children are different, and as they often spend a good deal of their time with practitioners, all aspects of their lives will be shared. In one day, practitioners could be celebrating a child's birthday, talking to a child about their new baby brother, helping a child put on her own coat, teaching maths, tending to a grazed knee, reassuring a parent, listening to children's jokes, making notes on a child protection case and practising for the nativity play. Few other careers are so varied. Incidentally, here is a joke I recently heard from a 3-year-old child,

> 'Knock, knock'. (Who's there?) 'Knock, knock'. (Who's there?) 'Knock, knock'. (Who's there?) 'Knock, knock'. (Who's there?) 'Orange!' (Orange who?) 'I didn't know you was a banana!' (Child dissolves into hysterical laughter!) Priceless!

5. Positive feedback and praise

Positive feedback is known to have an impact on people's emotions, motivation, and performance. In the early years, we use positive reinforcement to encourage the behaviour we want to see in children, but it is no less important for adults, too. Feedback from employers and service users (in this case, children and families) affects people's attitudes, providing recognition, encouragement, and support (Su and Xiao, 2022). Joel's response is an example of the value of positive feedback:

> It's compliments like that when I think, actually, yeah, this is a really good nursery, this is a really good setting. All of us get feedback from parents and stuff like that saying thank you for doing that, and it just makes it worth it.
>
> (Joel)

In an early years setting, positive feedback can come from a range of people, not just children and families. In the next example, Jake reflects on a recent visit from an early years advisor:

> We had the head of quality assurance round to look at our baby room, and she said I just wish I could bottle the atmosphere that you have here and take it round and just show everybody how it can be.
>
> (Jake)

A powerful message like this from an early years expert provides staff in a setting with much-needed encouragement and motivation to continue to do a great job. For managers, giving positive feedback to staff facilitates a happier, more supportive team.

 Individual activity

Identify which of the five themes is most important to you. Choose a relevant positive incident and reflect on how it made you feel.

Relationship-based early years practice

All of the themes listed at the start of the chapter have something in common: they are all concerned with relationships. Relationship-based practice is the guiding principle of Social Pedagogy. Stobbs et al. (2023), writing in support of social pedagogy in schools, explain that we should work together to develop healthy, inclusive settings 'built on the key social pedagogical foundations of positive relationships, democracy, inclusion, creativity and pedagogical love' (Stobbs et al., 2023, p. 3). This is arguably even more important for very young children in early years settings. Cliffe and Solvason (2023) point out that the implications of the Covid-19 pandemic on children's relationships have yet to be released and make relationships within early years settings even more crucial than ever before.

Reflective prompt - We probably all remember a teacher from our past who made us feel scared or stupid, but try to think back and reflect on an adult who had a positive impact on you as a child. What did they do that made them memorable to you? How can you be this to a child?

Mitigating stress and burnout

The fulfilment may help to safeguard practitioners against burnout. Stamm's (2013) deduction that people can be at high risk of experiencing burnout at the same time as experiencing satisfaction is reinforced by these results. Building upon the depictions of positive encounters and job satisfaction, there is the potential for positively impacting staff retention within the early years field. Jake's portrayal of his role as 'the best job in the world' serves as a motivating example. By pinpointing the factors that generate such sentiments, we can plan for a future characterised by a fulfilling and enriching professional journey.

These examples of empathy satisfaction support Figley's (2013) view that emotion work can have a positive impact and Morelli et al.'s (2014) conviction that empathy increases our concern for others. This could be a major motivation for remaining in a job which makes difficult emotional demands and provides little monetary reward. This is apparent in Solvason et al.'s (2020) research with early years practitioners, which identified descriptions of 'the relentless exhaustion of the role with their deep passion for it' (p. 198).

Building resilience

Cultivating resilience is the key to success; resilience enables us to maintain a constructive outlook even amidst challenges. Resilient practitioners develop problem-solving skills, recognise and manage their own stress levels, and maintain a good work-life balance. Stress has been identified as a worldwide problem, a major cause of disability and illness in the 21st century (WHO, 2020). Research by Hasan et al. (2022) aimed to evaluate a range of resilience-building strategies for early years practitioners. Strategies included:

- Personal growth programmes
- 20-minute group exercise (physical activity outdoors)
- Reflective group supervision
- Breathing exercises
- Mindfulness - group exercises
- Mindfulness - smart phone app
- Stress reduction online course
- Coaching each other within the staff team
- Yoga
- Stress management course at home via Zoom
- Journaling

Experiencing satisfaction through positive empathy, compassion 165

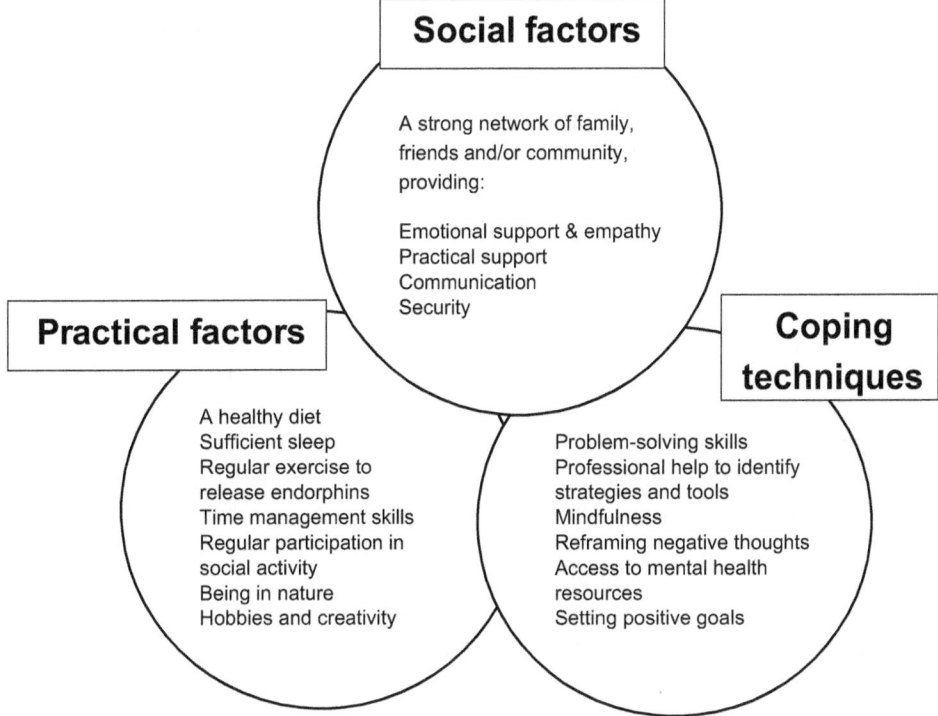

Figure 10.2 Protective factors

Hasan et al.'s (2022) research concluded that group strategies were the most likely to improve resilience among early years teams, although this was often difficult to organise within the working day. Figure 10.2 identifies some protective factors which help to build resilience.

 Individual activity

Look at the list of strategies taken from Hassan et al.'s research and in Figure 10.2. Which strategies do you think could work for you and your team? Can you identify what could work for you individually? How could you incorporate this in your week?

Self-actualisation

Self-actualisation is a psychological term that refers to achieving one's full potential; self-actualisation means being the best we can possibly be and being completely fulfilled creatively, socially, and intellectually. The term was originally introduced by Goldstein in 1940 and made popular by Maslow in 1943. Carl Rogers also wrote about self-actualisation in 1951. Table 10.1 shows their ideas.

Table 10.1 Theories of self-actualisation

	Kurt Goldstein (1940)	The desire for self-fulfilment is the goal of every living thing
	Abraham Maslow (1943)	The drive to self-actualise emerges when basic needs have met
	Carl Rogers (1951)	For self-actualisation, people need to be treated with empathy, congruence and unconditional positive regard

Maslow (1943) urges people to make the best use of their talents, saying, 'a musician must make music, an artist must paint, a poet must write, if he is to be ultimately happy'. However, this does not mean that things are always perfect; just that we are in the right place for us to feel fulfilled. In more recent times, in Sir Ken Robinson's book 'finding your element', Robinson (2009) urges people to follow their natural talents and true passion and to find their element, the place they should be, which allows them to fulfil their potential. Self-actualisation is different for different people; what a 60-year-old grandfather believes to be reaching his highest potential will be different from that of a 17-year-old single woman. Krems et al. (2017) suggest that age, sex, relationship, and parenting status all have an impact on people's view of self-actualisation.

  Individual activity

What do you think of these three ideas? Do you think that everyone strives for self-actualisation, to be the best they can be? Can we only reach self-actualisation when our other (physical, security, self-esteem, etc.) have been met? Or can we only reach self-actualisation when the people around us treat us with the core conditions? Reflect on what self-actualisation means to you and what you need to feel that you are fulfilling your potential.

To feel that we are reaching our potential and being the best version of ourselves, it is important, say Maunz and Glasser (2023, p. 349), 'to be authentic, to be able to follow our own ideas, goals and talents and express ourselves individually as we truly are [sic.]'. This can be difficult in the work environment when our personal values are not aligned with the values of the organisation. The following case study gives an example of this tension.

Case study – a difference of opinion in the baby room

Siân works in the baby room of a private day nursery, one belonging to a nursery chain. She has recently joined the nursery, having had a career break whilst raising her son, who is now two years old. There are usually two or three early years educators working in the room, depending on the number of babies each day. Siân enjoys her job and finds being with the babies and meeting the families rewarding; however, there has been some disagreement over some aspects of the care routines.

Siân practised 'attachment parenting' with her own son: carrying him in a sling, co-sleeping, and breastfeeding until he was two. She believes strongly that babies should be held and cuddled so that an emotional bond is formed that makes the baby feel secure. However, this does not match the philosophy of the nursery. The nursery manager believes that children need to learn to 'self-soothe' from a young age and that carrying a baby around is not practical in a nursery environment. Siân believes that this is an outdated view and that leaving babies to cry is never the right thing to do.

Having to leave babies to cry and not being allowed to carry and cuddle them is upsetting Siân. She feels that she is not doing a good job and she is not meeting the babies' needs. Siân is the only member of the baby room staff who is a mother herself, and she wonders if that is why she is getting upset about the situation. She feels that she needs to do something to promote a change of approach in the room, but as the newest member of staff, she is not sure what to do. She wonders whether to look for another job in a nursery that is better aligned with her views.

 Reflective prompt – Have you experienced a difference of opinion like this at work? What do you think you might do in Siân's position? How do you think it would affect you if you had to do something you didn't agree with? How might this affect your opportunity to self-actualise?

Reaching self-actualisation in your career

According to Maslow (1943), it is not possible to reach self-actualisation until all of our needs have been met. This makes sense; for example, if we are at work in a freezing cold environment, it is difficult to concentrate on anything else other than being cold.

 **Group activity**

Think about how your needs at each level are met within your workplace and complete Table 10.2. Use this as a prompt for discussion about what is going really well and how things might be improved.

Table 10.2 Are my needs being met? (Based on Maslow's hierarchy of need, 1943)

Physiological needs	Are you able to eat and drink regularly?
	Do you have times when you can rest?
	Do you have sufficient toilet breaks?
	Is the room warm enough and well-ventilated?
Safety needs	Do you feel physically safe at work?
	Are the security systems sufficient?
	Do you feel emotionally safe?
Belongingness needs	Do you have good relationships at work? Do you have friends at work?
	Do you have people at work that you can talk to?
	Do you feel like part of the team?
Esteem needs	Are you proud of the work you do?
	Do you feel that your work is appreciated? Do you feel that you are accomplishing something worthwhile?
	Do you feel respected?

There has been criticism of Maslow's hierarchy of need theory. Criticising Maslow's research methods and suggesting that the levels of need are not universal. There are cultural differences, for example, which mean that, for some people, socialisation is not an important precursor to success. Winter (2016) points out that 'there are many obvious cases of individuals whose primary interest is in painting or meditating all day long and they appear happy and fulfilled without having other basic needs fulfilled'. For these individuals, their art or their wellness activity is more important than some of the physiological needs. For some, higher-level needs may be more important. Tay et al. (2011) suggest that some higher-level needs, such as esteem and respect, are important even if lower needs are not being met.

Figure 10.3 identifies some of the ways that early years settings can create opportunities for self-actualisation for practitioners.

Experiencing satisfaction through positive empathy, compassion 169

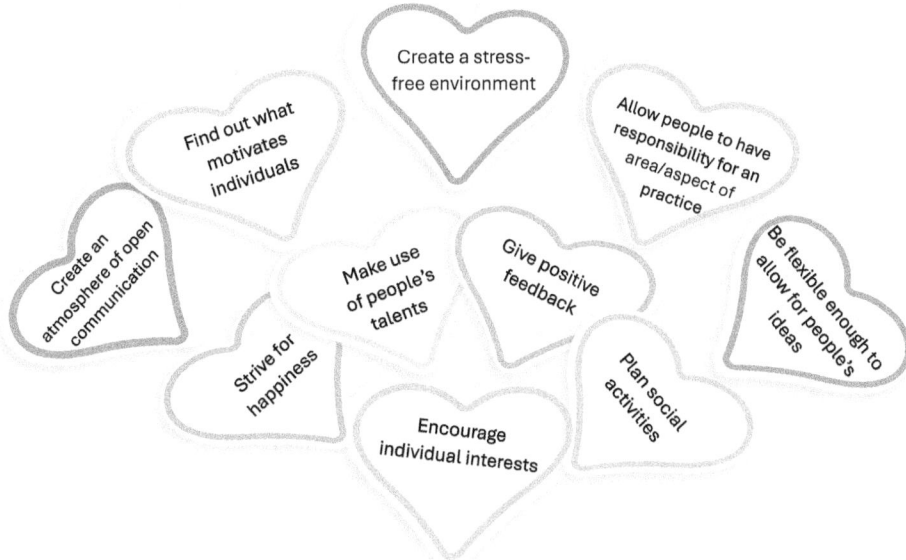

Figure 10.3 Ways of promoting self-actualisation

The power of compassion

Caring for others is a fundamental human need to join with others and a fundamental need to care for ourselves. Practising compassion is not only beneficial for others, but it is helpful for us, too. The Dalai Lama once said, 'If you want others to be happy, practice compassion. If you want to be happy, practice compassion' (The Dalai Lama and Cutler, 1998). Compassion for others and self-compassion are both rooted in empathy, so when you extend compassion to others, you can more easily empathise with yourself when you are suffering. Thus, 'compassion builds compassion'. Figure 10.4 outlines some personal advantages of compassion (developed from ideas by Compassionate Communities, 2023).

Personal growth

One of the advantages in Figure 10.4 is 'personal growth', which can be achieved through self-compassion. Personal growth means developing as an individual, moving forward, 'an active and intentional journey of self-improvement and self-actualization' (Ivtzan et al., 2011). Everyone's personal growth priority is different, and individual, just as self-actualisation means different things to different people. For one person, personal growth might mean achieving better work/life balance; for another, it might mean gaining promotion; for another, it might mean making new friends or living a healthier life.

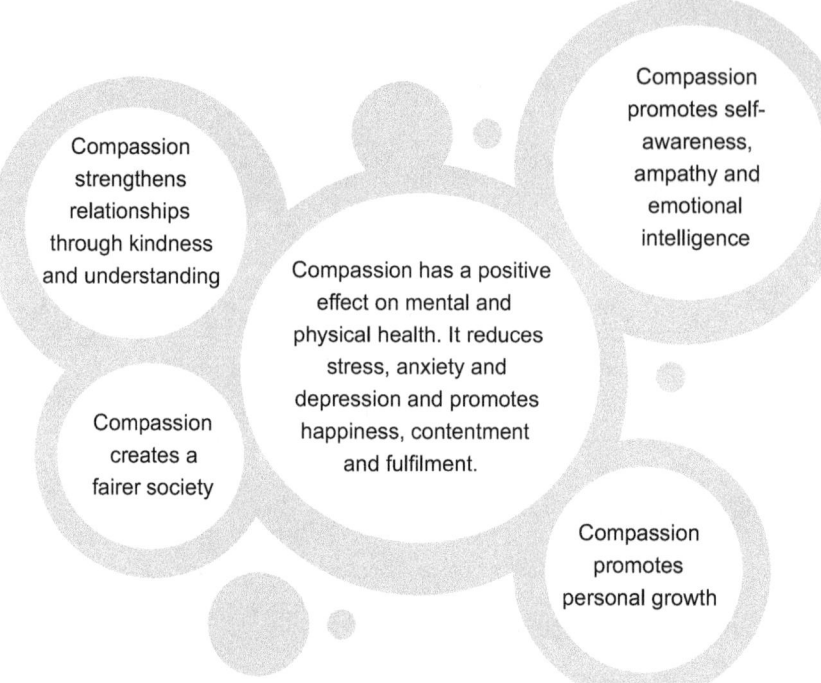

Figure 10.4 Personal advantages of compassion

Personal growth initiative (PGI) is an individual's active and intentional engagement in the growth process (Weigold et al., 2020). People with high PGI consciously seek development opportunities; Robitschek et al. (2012) identified four components of personal growth:

- **Readiness for change** - preparing for self-change, understanding the need for change, and motivation
- **'Planfulness'** - the knowledge and ability to plan for change, goal-setting
- **Using resources** - seeking resources and help needed for change
- **Intentional behaviour** - purposeful engagement in self-change behaviour

Here is an example of a personal growth plan based on learning to drive. The first stage, readiness for change, might be to think about the reasons for the plan and the benefits. If I learn to drive, I will be more independent, I won't have to ask people to give me lifts, I won't have to catch the bus and spend time waiting at bus stops in bad weather. The second stage, planfulness, is coming up with a realistic plan; this involves thinking and might include reading, researching, and investigating possibilities (for example, driving schools, costs, etc.). The third stage involves using the resources available; in this case, this would be arranging driving lessons; it may include asking friends or family for help (taking you out for practice drives, quizzing you on the highway code). The final stage is the action stage, booking those lessons and starting to learn to drive. This stage also includes measuring success and reflecting on your success.

Individual activity

Use the following prompts to identify, develop, and improve your Personal Growth Initiative (PGI).

Table 10.3 Personal growth activity

Component	Prompts	Your response
Readiness for change	→ Why do you want to improve yourself?	
	→ What might the benefits be?	
Planfulness	→ What will you need to do?	
	→ Do you need to set yourself goals?	
Using resources	→ What will you need in order to succeed?	
	→ Who will be able to help you?	
Intentional behaviour	→ What action can you start with?	
	→ How will you measure your growth?	

Career development

Few careers have more opportunities for progression than a career in the early years. The UK government's latest campaign to increase the numbers of early years practitioners has the strap line, 'make a difference that lasts a lifetime' (Gov.uk, 2024). The campaign focusses on the areas of practice that are under recruiting at present: working in private day nurseries, preschools, wraparound care, and childminding. Employment has changed over the last century; 'people no longer expect to find a "job for life" when leaving education' (Prowle and Hodgkins, 2020, p. 186); a career is now seen as 'the sequence of employment-related positions, roles, activities and experiences encountered by a person' (Arnold, 1997). Career development is not a priority for everyone, but for many people, growth and advancement is important.

Continuing Professional Development (CPD) is important for everyone, ensuring that practitioners' skills are up to date and to develop people's skills. Some CPD is mandatory (for example, safeguarding updates), whilst some opportunities are less formal. In many local authorities in the UK, funding cuts have meant that free training courses are much less likely to be available to practitioners, but it is possible to create ways of sharing expertise with others. Starting up a group with other local settings to discuss common issues and share ideas can be a great way of improving quality for all.

 **Group activity**

How could you share experiences and expertise with each other within the setting? What opportunities could there be to make links with other settings and learn from others within the early years community?

Chapter summary

In this chapter, we have explored the numerous positive aspects of working with children and families. We examined how job satisfaction is deeply tied to emotions, particularly compassion and empathic satisfaction. From the empathy research, five key themes related to job satisfaction emerged: enjoyment, fun and laughter, observing children's progress, pride in making a difference, pleasure in relationships, and receiving positive feedback and praise. These positive aspects are often rooted in relationships, a core principle of Social Pedagogy. Building close, supportive relationships with children and their families can be incredibly rewarding.

Evidence suggests that job satisfaction can mitigate stress and burnout; the more we enjoy our work, the better we can handle its challenges. This chapter also explores ways practitioners can build resilience to cope with their roles. The concept of self-actualisation was discussed through the theories of Goldstein (1940), Maslow (1943), and Rogers (1951). Self-actualisation involves realising one's full potential and working authentically according to personal values. Siân's case study illustrates the consequences when these conditions are not met.

To achieve self-actualisation, a practitioner's own needs must be met. We examined how well these needs are being met in your workplace. The benefits of compassion and its connection to personal growth were discussed alongside an activity based on Personal Growth Initiative (PGI), reflecting on your ability to achieve personal growth. The chapter concludes by highlighting the importance of continuing professional development in expanding knowledge and advancing career skills.

Key messages

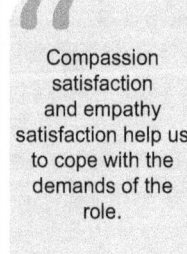
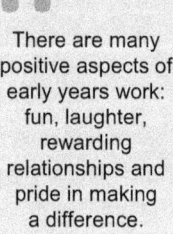
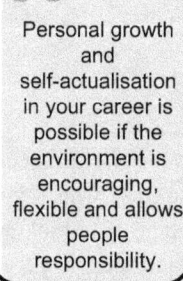
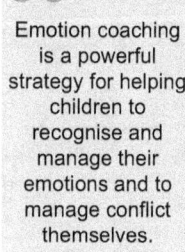

Figure 10.5 Key messages from Chapter 10

References

Andreychik, M. (2019) 'Feeling your joy helps me to bear feeling your pain: Examining associations between empathy for others' positive versus negative emotions and burnout', *Personality and Individual Differences*, 137, pp. 147-156.

Arnold, J. (1997) *Managing careers into the 21st century*, London: Paul Chapman.

Cao, F. and Zhang, H. (2020) 'Workplace friendship, psychological safety and innovative behaviour in China: A moderated-mediation model', *Chinese Management Studies*, 14(3), pp. 661-676.

Cliffe, J. and Solvason, C. (2023) 'What is it that we still don't get? – Relational pedagogy and why relationships and connections matter in early childhood', *Power and Education*, 15(3), pp. 259-273.

Compassionate Communities. (2023) *The power of compassion*, available at: https://compassionate communitiesni.com/the-power-of-compassion (accessed 1st November 2024).

Dalai Lama, H. and Cutler, H. (1998) *The art of happiness*, London: Hodder and Stoughton.

De Castella, T. (2020, January 28) 'Why we changed careers to work with children', *Children and Young People Now*, available at: www.cypnow.co.uk/content/features/why-we-changed-careers-to-work-with-children/ (accessed 1st November 2024).

Eichstellar, G. (2023) *The relational universe*, available at: wwFw.thempra.org.uk/social-pedagogy/key-concepts-in-social-pedagogy/relational-universe/

Elfer, P., Greenfield, S., Robson, S., Wilson, D. and Zachariou, A. (2018) 'Love, satisfaction and exhaustion in the nursery: Methodological issues in evaluating the impact of Work Discussion groups in the nursery', *Early Child Development and Care*, 188(7), pp. 892-904.

Elfer, P. and Page, J. (2015) 'Pedagogy with babies: Perspectives of eight nursery managers', *Early Child Development and Care*, 185, pp. 11-12.

Figley, C. R. (2013) *Treating compassion fatigue*, London: Taylor and Francis.

Galetz, E. (2019) 'The empathy-compassion matrix: Using a comparison concept analysis to identify care components', *Nursing Forum*, 54(3), pp. 448-454.

Goldstein, K. (1940) *Human nature*, Cambridge, MA: Harvard University Press.

Gov.uk. (2024) *Early years careers*, available at: https://earlyyearscareers.campaign.gov.uk

Hamilton, O., Virhia, J. and Almeida, T. (2022, October 31) 'Workplace friendships', *The British Psychological Society*, available at: www.bps.org.uk/psychologist/workplace-friendships

Hasan, R. A., et al. (2022) 'Resilience-building for mental health among early childhood educators: A systematic review and pilot-study towards an EEG-VR resilience building intervention', *International Journal of Environmental Research in Public Health*, 19, pp. 1-29.

Hodgkins, A. (2023) *Exploring early childhood practitioners' perceptions of empathic interactions with children and families*. PhD thesis, University of Worcester, available at: https://eprints.worc.ac.uk/13525/

Ivtzan, I., Chan, C. P. L., Gardner, H. E. and Prashar, K. (2011) 'Linking religion and spirituality with psychological well-being: Examining self-actualisation, meaning in life, and personal growth initiative', *Journal of Religion and Health*, 52(3), pp. 915-929. https://doi.org/10.1007/s10943-011-9540-2

Krems, J., Kenrick, D. and Neel, R. (2017) 'Individual perceptions of self-actualization: What functional motives are linked to fulfilling one's full potential?', *Personality and Social Psychology Bulletin*, 43(9), pp. 1337-1352.

Maslow, A. H. (1943) 'A theory of human motivation', *Psychological Review*, 50(4), pp. 370-396.

Maunz, L. A. and Glasser, J. (2023) 'Does being authentic promote self-actualization at work? Examining the links between work-related resources, authenticity at work, and occupational self-actualization', *Journal of Business and Psychology*, 38, pp. 347-367.

McIntyre, G. (2020) 'No two days are the same', *Get Into Teaching*, available at: https://getintoteaching.education.gov.uk/blog/no-two-days-are-the-same

Morelli, S., Rameson, L. and Lieberman, M. (2014) 'The neural components of empathy: Predicting daily prosocial behavior', *Social, Cognitive and Affective Neuroscience*, 9(1), pp. 39-47.

Pink, D. (2011) *Drive: The surprising truth about what motivates us*, New York: Cannongate Books.

Prowle, A. and Hodgkins, A. (2020) *Making a difference with children, young people and families: Re-imagining the role of the practitioner*, London: Red Globe Books, Bloomsbury.

Robinson, K. (2009) *The element: How finding your passion changes everything*, London: Penguin.

Robitschek, C., Ashton, M. W., Spering, C. C., Geiger, N., Byers, D., Schotts, G. C. and Thoen, M. A. (2012) 'Development and psychometric evaluation of the personal growth initiative scale-II', *Journal of Counselling Psychology*, 59(2), pp. 274-287.

Rogers, C. (1951) *Client-centered*, Therapy, pp. 515-520.

Solvason, C., Webb, R. and Sutton-Tsang, S. (2020) 'Evidencing the effects of maintained nursery schools' roles in Early Years sector improvements', *TACTYC*, available at: www.tactyc.org.uk (accessed 4th June 2024).

Stamm, H. (2013) 'Chapter 5: Measuring compassion satisfaction as well as fatigue: Developmental history of the compassion satisfaction and fatigue test', in Figley, C. (ed) *Treating compassion fatigue: Psychosocial stress series*, 2nd edn, London: Taylor and Francis, pp. 107–199.

Stobbs, N., Solvason, C., Gallagher, S. and Baylis, S. (2023) 'A human approach to restructuring the education system: Why schools in England need social pedagogy', *International Journal of Social Pedagogy*, 12(1), p. 8.

Su, W. and Xiao, F. (2022) 'Supervisor positive feedback and employee performance: Promotion focus as a mediator', *Social Behavior and Personality: An International Journal*, 50(2), p. e11135.

Weigold, I. K., et al. (2020) 'Personal growth initiative and mental health: A meta-analysis', *Journal of Counselling and Development*, 98(4), pp. 376–390.

Williams, C., Thomas, J., Bennett, A., Banks, G., Toth, A., Dunn, A., McBride, A. and Gooty, J. (2023) 'The role of discrete emotions in job satisfaction: A meta-analysis', *Journal of Organisational Behaviour*, 45(1), pp. 97–116.

Winter. (2016) *Praise & criticism: Hierarchy of needs (Maslow), human performance technology*, available at: https://blog.hptbydts.com/praise-criticism-hierarchy-of-needs-maslow

World Health Organisation (WHO). (2020) *WHO reveals leading causes of death and disability worldwide: 2000-2019*, available at: www.who.int/news/item/09-12-2020-who-reveals-leading-causes-of-death-and-disability-worldwide-2000-2019 (accessed 1st November 2024).

11
Guided reflections and future directions

This final section presents guided reflections on the key messages from each chapter of the book. These summaries aim to spark your reflections and highlight actionable strategies for improving early years practice within your setting. Each chapter's key messages will offer an overview of the lessons learned.

Crucial findings from the empathy research are examined to determine how these insights can be applied to foster more compassionate and effective interactions with children. Additionally, future research directions will be proposed, which aim to continue advancing our understanding of empathy in early years care and education.

Ultimately, this conclusion emphasises the profound impact of empathy and compassion, underscoring their essential roles in early years care and education. By reflecting on these insights, you and your setting can implement positive changes that nurture a more empathetic, supportive environment for all.

Guided reflections

Each chapter of this book concludes with two to four key messages, highlighting the main takeaways. In this final chapter, guided reflections offer an opportunity for deep and creative thinking around each message, aiming to inspire real change in early years settings. These guided reflections can be utilised in various ways:

- Individual Reflection: Use these prompts for reflective journaling to examine the chapter content and consider what the messages mean to you personally.
- Group Discussion: Use the prompts for discussion and debate in team meetings or CPD sessions to explore what the messages mean for your setting.
- Training Purposes: Integrate these prompts into college or university courses, conference symposia, or workshops to explore the messages collectively as a group of practitioners.

The reflections can be used individually or in small or large groups. They are merely a guide, so feel free to adapt them to suit your needs. Take what is useful for your particular circumstances and requirements.

DOI: 10.4324/9781003464686-11

Chapter 1 Introducing the philosophical foundations of the book

Key message 1: Remember that working in the early years is important and worthwhile. Although it can be tough, it is also incredibly rewarding.

Guided reflection:

How do you remind yourself of the importance and worthiness of your work in early years care and education, especially during tough times? Can you share an example where reflecting on the significance of your role helped you stay motivated? What aspects of your work do you find most rewarding despite the challenges?

Key message 2: The core conditions of empathy, congruence, and unconditional positive regard are essential in working with children and families.

Guided reflection:

How do you demonstrate empathy and congruence (being genuine and authentic) in your interactions with children and families? Can you share an example of where these core conditions helped build trust and understanding? How do you practice unconditional positive regard (accepting and valuing others without judgement) in your work? Can you describe a situation where this approach positively impacted your relationship with a child or family?

Key message 3: A shared philosophy, created through critical reflection and based on positive values and a strength-based approach, should underpin the practice of your setting.

Guided reflection:

How do you engage in critical reflection to help create a shared philosophy based on positive values in your setting? How do you incorporate a strength-based approach into your practice? Can you describe a situation where focusing on the strengths of children, families, or colleagues led to positive outcomes?

Chapter 2 Understanding empathy and compassion

Key message 1: Empathy and compassion are two different concepts. Compassion is a result of empathy. Both are fundamental to working with young children and their families.

Guided reflection:

How do you personally define empathy and compassion?

Can you recall a situation where you felt empathy for someone? How did it make you feel?

How did your empathy lead to compassionate actions in that situation?

If you are in a group, how do your peers' experiences compare to your own?

What new strategies can you adopt from this discussion to enhance your practice?

Key message 2: Two types of empathy (cognitive and affective) are present in early years practice.

Guided reflection:

How do you use cognitive empathy (understanding another's perspective) in your interactions with young children? Can you provide an example of where this type of empathy helped you address a child's needs?

How do you experience and express affective empathy (sharing another's emotions) in your practice? Can you recall a situation where feeling what a child felt led to a meaningful response?

Key message 3: Early Years practitioners use intuition, which draws on expertise, training, and sensitivity. Intuitive feelings tend to be accurate.

Guided reflection:

How do you believe your intuition is influenced by your training and expertise in early years practice? Can you recall a specific instance where your intuitive feelings guided you to make an accurate decision?

How does your sensitivity to children's needs enhance your intuitive decision-making? Can you provide an example where your intuition, supported by your sensitivity, led to a positive outcome for a child or family?

Chapter 3 Building empathic relationships with young children

Key message 1: The skills and qualities required to work with young children have historically been grounded in gendered assumptions.

Guided reflection:

How do societal perceptions of early years work as 'vocational' impact the professional status and pay of early years practitioners, and what strategies can be implemented to better recognise and value their skills and emotional qualities within the profession and by society at large?

Consider the importance of empathy, caregiving, and pedagogical skills, and think about the steps that can be taken to promote a progressive understanding of caregiving roles to ensure all practitioners feel valued and supported.

Key message 2: Relationships between practitioners and children, based on understanding, trust, and empathy, are the most important aspect of practice.

Guided reflection:

Can you share a specific experience from your practice that highlights the importance of relationships in early years settings, describe a challenging situation where building trust with a child was difficult and the steps you took to address it and explain how different children's responses to relationship-building efforts have influenced your approach?

Key message 3: Attachment and transitions necessitate careful planning and empathy for all involved.

Guided reflection:

How can early years practitioners balance the need for secure attachments with the practical challenges of staff changes and rota systems while demonstrating empathy and compassion to support children during transitions? Consider specific actions and behaviours that can help children navigate changes smoothly and think about the importance of personalised care in influencing a child's sense of security and confidence.

Key message 4: Professional love, care, and touch are all important aspects of a child's experience away from home.

Guided reflection:

How can early years practitioners balance the need for professional boundaries with the importance of showing love and affection to children, and what strategies can be implemented to ensure children receive the emotional support they need while maintaining professional standards? Consider how early years settings can develop clear guidelines and training to support practitioners in showing appropriate affection while safeguarding children. Think about the importance of having well-defined boundaries and regular training to help practitioners feel confident in their interactions with children.

Chapter 4 Extending empathy and compassion to parents, carers, and families

Key message 1: Parents/carers are the child's first educators, and, as such, relationships with families must be based on respect, support, and partnership.

Guided reflection:

How do you demonstrate respect and build partnerships with parents and carers in your daily practice?

In what ways do you support parents and carers as the child's first educators? How do you ensure that your interactions with families foster a collaborative and supportive environment?

Key message 2: Getting to know parents/carers as individuals is vital In understanding the child and family holistically.

Guided reflection:

How do you make an effort to get to know parents and carers as individuals? Can you share an example where understanding a parent's or carer's unique background and perspective helped you better support their child?

Chapter 5 Fostering empathic and supportive teams

Key message 1: A supportive team, built on trust, respect, empathy, and compassion, can be a secure base for practitioners.

Guided reflection:

How do you contribute to building trust and respect within your team? Can you share an example where a supportive team environment positively impacted your practice or wellbeing?

In what ways do empathy and compassion play a role in your interactions with colleagues? Can you describe a situation where these qualities helped create a secure and supportive team dynamic?

Key message 2: Negativity within teams must be addressed by developing resilience and a growth mindset.

Guided reflection:

How do you approach and address negativity within your team? Can you provide an example of where developing resilience and a growth mindset helped you or your team overcome challenges and foster a more positive environment?

Key message 3: A staff team is a 'relational universe', where everyone is connected. Celebrating the diversity of a team is a strength.

Guided reflection:

How do you recognise and celebrate the diversity within your team? Can you share an example where valuing diverse perspectives and backgrounds strengthened your team's connections and effectiveness?

Key message 4: Compassionate leadership motivates and empowers. Appreciating the work and commitment of staff benefits everyone.

Guided reflection:

How does compassionate leadership in your team motivate and empower you and your colleagues? Can you share an example where a leader's compassion positively influenced your work or morale? In what ways does appreciating the work and commitment of staff benefit the entire team?

Chapter 6 Supporting and promoting positive behaviour

Key message 1: 'Behaviour management' is an outdated term; we should be helping children to understand and manage their emotions.

Guided reflection:

How do you help children understand and manage their emotions in your practice? Can you share an example where guiding a child through their emotions led to a positive behaviour outcome?

How have you adapted your approach from traditional 'behaviour management' to focusing on emotional understanding and regulation? What challenges have you faced, and how have you overcome them? (if not, how might you go about this, and how might you pre-empt and manage challenges?)

Key message 2: Empathy helps us to 'tune into' the emotional worlds of children and to interpret their behaviour. All behaviour is communication.

Guided reflection:

How does empathy help you interpret the behaviour of the children in your care? Can you share an example where tuning into a child's emotional world helped you understand and respond to their behaviour effectively?

Can you describe a situation where recognising the idea that 'all behaviour is a form of communication' helped you address a child's needs more appropriately?

Key message 3: The bio-ecological framework explains the influences of a range of factors on children. Relationships between the setting and family are a key aspect of the bio-ecological framework.

Guided reflection:

How do you see the various factors within the bio-ecological framework influencing the children in your care? Can you provide an example of where understanding these influences helped you support a child's development? Can you share an instance where a positive relationship with a family enhanced a child's experience and growth?

Key message 4: Emotion coaching is a powerful strategy for helping children to recognise and manage their emotions and to manage conflict themselves.

Guided reflection:

How do you incorporate emotion coaching into your practice to help children recognise and manage their emotions? Can you share an example of where this strategy led to a positive outcome for a child?

Can you describe a situation where emotion coaching empowered a child to resolve a conflict independently?

Chapter 7 Embracing empathy and compassion in challenging situations

Key message 1: Recognising the obstacles to and challenges of empathy helps us to find ways of removing and managing them.

Guided reflection:

What are some common obstacles or challenges you face when trying to empathise with children and their families? How do you manage the challenges of maintaining empathy in difficult situations? Can you describe a strategy or approach that has been effective for you in removing or managing these obstacles?

Key message 2: Stereotypes and assumptions can be very damaging. Always make efforts to understand the points of view of others.

Guided reflection:

How do you actively challenge stereotypes and assumptions in your practice? Can you share an example where making an effort to understand someone else's point of view led to a more positive and inclusive outcome?

Key message 3: Courageous conversations are an inevitable part of Early Years practice. Approaching these with empathy and compassion encourages cooperation.

Guided reflection:

How do you approach courageous conversations with empathy and compassion in your practice? Can you describe a situation where this approach led to a positive resolution?

Chapter 8 Developing and enhancing empathy skills

Key message 1: Empathy is a skill that develops throughout our lives, but it can be increased through experience and reflection.

Guided reflection:

How have your experiences in early years practice contributed to the development of your empathy? Can you share an example where reflecting on a particular experience helped you become more empathetic?

What specific actions or reflections have you found effective in increasing your empathy towards children, families, or colleagues?

Key message 2: It is important to be aware of the emotional labour involved in the Early Years and the emotional burden this can cause.

Guided reflection:

How do you recognise and acknowledge the emotional labour involved in your role as an early years practitioner? What strategies do you use to cope with the emotional burden that comes with your work? Can you describe a situation where these strategies helped you maintain your wellbeing and continue to provide high-quality care?

Chapter 9 Understanding and managing empathic distress

Key message 1: Empathy can affect people in different ways. Being aware of this, and aware of your own wellbeing, will enable you to practice self-care.

Guided reflection:

How does empathy affect you personally in your role as an early years practitioner? What self-care strategies do you use to maintain your wellbeing? Can you describe a situation where prioritising your own wellbeing enabled you to continue providing empathetic care to others?

Key message 2: Emotional labour is intrinsic to your role. However, stress and burnout can be debilitating. It is important to seek support if stress becomes unmanageable.

Guided reflection:

How do you recognise the signs of stress and burnout in yourself as an early years practitioner? Can you share an example where acknowledging these signs helped you take steps to manage your stress?

What support systems or resources do you rely on when stress becomes unmanageable?

Key message 3: Consider which self-help strategies work for you and prioritise your own wellbeing. You cannot care for others if you are not emotionally strong yourself.

Guided reflection:

What self-help strategies have you found most effective in maintaining your emotional strength and wellbeing? How do you balance caring for yourself with caring for others in your role? Can you describe a situation where focusing on your own wellbeing enabled you to provide better support to those around you?

Key message 4: Working in the Early Years is emotionally draining. Ensure that these are opportunities for talking to colleagues and supporting each other.

Guided reflection:

How do you create opportunities for open conversations and mutual support among colleagues in your early years setting? What strategies do you use to foster a supportive environment where colleagues feel comfortable sharing their experiences and challenges? Can you describe a situation where this approach led to a stronger, more resilient team?

Chapter 10 Experiencing satisfaction through positive empathy and compassion

Key message 1: Compassion satisfaction and empathy satisfaction help us to cope with the demands of the role.

Guided reflection:

How does experiencing compassion satisfaction (the pleasure derived from helping others) help you cope with the demands of your role as an early years practitioner? Can you share an example where this satisfaction positively impacted your wellbeing? In what ways does empathy satisfaction (the fulfilment from understanding and connecting with others) support you in managing the challenges of your work? Can you describe a situation where feeling empathy satisfaction helped you navigate a difficult situation?

Key message 2: There are many positive aspects of early years work: fun, laughter, rewarding relationships, and pride in making a difference.

Guided reflection:

Can you think of an example where a joyful moment with the children reinforced your passion for your role? How do the rewarding relationships you build with children and their families bring you pride and a sense of accomplishment? Can you describe a situation where making a difference in a child's life brought you a deep sense of fulfilment?

Key message 3: Personal growth and self-actualisation in your career are possible if the environment is encouraging, flexible, and allows people responsibility.

Guided reflection:

Can you share an example where an encouraging, positive environment allowed you to take on responsibility and grow in your career? In what ways has being given responsibility in your role helped you achieve personal growth and self-actualisation? Can you describe a situation where taking on new responsibilities led to significant professional development?

Concluding the empathy research

Throughout this book, there have been references to a research project on early years practitioners' empathy. Examples from participants have been used to illustrate all chapters. The research was carried out between 2019 and 2023 and was conducted for a PhD study (Hodgkins, 2023).

The principal objective of this research project was to examine *'Early Childhood Practitioners' Perceptions of Empathic Interactions with Children and Families'*. A prior interest in the subject of empathy had identified it to be an essential skill in relationships, particularly in helping relationships. In the early childhood profession, an 'ethic of care' (Noddings, 2013) is well-established, and practitioners are required to demonstrate empathy and compassion in their interactions with children and families. This study set out to investigate how early childhood practitioners in England perceive empathy within their practice, examine empathic interactions in detail, and ascertain any impact on practitioners. There are various kinds of impact that can originate from the research of this kind, including attitudinal impact, awareness, economic impact, social impact, influencing policy, and cultural influence (Rapple, 2019). Three main recommendations for practice arose from the research:

- **Recommendation one:** Raise awareness of the emotional impact of close empathic relationships on practitioners
- **Recommendation two:** Promote reflective supervision in early years settings, where practitioners can openly share their emotions
- **Recommendation three:** Endeavour to address the particular needs of early years managers

The study, however, does have limitations. The small sample size, consisting solely of participants from England, restricts the generalisability of the findings. Future research involving a larger and more geographically diverse sample would be beneficial in producing more transferable results.

Conclusion

It is hoped that this book will go some way towards meeting the recommendations listed previously. In the ever-evolving landscape of early years care and education, there is a conspicuous absence of research and resources dedicated to practitioner empathy. This gap is particularly striking, considering the pivotal role empathy plays in nurturing profound relationships with both children and families. As the early years profession grapples with recruitment challenges stemming from stress, emotional labour, and unfavourable work conditions, a fresh approach is urgently needed. The aim of this book is not only to address the ongoing crisis but also to celebrate the inherent joy and fulfilment in working with young children while fostering a culture of compassionate and positive practice.

 Final group activity

Drawing on all the insights and knowledge gained from the activities in this book, collaboratively create a group ethos or mission statement that clearly and powerfully articulates the core values of your organisation.

References

Hodgkins, A. (2023) *Exploring early childhood practitioners' perceptions of empathic interactions with children and families*. PhD thesis, University of Worcester, available at: https://eprints.worc.ac.uk/13525/

Noddings, N. (2013) *Caring: A relational approach to ethics and moral education*, 2nd edn, CA: University of California Press.

Rapple, C. (2019) 'Research impact: What it is, why it matters, and how you can increase impact potential', *Kudos*, available at: https://blog.growkudos.com/research-mobilization/research-impact-what-why-how (accessed 14th November 2024).

Further reading

A range of publications relating to this research have been published and may be of interest:

Boddey, J. and Hodgkins, A. (2022, November–December) 'Supporting your families', *Under 5*, pp. 14-15.

Hodgkins, A. (2019, April 1) 'With feeling', *Nursery World*.

Hodgkins, A. (2021) 'Early years practitioners need emotional support too', *Nursery Management Today*, 21(2), p. 33.

Hodgkins, A. (2022a) 'Chapter 5: Empathy, compassion and emotion', in Richards, H. and Malomo, M. (eds) *Developing your professional identity: A guide for working with children and families*, St Albans: Critical Publishing.

Hodgkins, A. (2022b) 'Exploring early childhood practitioners' perceptions of empathy with children and families: Initial findings', *Educational Review*, 76(2), pp. 223-241.

Hodgkins, A. (2023) 'Chapter 4: Appreciating and practicing empathy', in Solvason, C. and Webb, R. (eds) *Exploring and celebrating the early childhood practitioner: An interrogation of pedagogy, professionalism and practice*, London: Routledge.

Hodgkins, A. and Boddey, J. (2023) 'Supporting parents with empathy and compassion', *International Journal of Birth and Parent Education*, 10(2), pp. 29-33.

Hodgkins, A., Gossman, P., Paige, R. and Woolley, R. (2023) 'We cry together every day' - expressing emotion in early childhood empathy research', *Early Years*, 44(3-4), pp. 903-917.

Hodgkins, A. and Groom, J. (2025) 'The cost of caring: Empathic relationships and emotional labour in early years management', *Journal of Early Childhood Education Research*, (Finland) (currently in production).

INDEX

absenteeism 90
abuse 23, 44, 45, 114, 115, 129
advanced empathy 26, 87, 121, 129-131
adversity 7, 36, 40, 114-115, 129
affective empathy 11, 16, 21-22, 60, 115, 123, 129, 131, 139, 142
aggression 92, *103*, 107-108, 112
Ainsworth, Mary 37-49
appreciation of staff 1, 29, 59, 82-84
attachment: difficulties 38-41, 44, 114, 148; relationships 28, 34, 37-38, 77-78, 93, 178
attachment parenting 167
attachment types 38
authenticity 5-7, 55, 63-64, *112*, 147, 166
avoiding empathy 144

befriending model 63-64
behaviour, children's 20, 24, *27*, 39-44, 60-61, 97, 106-107, 163, 180-181
behaviour management 92-93, 99, 180
behaviour policy 99
beneficence 11
bias 102-104, *127*, 152
bio-ecological systems theory 86-90, 181
body language 27, 87, 129-130; *see also* non-verbal communication
boundaries 34, 45, 90, 115, 178
Bowlby, John 38-40
brain development 21, 30, 40, 100, 115, 124, 135
Bronfenbrenner, Urie 86-88
bullying 70, 79, 117, 150
burnout 126, 131, 139-145, 164, 183

career development 2-5, 162, 167, 171-172, 184
challenging partnerships 57-59
challenging situations 102-118, 146, 181
change: making positive change 110-111, 126, 161, 167, 170-175; in the sector 2, 35, 115, 153; in staff 54, 70, 74, 105-106, 124

Children Act, The 63, 110
children's rights 29
Claxton, Guy 25-27, 87, 130
coaching 126, 151, 164
cognitive empathy 18-22, 123, 139, 152, 177
collaboration 12, 76, 90, 179, 185
communication barriers 112-114
community 29, 56, 88-91, 115, 161, *165*
compassion 16-32
compassionate environment 29-31
compassionate pedagogy 29-31
compassion fatigue 146, 159
compassion satisfaction 159, 184
conflict: between children 97, 125, 181; with parents/carers 107; self 131; between staff 79-81, *103*, 104, 107
conflicting values 61, 63, 69, 143-145
congruence 5, *8*, 16-17, 30, 53, 55, 63, 107-108, 166, 176
Conkbayir, Mina 40
consequences of empathy 17, 139, *140*
constructs 35, *36*
Continuing Professional Development (CPD) 171, 175
core conditions 5-6, *8*, 17, 53-56, 62, 63, 71, 73, 107-108, 166, 176
courageous conversations 61, 65, 108-109, 182
Covid-19 1-3, 42, 51, 163
critical reflection 7, 176
cultural differences 52-53, 92, 113
culture 9, 30, 72, 77, 88

Dachyshyn, Darcey 28, 125
decline of empathy 117-118
deep acting 131-132
democratic leadership 76
developmental psychology 17
development of empathy 121-135
diamond model 98-99
disadvantage 36, 106
discrimination 60, 61, 69, 72, 104-105

distributed leadership 76
diversity 52-54, 71-73, 104, 125, 180
double loop learning 7
driving and resisting forces 3-4

Elfer, Peter 12, 20, 36-43, 75, 82, 134, 142, 145-146, 159
emotional contagion 122
emotional impact 7, 11, 20, 128, *144*, 146, 151, 185
emotional labour 131-132, 143-146, 182-183
emotional security 77
emotion coaching 86, 95-97, 142, 181
empath 124
empathic and compassionate leadership 74-76
empathic distress 21, 23-24, 63, 110, 128, 139-155, 159, 183
empathy gap 103-104
empathy overload 143, 196
empathy satisfaction 158-163
empowerment 6, 76-77, 98-99, 158
English as an additional language 73, 113-114
enjoyment, fun 159-161
environment: for children 4, 29-31, 114, 115; influence of 88, 123-124, 109, 123; work 153, 158, 160, 166-169, 179-184
ethical dilemma 63, 143
ethical research 11
ethics 6, 30
ethnocentric 77
exhaustion 2, 11, 74, *103*, 140, 143-145, 164
expertise *26*, 59, 171, 177
expert model 64

factors influencing behaviour 86, 88-92, 181
family structures 50, *51*, 54
fathers 53-54, 72
fatigue 139, 146, 159
feedback 75, 78, 113, 116, *127*, 148, 154, 160, 163
feeling 'known' 37, 77
female 2, 35-36, 54, 72-73, 132
friendship 77-79, 99, 160

gender 36, 54, 65, 72-73, 77, *88*, 105, 107, 177-178
Goleman, Daniel 95, 154
graduate-led workforce 2, 35
growth mindset 70, 179-180
guided reflection 175-185
guilt 45, 62-63, 143, 145, 151

heartful practice 28
hierarchy of needs 7, 77-79, 168
Hochschild, Arlie 131, 145

ideal parent 52, 58
implicit learning 25-26, 151
increasing empathy 126-127, 160, 182
individualised care 42, 111
innate empathy 121-124
inspection 111-112, 116
interpersonal self-awareness 147-148
interpersonal skills 17, 74, 104, 125, 154
intrapersonal self-awareness 147-148
introvert 104, 126
intuition, gut feeling 25-26, 87, 121, 125, 128, 177
intuitive empathy 25, 129-131

job crafting 79
Johari window 147-148
judgement 8, 25, 55-56, 78, 87, 91-92, 99

key worker/ key person 6, 37, 40, 43, 111

language 35, 45-46, 52, 62, 73, 122, *127*
language barriers 103, 112-114
leader / leadership 2, 68, 74-76, 81, 84, 124, 180; types 76
LGBTQIA+ community 73
listening: active 24, 107, 133; to adults 74, 87, 131; to children 29, 125
locus of control 91-92, 99
love 29, 34, 44-46, 95, 114, 132, 145, 163, 178

making a difference 115, 160-162
management 62, 68, 74-84, 153
Maslow, Abraham 7, 77-78, 165-167
mental health: adults 23, 43, 59, 70, 74, 80, 83, 128-129, 140-141, 46, 152-153, *165*; children 36, 40, 56, 59, 114-115
mentoring 126
mesosystem 88-90
mirror neurons 124
mothering/maternal 2, 35
motivation 23, *70*, 76-77, 125, *141*, 158, 161-164, 170
multiple adversity 114

negativity 69-70, 81, 179-180
neurodiversity 88
neuroscience 16-17, 40
non-verbal communication 129

obstacles to empathy 7, 103, 182
Ofsted 7, 82, 111-112, 116

Page, Jools 34, 44-46, 146
parent partnership 50-52, 63-64
parental engagement 56
parenting culture 52

Index

parents/ carers 34, 50, 57-59, 62-65, 88, 108-110, 116, 179
partnership models 63-64
personal growth 5, 164, 169-172, 184
personality 9, *19*, 78, 117
personal philosophy 9-12
person-centred practice 5-6, 53
perspective taking 17, *122*
philosophy (of the book) 3-4
philosophy (setting) 30, 167, 176
Planfulness 170
positive feedback 160, 163
poverty 6, 56-57, 114
power 70, 74, 126, 162, 169; imbalance 50; lack of 132, 143
praise 93-94, 160, 163
prejudice 56, 73, 104-105
pre-requisites for empathy 123
presenteeism 150-151
pride 158-161, 144, 184
'problem families' 57-58
professionalisation 2, 44
professionalism 2, 121
professional love 34, 44-46
progress: children's 35, 61, 62, 75, 159-160; staff 28, 77
progression/ career progression 2-3
protective factors 165

qualifications/ training 2-4, 26, 35
qualities 11, 34-36, 46, 78, 145, 177-179
quality 35, 59, 74, 124, 160-161
quality improvement 74, 151, 171

rational compassion 152
recognising emotion 24, 87
reflective practice 7-9, 121, 134-135
Reggio Emilia 30, 124
relational universe 71, 75, 180
relationship-centred practice 71
resilience 6-7, 70, 124, 140, 158, 164-165, 179-180
respect 5, 50-52, 64, 68-69, 78, 107-114, 117, 151, 168, 179
reward charts 93-94
reward/ rewarding 1-2, 35, *69*, 110, 152, 158, 161-162, 167, 176, 184
Rogers, Carl 5, 11, 17, 43, 71, 87, 123, 165-166
role model 4, 26, 74, 122, 124, 126
rules 63, 89-93, 109, 115, 131, 143-146

safeguarding 34, 45, 61, 102, 109-112, 153, 171, 178
secure attachment 37-45, 179
security 7, 9, 38, 40, 46, 77-78, *165*, 166, 168, 178
self-actualisation 7, *77*, 78-82, 165-169, 184

self-awareness 121-125, 147-148, *170*
self-belief 7, 78
self-care 148-153, 183
self-concept 78
self-confidence 39, 45, 92, 178
self-efficacy 78
self-esteem 7, 39, 45, 78-82, 158-161, 166
self-fulfilling prophecy 106
self-image 78
self-perception 73
self-regard 78
sensitivity 25, 35, 72, 124, 132, 145, 177
servant leadership 76
sex 5, 36, *51*, 53-54, 60, 72-73, 77
situational leadership 76
social pedagogy 70-71, 97-99, 125, 162-163
social psychology 17
special educational needs 59, 107
stereotypes 65, 72, 82, 104-105, 182
strength-based practice/ approach 4, 6-7, 74-75, 110, 176
stress: children 40-41; practitioners 2, 53, 74, 78, 82-83, 117, 126, 131, 134, 139-146, 148, 153, 160, 164, 170, 183-185
supervision 7, 11, 121, 151, 159, 164, 185
supporting families 56
support systems 183
surface acting 131, *132*

Taggart, Geoff 28-30
'tantrum' 87, 100
teaching 3-4, 34-35, 125, 126, 161-162
teaching empathy 126
teamwork 68
theory of mind 122
time out 94-95
touch 28-29, 34, 45-46, 153, 178
toxic stress 40-41
transformational leadership 76
transitions 34-37, 41, *88*, 142, 178
trauma 23, 70-71, 78, 114-115, 121, 128-129, 151
triangle of care 51, *52*
tuning in 26, 80, 181

unconditional positive regard 5, *8*, 17, 53-55, 107-108, *166*, 176
unique child 42

values 3-9, 30, 55, 61, 63, 68-70, 88, 91, 105, 143, 147, 166
vicarious trauma / secondary trauma 115
virtuous research 11

ways of knowing 25-28, 87
work discussion groups 134-135, 151
wounded healer 22-23, 121, 129

For Product Safety Concerns and Information please contact our EU
representative GPSR@taylorandfrancis.com
Taylor & Francis Verlag GmbH, Kaufingerstraße 24, 80331 München, Germany

www.ingramcontent.com/pod-product-compliance
Lightning Source LLC
Chambersburg PA
CBHW082100230426
43670CB00017B/2903